CAMBRIDGE

Official Cambridge Exam Preparation



# PREPARE

STUDENT'S BOOK WITH EBOOK

B1

LEVEL 5

Niki Joseph
Helen Chilton

Second Edition

**Cambridge University Press**
www.cambridge.org/elt

**Cambridge Assessment English**
www.cambridgeenglish.org

Information on this title: www.cambridge.org/9781009032117



First published 2015
Second Edition 2019
Second Edition update 2021

20 19 18 17

Printed in Dubai by Oriental Press

*A catalogue record for this publication is available from the British Library*

ISBN 978-1-00-903211-7 Student's Book with eBook
ISBN 978-1-00-903212-4 Workbook with Digital Pack
ISBN 978-1-00-903213-1 Teacher's Book with Digital Pack

# CONTENTS

| LISTENING | SPEAKING | WRITING | VIDEO |
|---|---|---|---|
| | | A short text | |
| A talk about a quiz<br>Listening Part 3 | Talking about yourself<br>Speaking Part 1 | | Best friends forever |
| | | | Shopping in London |
| | | An online comment | Fun and games |
| An interview about being lost on a mountain<br>Listening Part 4 | Talking about past experiences<br>Speaking Part 1 | | |
| | | A story (1)<br>Writing Part 2 | You made it! |
| Seven short conversations<br>Listening Part 1 | Discussing options (1)<br>Speaking Part 3 | | |
| | | | Sports in Canada |
| | | An email (1)<br>Writing Part 1 | |
| Six short conversations<br>Listening Part 2 | Describing a picture (1)<br>Speaking Part 2 | | Amazing architecture |
| | | An article (1)<br>Writing Part 2 | |
| A video call about a homework project | Discussing a topic (1)<br>Speaking Part 4 | | Animals in danger |
| | | | Only in Australia |

**Key to symbols:**
*B1 Preliminary for Schools* exam task    Video

| LISTENING | SPEAKING | WRITING | VIDEO |
|---|---|---|---|
| | | A story (2)<br>✔ Writing Part 2 | ▶ Off to school |
| An announcement on a flight<br>✔ Listening Part 3 | Talking about travel<br>✔ Speaking Part 1 | | |
| | | | |
| | | | |
| | | An online review | ▶ #NoFilter |
| Seven short conversations<br>✔ Listening Part 1 | Discussing options (2)<br>✔ Speaking Part 3 | | |
| | | | ▶ Social media detox |
| | | An email (2)<br>✔ Writing Part 1 | |
| Six short conversations<br>✔ Listening Part 2 | Describing a picture (2)<br>✔ Speaking Part 2 | | ▶ Lights, camera, action! |
| | | | |
| | | | |
| | | An article (2)<br>✔ Writing Part 2 | ▶ Getting the message |
| An interview about fame<br>✔ Listening Part 4 | Discussing a topic (2)<br>✔ Speaking Part 4 | | ▶ We love celebs! |
| | | | ▶ Collectors |
| | | An email (3)<br>✔ Writing Part 1 | |
| A radio programme | Discussing options (3)<br>✔ Speaking Part 3 and Speaking Part 4 | | |

# WELCOME TO PREPARE

## LEARN ABOUT THE FEATURES IN YOUR NEW STUDENT'S BOOK!

### ABOUT YOU

Start each unit by talking about you, your life and the unit topic

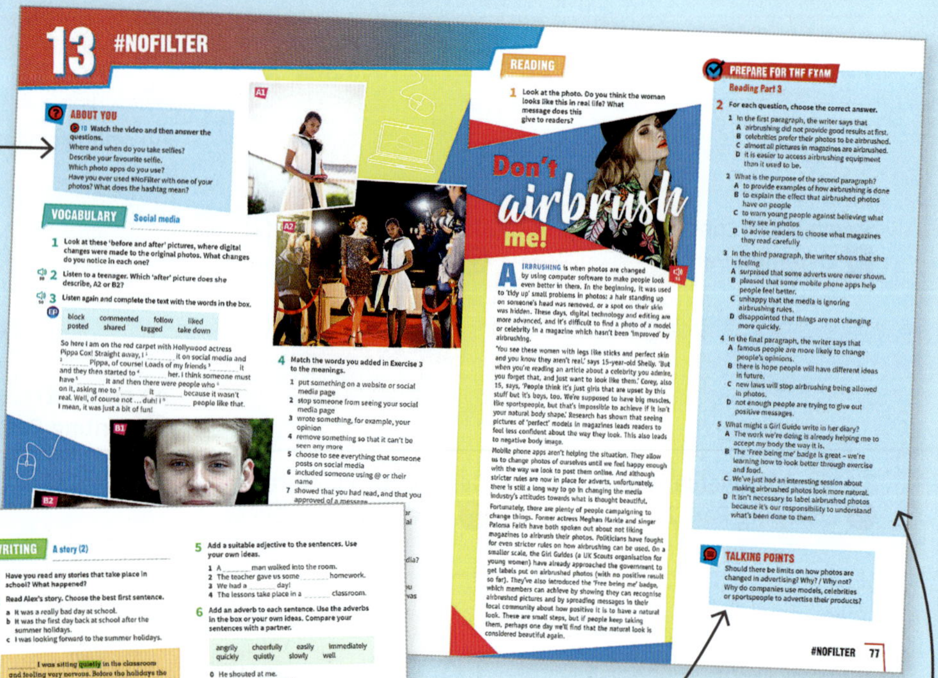

### PREPARE TO WRITE

Learn useful tips to help you prepare, plan and check your writing

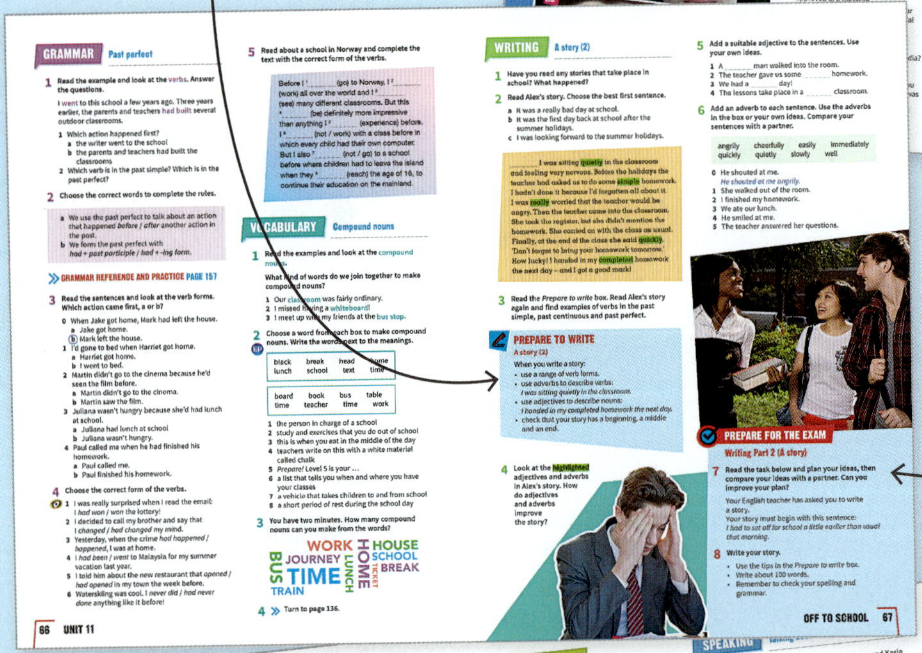

### TALKING POINTS

Say what you think about the topic in the text

### PREPARE FOR THE EXAM

Easy to find exam tasks to get you ready for the exam

### PREPARE TO SPEAK

Learn useful words and phrases for effective communication

### VIDEO

Watch interviews with teenagers like you

## LIFE SKILLS

Develop important skills that you can use in your daily life

## CULTURE

Learn about the culture of English-speaking countries and the wider world

## VIDEO

Watch interesting documentaries about the culture topics

## PREPARE FOR THE EXAM

Read useful tips, learn exam techniques, then try a practice exam task

## VIDEO

Watch teenagers doing speaking tasks in an exam situation

## PROJECT

Work together to create something fun and expand your learning

## REVIEW

Check your progress

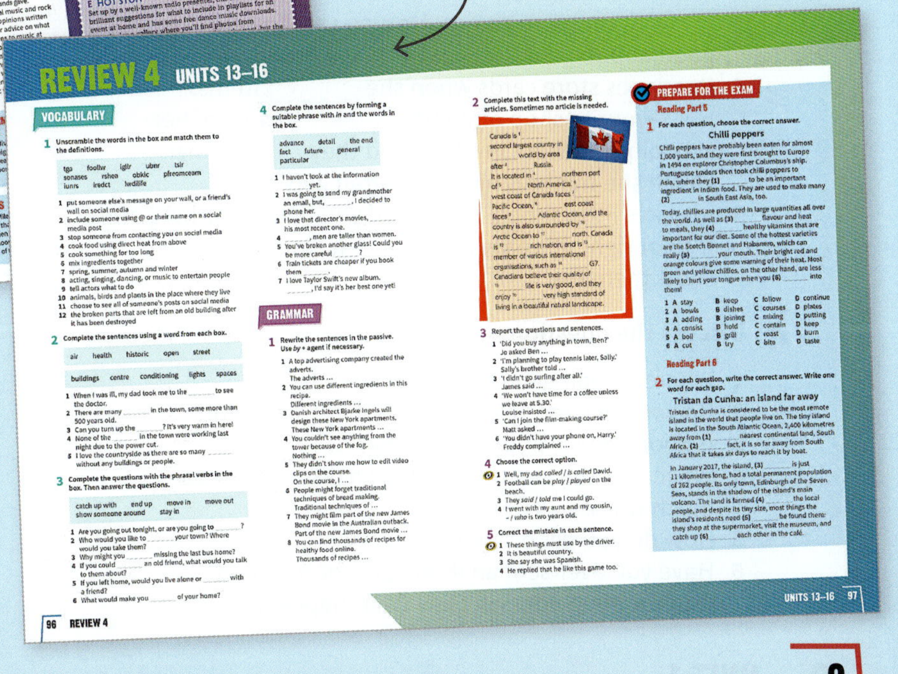

# 1 GOING SHOPPING

## ABOUT YOU

Where do you usually go shopping?
Which is your favourite shop?
Which is better: going to shops or shopping online?

## VOCABULARY Shopping

**1** **Look at the photos. What different things can you buy in these places?**

**Compare your answers with your partner.**

01 **2** **Listen to five teenagers talking about these different places to shop. Match each speaker to one of the photos.**

Daisy ☐ Sean ☐ Alec ☐ Rose ☐ Iris ☐

01 **3** **Complete the sentences with the words in the box. Then listen again and check.**

EP

| | | | |
|---|---|---|---|
| charge | charges | discount | exchange |
| online shopping | | promotions | purchases |
| receipt | refunds | send … back | serve |
| service | shop | spend | |

1 Daisy says that markets are probably her favourite place to ______. She says you don't have to ______ much money there. But if you're a tourist, sometimes they can ______ you high prices.
2 Sean thinks that ______ is the best thing ever. He says if you spend a certain amount, you don't have to pay the delivery ______. If the item isn't right, you can usually ______ it ______.
3 Alec's favourite department store was offering a 10% ______ on some games. He also says they are really good about ______.
4 Rose uses store cards when she ______ items. Her favourite shop often has ______. Some of her schoolmates work in shops and they ______ her, which she thinks is nice. She often gets good ______.
5 Iris likes little shops. She says if you buy something and it's not right, it's easy to ______ it. You just have to show them the ______.

**4** **Discuss the questions.**

1 Where do you generally shop?
2 Do you keep receipts? Why are they important?
3 Is good service important? Why?
4 When was the last time you got a discount? How much was it?
5 How do you get discounts?
6 Have you ever sent an item back, or returned it to the shop yourself? Say what happened.

# READING

**1** **Read the title and first line of the article. What do you think Olivia and her friends do in town? Read the article quickly to check.**

## SHOPPING: TEEN TRENDS

02

**It's Saturday morning and Olivia, 16, is going into town with some friends like they usually do.**

Their day begins in a coffee shop. 'We have frappuccino coffees and chat,' Olivia says. 1 ______ 'We like finding the latest fashions on Pinterest or Instagram.' Like adults, many teens want good value for money. 'If there's something new I want, but it's too expensive, like these cool trainers I saw the other day, I won't get them till they're on sale a few weeks later. 2 ______ And you can sometimes get discounts at the checkout when you're paying,' says Olivia. Although girls are more likely to spend money on jewellery or make-up, both sexes are into looking good and buy high-quality hair and body products. 3 ______ This means downloading apps is a favourite activity.

Teens shop on the internet because 'online companies don't always charge you as much money and it's easy,' says Olivia. 4 ______ 'For example, sometimes we go to a gaming store and try out several new games. A lot of games cost more than we can afford, so we wait until there's a special offer, when you can get two games for the price of one and that kind of thing. 5 ______ There's no brand new stuff on them but you can save a lot of money.'

After that, Olivia and her friends go for lunch. 'I love any healthy food, especially organic stuff,' says Olivia. 'We go anywhere that serves it – plenty of places do, but it can be expensive. After that, I don't usually have any money left!' laughs Olivia.

## PREPARE FOR THE EXAM

### Reading Part 4

**2** **Read the article again. Five sentences have been removed from the text. For each space choose the correct sentence. There are three extra sentences which you do not need to use.**

**A** Some people I know send everything back.
**B** While they're there, they also do some online shopping.
**C** They're also keen on keeping their mobile technology up to date.
**D** You can usually get anything new that way if you're prepared to wait!
**E** You can get refunds online but it takes longer.
**F** There are plenty of second-hand websites, too, where stuff's even cheaper.
**G** I'm not really interested in buying things like that.
**H** But they still enjoy looking around the shops.

» PREPARE FOR THE EXAM PAGE 124

**3** **Match the highlighted words and phrases in the article to the meanings.**

1. have enough money to buy something
2. where you pay for your goods
3. not new; already used in the past by someone else
4. a price that is lower than usual
5. the amount you paid for something was right
6. very interested in or enthusiastic about something

## TALKING POINTS

Do you think people spend too much time looking at things they'd like to buy online?

Do you think it is important to buy good-quality products which are more expensive, rather than buying cheaper items? Why? / Why not?

## GRAMMAR Determiners

**1** **Read the examples and look at the nouns after the words. Which are countable and which are uncountable?**

1 Olivia, 16, is going into town with **some** friends.
2 After that, I don't usually have **any** money left!
3 There's **no** brand new stuff on them.
4 They don't charge you as **much** money.
5 Like adults, **many** teens want good value for money.
6 There are **plenty of** second-hand websites, too.
7 Sometimes we go to a gaming store and try out **several** new games.
8 **A lot of** games cost more than we can afford.

**2** **Complete the table with the words in the box. Use the examples in Exercise 1 to help you.**

| ~~some~~ | ~~any~~ | a lot of | many |
|---|---|---|---|
| much | plenty of | no | several |

| | Countable | Uncountable |
|---|---|---|
| **Positive** | *some* | |
| **Negative** | | *any* |
| **Questions** | | |

» GRAMMAR REFERENCE AND PRACTICE PAGE 147

03 **3** **Listen to the short conversations. Add more determiners to the table.**

**4** **Choose the correct word to complete the sentences.**

1 Last weekend I got *a / some / any* great discounts on clothes.
2 My brother buys *much / a lot of / many* clothes online.
3 I got a discount on *a / some / no* headphones online.
4 I bought *a / some / much* jeans yesterday.
5 Have you got *any / much / several* BeBop trainers?
6 We don't eat *some / any / no* special food.

**5** **Complete the conversation with the words in the box.**

| any | many | much | no |
|---|---|---|---|
| plenty | several | some | ~~some~~ |

**A:** What are you doing?
**B:** I'm looking for [0] *some* information about [1] ______ trainers. I looked on a few websites but there weren't [2] ______ in my size – not even one pair!
**A:** I'm surprised. There are [3] ______ of websites where you can buy trainers. Have you tried this site?
**B:** Not yet! I can't see [4] ______ places that sell the trainers I want!
**A:** Look here. It looks like there are [5] ______ models listed here in fluorescent green. How [6] ______ money were they in the shop?
**B:** About £50, I think.
**A:** Oh dear, there are [7] ______ trainers in your size!

**6** **Complete the questions with the correct words. Then ask and answer the questions with a partner.**

1 How ______ pairs of trainers do you have?
2 Do you have ______ sunglasses?
3 How ______ time do you spend shopping online?
4 Do you know ______ websites where you can get discounts?

## VOCABULARY any

**1** **Read the examples. Complete the rules with the words in the box.**

1 They aren't doing **anything**.
2 We go **anywhere** that serves healthy food.
3 Has **anyone** seen my new trainers?

| negative | positive | question |
|---|---|---|

a With a ______ verb, *any* has a positive meaning.
b With a ______ verb, *any* means the same as *no*.
c Use *any* in a ______.

**2** **What other words or phrases do you know with *any*?**

**3** **Complete the sentences with the words and phrases in the box.**

EP

| ~~any~~ | any better | any good |
|---|---|---|
| any longer | any more | anyone |
| anything | anywhere | |

0 I don't mind what colour the trainers are – *any* colour will do.
1 Maria doesn't work in this shop ______.
2 Is there ______ in this shop that would be a good present for your mum?
3 This book isn't ______ – it's so boring. I won't finish it.
4 Has ______ got David's number? I need to call him today.
5 Tony isn't feeling ______ today – the boss wants me to work this afternoon.
6 Is there ______ near here where I can buy some speakers?
7 I can't eat ______. I'm full. That was delicious!

**4** » **Work in pairs. Turn to page 135.**

## WRITING A short text

**1** **Read the introduction to the magazine competition. What do you have to write about?**

# COMPETITION!

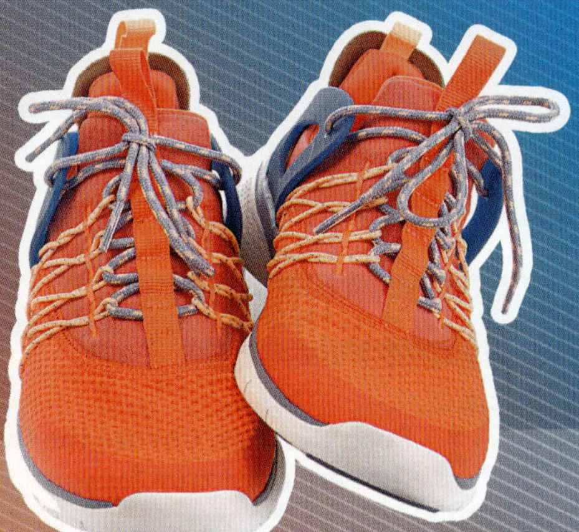

Tell us about the last cool thing you bought. Where did you buy it? Do your friends like it? Email us at itsallaboutyou@weareteens.co.uk. We'll include the best stories in our magazine next month!

**Maksim, Russia**

Last week, I bought some really cool sunglasses from a shop in my town called Eyewear. It's a great shop that only sells sunglasses. There are a lot of styles to choose from but I chose these ones because I just loved them! There was a promotion that day and I got a 10% discount. I forgot the receipt, so I went back to get it and the assistant gave me a free case to keep them in. Great customer service!

**Emily, Ireland**

Mum was going to get these cute trainers for me at the end of the month, but I couldn't wait any longer, so I bought them myself. I got them from the local sports shop near my house. Several of my friends already had pink ones, but I wanted to be different. So I got some orange and blue ones! Plenty of people have asked me where I got them, but I'm not telling anyone my secret store!

**JD, UK**

Last week, I was at the shopping centre and I went into Soundz, which is my favourite shop. They have an online store, but I prefer to go to the shop so I can try the things on sale. You can find a lot of cool stuff there like headphones, speakers and MP3 players. I saw these great Bluetooth headphones. I put them on and listened to several songs from my phone. They were expensive, but I got a 10% discount because of a promotion. My friend is saving up for a pair now!

**2** **Read the three texts. Which thing do you think is the coolest?**

**3** **Read the *Prepare to write* box. Read the texts and underline the following in each one:**

| | |
|---|---|
| Maksim's message: | shopping vocabulary |
| Emily's message: | all the determiners from page 12 |
| JD's message: | two different tenses |

**4** **Read JD's text again. Underline the sentences that answer the competition questions. What extra information does she add?**

**5** **Read about the competition again. You are going to write a short text about something you bought recently. Plan your ideas and make some notes. Here are some ideas to help you.**

- What is the last thing you bought?
- Where did you buy it?
- Why did you choose it?
- What do your friends think?
- Extra information?

**6** **Write your own short text.**

- Use the tips in the *Prepare to write* box.
- Write about 80 words.
- Remember to check your spelling and grammar.

### PREPARE TO WRITE
**A short text**

When you write an answer to something:

- answer all the questions.
- add some extra information.
- use a range of different tenses and structures.

# 2 BEST FRIENDS FOREVER

## ABOUT YOU

01 **Watch the video and then answer the questions.**
How important are friends to you?
What makes a good friend, in your opinion?

## VOCABULARY Personality adjectives

**1** **Read the quiz. Choose the five sentences that are most true for you.**

### WHAT KIND OF A FRIEND ARE YOU?

- I sometimes feel a bit **anxious** in situations where there are lots of people.
- When my friends are **annoying**, I tell them. But I am **sensitive** to their feelings.
- I hang out with my friends if I have spare time.
- I love hanging out with a big group of friends.
- If my friends have a problem, then I'll listen.
- My friends trust me with their secrets.
- I love laughing, especially when I feel **silly**!
- I love my friends, but I really love being on my own.
- I don't like planning too much. Let's just see what happens!
- I'd do anything to help my best friends.
- I prefer to listen to other people's ideas, although I sometimes have good ideas too.
- I have lots of best friends – girls and boys!

**2** **Read the descriptions. Do you agree with what the quiz says about you?**

### 1 MOSTLY ORANGE Brilliant best friend

You're a **reliable** best friend. And you're also kind, honest and caring, and your friends know how **sensible** you are! You're a **thoughtful** and sweet person, and it's no surprise that you love having people around you.

### 2 MOSTLY YELLOW The cheerful chum

You've got loads of friends and you're **easygoing**! You love having fun and you'd never be cruel to anyone. You are never **jealous** of other people, and everyone likes that! People love having you at parties! Go, **sociable** you!

### 3 MOSTLY GREEN The perfect pal

You prefer to have a few close friends rather than lots of friends. You're confident, **talented** and **loyal** to your friends. You love hanging out with your friends but you also like to spend time alone.

**3** **Match the words in Exercises 1 and 2 to the meanings.** EP

1 making you feel angry
2 someone you can trust and/or believe
3 behaving in a careful way that shows good judgement
4 enjoying being with people
5 worried and nervous
6 relaxed and calm
7 behaving in a way that is funny and not serious
8 having a natural ability to do something
9 always supporting and liking someone
10 thinking about how you can help other people
11 wanting something that someone else has
12 being easily upset by things other people say or do to you

04 **4** **Listen to Sophie and Ben talking about the quiz. Which of the adjectives from Exercises 1 and 2 would you use to describe them?**

**5** **Discuss the questions. Use the adjectives in Exercises 1 and 2.**

1 How would you describe yourself? What is your best personal quality?
2 What qualities does your best friend have?

## READING

**1** Make a list of the differences between your online friends and your real friends.

**2** Read the article quickly. Were any of your ideas mentioned?

# FRIENDSHIP IN THE 21st century

05

ENTERTAINMENT | STYLE | HEALTH & FITNESS | TECH | RELATIONSHIPS

**Scientist Dr Russell Carley is interested in finding out about friendship in the 21st century. He started by trying to answer the question: Can online friends be as good as face-to-face friends?**

Surprisingly, he found that the answer is a big YES! A friend is someone who gives you honest advice and support, and, of course, an online friend can do that. Online friends can also be close friends. Our real friends can't be with us 24 hours a day, but the online community never sleeps! When you feel anxious in the middle of the night, there's always someone who can give you support through a text, a message or just a 'like'. Having online friends is good for your memory, too. There's a lot of information to check every day. When you see an interesting holiday picture, you make a note in your mind to ask your pal about it next time they're online, or when you're together in person.

Also, you can find friends who have the same interests as you more easily. If you're interested in Japanese comics, there will be plenty of people who love that too. For most of us, the online community provides support, it builds our confidence, and we feel loved.

So, if online friends are so good, do we need real friends? Interestingly, Dr Carley's research suggests that we do. As he points out, with your real friends, you are in the same physical space; you create memories together as you experience and enjoy doing things with each other. You have to be more responsible with your real friends, as you can't just 'unfriend' them if you disagree with them!

Dr Carley explains the science. 'When you are with your friends, you get hugs and high fives. Hugging is good for us because our body produces a chemical called oxytocin that makes us feel good and we also feel trust and love. Chatting to your best pals, you copy their words and gestures. When they smile, you smile too! So, in conclusion, both real friends and online friends are great – they just help us in different ways.'

**NEXT WEEK:** Are you good at staying in touch with your friends?

**3** Read the article again. Answer the questions.

1. How can an online friend support you at night?
2. How do online friends help your memory?
3. What happens when you hug a friend?
4. What happens when you talk to people face-to-face?
5. According to the article, which are best for you: online or face-to-face friends? Why?

**4** Match the highlighted words in the article to the meanings.

1. friend
2. movements of your hands, arm or head to show a feeling
3. remove someone from your social media account
4. when you put your arms around someone because you like them
5. getting more information about something

### TALKING POINTS

Do you think you will have the same online friends in five years' time? Why? / Why not?

Do you think you will have the same real friends in five years' time? Why? / Why not?

What are the disadvantages of having online friends?

## GRAMMAR *-ing* forms

**1** **Match the examples to the rules.**

1 He enjoys **finding out** about friendship in the 21st century.
2 **Hugging** is good for us.
3 Are you good at **keeping** in touch with your friends?

a After some verbs such as *enjoy* and *hate*, we use the *-ing* form.
b Some adjectives are followed by a preposition and then by the *-ing* form.
c We can use the *-ing* form as the subject of a sentence.

» GRAMMAR REFERENCE AND PRACTICE PAGE 148

**2** **Complete the sentences with the *-ing* form of the verbs in the box.**

| go | learn | prepare |
|---|---|---|
| read | visit | work |

1 I don't mind ________ to the cinema with my parents and their friends.
2 ________ English is easy, especially when I'm with my friends.
3 The girls enjoyed ________ a presentation together for their English class.
4 David can't stand ________ in groups in class, as he always disagrees with the other people.
5 Pablo is interested in ________ more articles about friendship in the 21st century.
6 ________ museums is part of our history class.

**3** **Match the sentence halves.**

1 Jo is afraid
2 Mike is good
3 Jackie is keen
4 Nina is crazy
5 Phil is interested

a about playing online games with her friends.
b of disappointing her friends.
c on going to football matches with friends.
d in making music in the school band.
e at listening to other people's problems.

**4** **Correct the mistakes in the sentences.**

1 I really like see my friends after school.
2 Mike loves go shopping with his parents.
3 Susan really enjoyed to visit the museum.
4 Play a musical instrument is fun.
5 Our teacher is good at teach us English.
6 Are those boys afraid to watching horror films?
7 My parents are interested in visit Slovakia.

**5** **Complete the sentences so they are true for you. Compare your sentences with your classmates. Find someone who has similar ideas.**

*I'm good at scoring goals!*

1 I'm good at …
2 I'm afraid of …
3 I really like …
4 … football is …
5 I'm keen on …
6 I'm crazy about …
7 I'm tired of …
8 I'm interested in …
9 I really enjoy …
10 … is boring for me

## VOCABULARY Prefixes: *un-* and *dis-*

**1** **Read the examples. How do *un-* and *dis-* change the meaning of the words? Which prefix do we often add to verbs?**

1 Talking about friends is really **interesting**! We'll probably **agree** about a lot of things.
2 Talking about friends is really **uninteresting**! We'll probably **disagree** about a lot of things.

**2** **Write the correct negative form of the words. Use *un-* or *dis-*.**

1 pleasant
2 like
3 kind
4 appear
5 lucky
6 reliable
7 happy

**3** **Complete the text with the words in the box. Add a negative prefix to the words if necessary.**

EP

| agree | appeared | interesting |
|---|---|---|
| kind | lucky | pleasant |

# Online friendships

Many people have an opinion about online friendships, especially parents. It can be really boring and [1] ________ to talk about it. They always say the same thing! Last year, Mum had an [2] ________ surprise – an old classmate contacted her and started posting old photos of her online. My sister and I thought it was funny, but Mum didn't! Fortunately, Mum just closed her page and the classmate [3] ________. Another friend told me about someone who was writing [4] ________ things about her on her wall. That's not nice! I'm very [5] ________ because nothing like that has happened to me. But I [6] ________ when people say you have to be careful about the online world.

# LISTENING

**1** Have you ever written a quiz? Who was it for? What did you ask?

## PREPARE FOR THE EXAM

### Listening Part 3

**2** Read the notes. What are they about? What kind of information is missing in each space?

**Notes for WRITING A QUIZ**

The name of the quiz is '**(1)** ________'.

The quiz should not just include questions about **(2)** ________ such as people's interests.

Write ten questions using a different **(3)** ________ each time.

Write options for people to select, which show whether a person is **(4)** ________ or shy, for example.

Give the finished quiz to the teacher by **(5)** ________ July.

Email the teacher at **(6)** ________ @ourschool.uk with any questions.

06 **3** Listen and complete the notes in Exercise 2. For each question, write the correct answer in the gap. Write one or two words or a number or a date or a time.

» PREPARE FOR THE EXAM PAGE 130

# SPEAKING Talking about yourself

07 **1** Listen to an interview with Ahmed and Sandrine. Tick (✓) the questions that they answer. Do they just answer *yes* or *no*, or do they add more information?

| | | A | S |
|---|---|---|---|
| 1 | What's your name? | | |
| 2 | How old are you? | | |
| 3 | What's your surname? | | |
| 4 | Who do you sit next to in English? | | |
| 5 | Where do you live? | | |
| 6 | Do you study English? | | |
| 7 | Do you like studying English? | | |
| 8 | Do you listen to music? | | |
| 9 | What's your favourite kind of music? | | |
| 10 | Do you get up early or late? | | |
| 11 | How often do you go to the cinema? | | |

07 **2** Read the *Prepare to speak* box, then listen again. Which phrases do Ahmed and Sandrine use?

## PREPARE TO SPEAK

### Talking about yourself

**Likes and dislikes**
I like it because …
I don't like it because …
I prefer …

**Talking about habits**
I usually …
I sometimes …

**Giving your opinion**
I think it's …

## PREPARE FOR THE EXAM

### Speaking Part 1

**3** Ask and answer the questions with a partner. Use phrases from the *Prepare to speak* box to add more information.

1 What's your surname?
2 Where are you from?
3 What's your house like?
4 Do you play sports? Why? / Why not?
5 What time do you go to bed?
6 Do you enjoy reading books? Why? / Why not?

» PREPARE FOR THE EXAM PAGE 131

# CULTURE

## SHOPPING IN LONDON

**1** **Read the texts on the opposite page. Which place would you most like to visit? Where should people go in London if they …**

**1** would like to go shopping for toys?
**2** are looking for second-hand clothes?
**3** plan to shop and then see a film?

**2** **Are the sentences true or false? Correct the false sentences.**

**1** Most Oxford Street shops are unusual and quite expensive.
**2** Camden would be a nice place to go shopping on a sunny day.
**3** Camden is good for people who like to dress differently.
**4** There is often a lot of traffic on Carnaby Street.
**5** Carnaby Street first became popular for modern fashion.
**6** There are football fields in the Westfield shopping centre.

**3** **Match the highlighted words in the text to the meanings.**

**1** new, modern and in fashion
**2** for people who are walking
**3** very bad, terrible
**4** extremely large
**5** tables to sell things, often outdoors

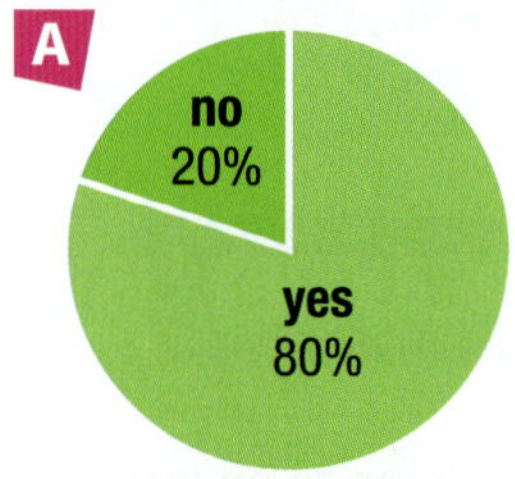


08 **4** **Listen to a report on teenagers' shopping habits in the UK. Number the questions in the order you hear them.**

....... Have you bought anything online in the last three months?
....... Where do you usually get the money from when you go shopping?
....... How often do you go shopping?
....... Do you count shopping as one of your hobbies?
....... Do you shop more in-store or online?
....... What do you buy when you go shopping?

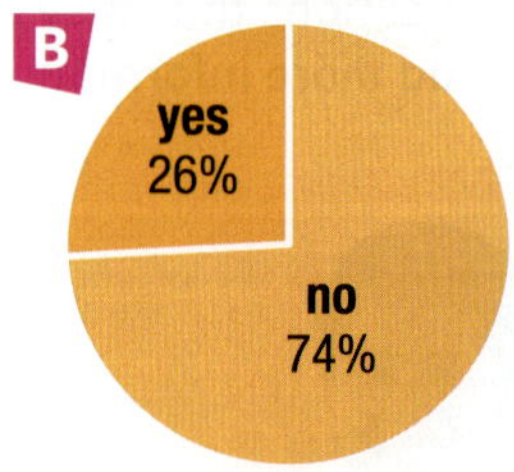


08 **5** **Listen again and match the pie charts to five of the questions (1–6) in Exercise 4.**

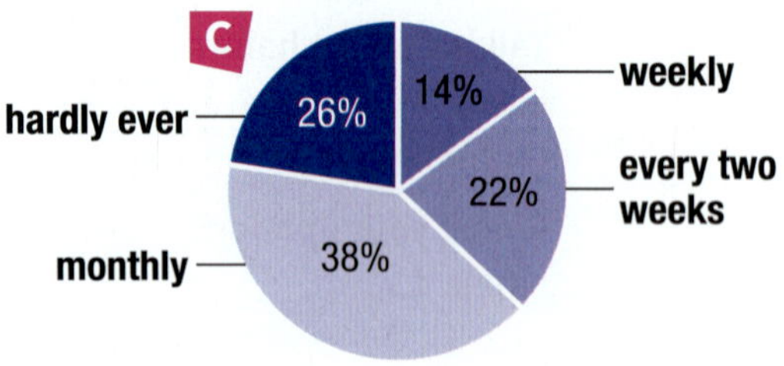


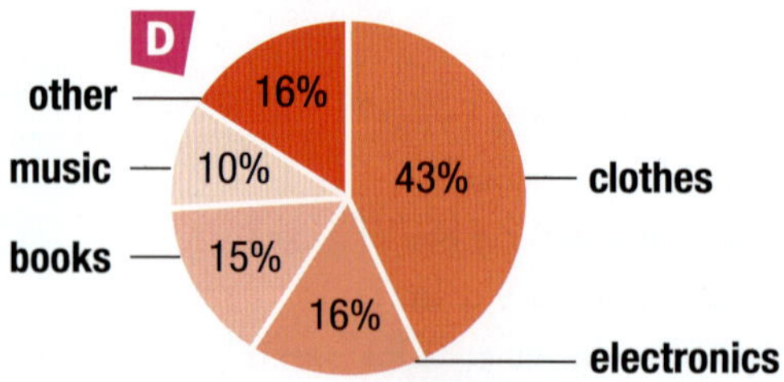


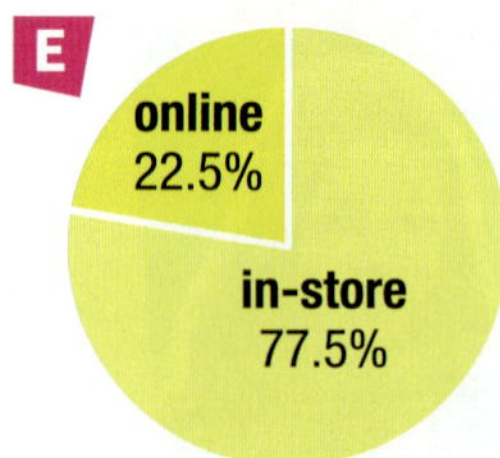


**6** **Read the *Useful language* phrases. Complete them with the words in the box.**

| amazing | example | next |
|---|---|---|
| questions | shopping | surprised |

### USEFUL LANGUAGE

**Doing a survey and presenting the results**

**1** I'm doing a survey about …
**2** Can I ask you a few …?
**3** The first / … / last question is …
**4** Can you give me an …?
**5** An … 80% said yes!
**6** This really … me.

# SHOPPING IN LONDON!

## What do you say?

We asked our London Life readers about their favourite places to go shopping in London. Here are some of their answers!

09

I love shopping with friends in Carnaby Street, near Oxford Circus. It's a **pedestrian** area, so there aren't any cars. Carnaby Street became famous for its **trendy** shops selling new, modern fashion in the 1960s, but now you can find all types of clothes and accessories there. If you get hungry, there are also lots of cafés and restaurants. While you're in the area, you can also visit Hamleys on Regent Street. It's the largest and oldest toy shop in the world. The first Hamleys shop opened more than 250 years ago!

*Paula*

My all-time favourite place for shopping in London is Oxford Street. It's got more than 300 shops, including the most typical high street brands. There are also some **huge** department stores, too. They sell everything from clothes and shoes to electronics and books, and the prices are quite good. The only problem with Oxford Street is that it's always really busy. About 500,000 people go there every day!

*Melissa*

When the weather is **awful**, I prefer to shop indoors where it's warm and dry. My favourite place to go is Westfield, in White City. It's the largest shopping centre in London, with 150,000 $m^2$ of shops. That's about the size of 30 football pitches! There are also four food halls with more than 80 different places to eat, including fast food and international restaurants. After you finish shopping you can also see a film at the 14-screen cinema. Don't forget to buy popcorn!

*Jon*

If you're into alternative fashion, then Camden is one of the best places to go in London. It's a historic neighbourhood near Regent's Park and not far from King's Cross Station. Camden is famous for its open-air markets, which have many shops and **stalls**. There are lots of second-hand clothes for sale and some shops also specialise in punk, goth or retro fashion.

*Kyle*

## PROJECT

*An interview about shopping habits*

**Create a survey to interview your friends about their shopping habits. Write questions about the topics below and your own ideas.**

- who people go shopping with
- how often people go shopping
- where people get their money
- if people prefer to shop online or in-store
- things that people usually buy
- how much people spend a week
- when people usually go shopping

**Interview at least 10 friends and take notes. Make pie charts and present your results to the class.**

02 NOW WATCH THE CULTURE VIDEO

# 3 FUN AND GAMES

## ABOUT YOU

03 **Watch the video and then answer the questions.**

Do you prefer team sports or individual sports? Why?

Which new sport or activity would you like to try?

How important is it to do sport regularly?

Why do you think people like to take part in sports competitions?

## VOCABULARY Sports phrases

**1 Look at the photos. Discuss the questions.**

1 Which are individual sports? Which are team sports?
2 Which of these sports can you do at your school?

10 **2 Listen to three people talking about sport. Which sports do they talk about?**

10 **3 Listen again. Choose the correct words to complete the phrases.**

EP

1 enter / join a competition or tournament
2 win / score a prize, medal, game or match
3 score / win a goal or point
4 give / lose a game or match
5 win / beat the other team
6 have / join a go at something
7 join / enter a club
8 give / join (someone) the chance
9 miss / enter an opportunity to do something

**4 Complete the email with some of the phrases from Exercise 3.**

Hi Helen,

I've just got more information about the tournament at the local tennis club next week. I think I'm going to [1] ________ the ________ because I like tennis, and it looks like fun. The tournament isn't only for people who are good at tennis. They want to [2] ________ people the ________ to play, even if they aren't very good at it. Why don't you [3] ________ a ________ at playing a few matches? It's all friendly and just for fun, so it doesn't matter if you [4] ________ all your ________. But if you do very well, you might [5] ________ a ________!

I think they're looking for members for their club, too. I hope you can make it – we don't want to [6] ________ the ________ to take part.

Text me if you want to know more.

Emma

**5 Discuss the questions.**

1 Have you ever won a medal? How did you feel?
2 Have you ever scored a goal or a point in a game? How did you feel?
3 Which clubs have you joined or would you like to join? Why?

## READING

**1** **Look at the photo of Ntando Mahlangu. What does he do? Read the article quickly and check your ideas.**

# MEET Ntando Mahlangu, PARALYMPIAN

In 2016, aged 14, Ntando Mahlangu, an amputee runner, did what many people his age would love to do: he became a silver medallist at the Paralympics in Rio. Ntando is from South Africa, where, in 2012, he received his first blades – the equipment he wears which helps him run – from Jumping Kids. This organisation gives young people like Ntando the chance to do something they were unable to do before.

In an interview Ntando says his disability has never been a problem for him: 'I was always active.' But before he got his running blades, Ntando couldn't walk for long distances. He played football with his friends, but he was shorter than them 'and sometimes there were disadvantages,' he says. Just four years after getting his blades, however, Ntando was one of the youngest competitors at the Rio Paralympics and he now often takes part in competitions for para-athletes.

Ntando has been very successful. He's won several medals and has broken a world record in his sport. Although he's making excellent progress at the moment, Ntando doesn't like to say much about his talent. 'If I achieve my goals, I always say that I am honoured to do that,' he says. Ntando knows that some sportspeople would love to reach their goals but aren't able to. Ntando could do even better in future Paralympics in Tokyo and Paris. He would love to get there and win more medals but is realistic. He understands that there is always the possibility of injuring himself beforehand, like there is for any athlete. Some athletes say they're definitely running at the next Paralympics, but this is something Ntando doesn't say: he knows he can't be sure of that.

For Ntando, it's people who are more important than medals. He wants to show people that he respects others. If he can respect the person he's running next to, he says, then everyone watching him on TV at home can respect each other, too. Ntando believes anyone can make a change in society and that it isn't necessary to be the president of a country. At the time of writing, Ntando is planning to compete at another important para-athletics competition.

**Good luck, Ntando!**

## PREPARE FOR THE EXAM

### Reading Part 3

**2** **Read the article again and the questions below. For each question, choose the correct answer.**

**1** What do we find out about Ntando in the first two paragraphs?
**A** He feels upset that he can't do some activities.
**B** He does not let challenges worry him.
**C** He feels grateful for opportunities he is given.
**D** He would prefer to enter big competitions than small ones.

**2** What does Ntando say about his success?
**A** He prefers not to talk about it.
**B** He likes to share it with other athletes.
**C** He never expects to win a competition.
**D** He wants to encourage other people to do well, too.

**3** What is Ntando's attitude towards competing at future Paralympics?
**A** He hopes that he will not hurt himself there.
**B** He is unsure whether he wants to compete there.
**C** He wants to beat his last achievement there.
**D** He accepts that he may not get there.

**4** In the final paragraph, Ntando says he hopes
**A** to have an important role in his country one day.
**B** other people will follow his good behaviour.
**C** to run in as many competitions as he can.
**D** his fans will support his plans for the future.

**5** What would another athlete say about Ntando?
**A** He's good at all kinds of sports.
**B** He is disappointed when he doesn't win.
**C** He's a talented guy and nice, too.
**D** He'll improve even more with new blades.

» PREPARE FOR THE EXAM PAGE 122

**3** **Match the highlighted words in the article to the meanings.**

**1** people who are in a competition
**2** participates in an activity with other people
**3** has done something better than anyone has done before
**4** doing a lot of things or moving around a lot
**5** be in a race or competition

## TALKING POINTS

Why is it useful to have a positive attitude in life?
Do you think it's important to be competitive? Why?
What do you think makes someone want to be the best at something, such as a sport?

## GRAMMAR Present simple and continuous

**1** **Match the examples to the rules.**

1 This organisation **gives** young people like Ntando the chance to do something …
2 Some athletes say they**'re** definitely **running** at the next Paralympics.
3 He now often **takes** part in competitions for para-athletes.
4 He**'s making** excellent progress at the moment.
5 He **wants** to show people that he respects others.

We use the present simple:
**a** to talk about something that we do regularly.
**b** to talk about a fact, system or process.
**c** with state verbs (*want*, *like*, *love*, etc.) which describe what we like, think and feel.

We use the present continuous:
**d** to talk about things that are happening now.
**e** to talk about future plans and arrangements that we are sure about.

GRAMMAR REFERENCE AND PRACTICE PAGE 149

**2** **Choose the correct verb forms.**

1 Most athletes *begin* / *are beginning* their day with exercise.
2 Wow! This is an exciting final. Everyone *is playing* / *plays* so well.
3 I *meet* / *'m meeting* Maria later today.
4 I usually *am getting up* / *get up* at about 7 o'clock.
5 The new fitness coach speaks French and *is coming* / *comes* from Canada.
6 Our class *is visiting* / *visits* a castle tomorrow.
7 *Do you think* / *Are you thinking* you really know all your friends on your social media sites?
8 My brother *likes* / *is liking* the same music as you.

**3** **Read the sentences. Which have a mistake? Correct the mistakes.**

1 Tonight we go to the cinema.
2 I'm writing to invite you to a picnic in the park on Saturday.
3 Those flowers are smelling really lovely.
4 That's the reason why I speak to you today.
5 I'm really pleased you are visiting my country.
6 Su-Jay is wears his new trainers today.
7 This evening, I'm going to a beach party with my friends.
8 My dad's company is producing material for NASA.

**4** **Think about a famous sportsperson. Find out about him or her and make some notes. Present your sportsperson to the class. Try to use the present simple and continuous.**

*Garbiñe Muguruza is from Venezuela but now lives in Switzerland. She is a famous tennis player and plays for Spain because her father is Spanish. She posts regularly on her Instagram account and you can also follow her on Facebook. Next month, she's taking part in an important international tennis competition.*

## VOCABULARY Suffixes: *-ist*, *-er*, *-or*

**1** **Read the sentences and complete the words.**

1 Ntando runs. He is a runn____.
2 He competes in the Paralympics. He's a competit____.

**2** **Choose the correct suffix to make the words into nouns for people. Sometimes the spelling of the word changes when the suffix is added.**

| canoe | climb | football | sail |
|---|---|---|---|
| spectate | surf | swim | win |

-er    -ist    -or

**3** **Complete the words with the correct suffix.**

1 My sister is a soccer play____.
2 My dad was the oldest competit____ in the swimming race.
3 Every Sunday a group of cycl____ ride past our house.
4 We didn't win the game. We were the los____.
5 Thousands of football support____ travelled to London last week for the cup final.

**4** **Choose the correct word to complete the sentence.**

1 Shh! I'm watching the *final* / *finalist* of the rugby world cup. It's so exciting!
2 Even if I didn't win the competition, I was proud that I was a *final* / *finalist*.
3 He won the silver *medal* / *medallist*, but wanted the gold.
4 At the London Olympics, Gemma Gibbons became a silver *medal* / *medallist* in judo.

## WRITING An online comment

**1** **Ntando received his first blades from an organisation called Jumping Kids. There are many organisations that do similar work. Read a post on a school website about Runners Inc. What is it? Don't read the comments yet.**

# RUNNERS INC.

Runners Inc. gives children with leg amputations the chance to lead full and active lives by giving them special equipment to help them walk and run. At our school we're trying to raise £1,000 by the end of the year to donate to the organisation. What do you think we could do to raise the money? Post your ideas.

## COMMENTS

### ZOE

Why don't we organise a non-uniform day? We each donate £1 so that we don't have to wear our school uniform for one day. It's a great way to raise money for Runners Inc. and we get to wear our own cool clothes as well! In addition, we could all wear something green, because that's the organisation's colour. I'd really recommend that.

### NAT

Why not encourage people to do an activity like a sponsored run? We can ask our family and neighbours to give us £1 for each time we run around the school sports field. There are lots of runners in my school and most people like doing something for charity. Also, it's a really good way of telling the community about Runners Inc. What about posting it on social media? That would be helpful as well, in my opinion.

**2** **Read Zoe's and Nat's online comments. Then answer the questions.**

1. What does Zoe suggest?
2. What extra suggestion does she make?
3. How does she link her suggestions?
4. Which activity does Nat mention?
5. How many reasons does he give for his idea?
6. How does he link his reasons?

**3** **Read the *Prepare to write* box. What phrases do Zoe and Nat use to make suggestions? What other phrases could you use to suggest something?**

### PREPARE TO WRITE

**Suggestions and comments**

When you post your ideas online:

- explain your ideas and reasons clearly and link them, using phrases like *in addition*, *also*, *as well*.
- use different phrases for making suggestions.
- use positive words and phrases to recommend something.

**4** **Read the task below and plan your ideas.**

**We're planning a new sports club in this town.**

**We want ideas for sports for teenagers to do.**

- Suggest one sport the club should offer for teenagers.
- Explain why you think teenagers would enjoy this sport.
- Say why this sport would be good for the club.

**Send us your ideas today!**

**5** **Write your comment.**

- Use the tips in the *Prepare to write* box.
- Write about 70 words.
- Remember to check your spelling and grammar.

# 4 EXTREME WEATHER

A

B

C

D

## ABOUT YOU

What kinds of weather do you like/dislike?
How do you or your family check the weather forecast?
What is the weather usually like at this time of year where you live?

## VOCABULARY Extreme weather

**1** **Look at the photos. What is happening in each one? Which do you think is the scariest? Why?**

12 **2** **Listen to four people talking about extreme weather. Match each person to a photo.**

12 **3** **Listen again. Complete the sentences with a word from one of the boxes.**

EP

earthquake flood lightning snowstorm tornado

blew fell down flowed poured rose shook

**Speaker 1**

**1** The speaker talked about a ______.
**2** There was no power in the city possibly because the wind ______ so hard.

**Speaker 2**

**3** There was a ______ storm.
**4** The speaker saw a fire ______.

**Speaker 3**

**5** There was a ______ where the speaker lives.
**6** There was so much rain that the river ______ by two metres.
**7** It ______ for hours.
**8** Dirty water ______ along the street.

**Speaker 4**

**9** The speaker experienced a big ______ a few years ago.
**10** The ground ______ violently.
**11** Many buildings ______.

**4** **Match some of the words in Exercise 3 to the meanings.**

**1** rained a lot
**2** when wind moved and made currents of air
**3** bright light that you see in the sky during a storm
**4** when it snows very heavily
**5** a large amount of water covering an area in a way that is a problem
**6** an extremely dangerous wind that moves in a circle
**7** moved quickly from side to side
**8** (water) increased in level

**5** **What are the infinitives of *blew*, *fell down*, *rose* and *shook*?**

**6** **Discuss the questions.**

**1** What should you do in case of a flood, fire and earthquake?
**2** What was the last extreme weather event in your country?
**3** Have you ever been in an extreme weather event? What happened?

## READING

**1** **Read the fact file about bush fires in Australia. Answer the questions.**

1. When and why do bush fires happen?
2. How are the fires important to Australia?

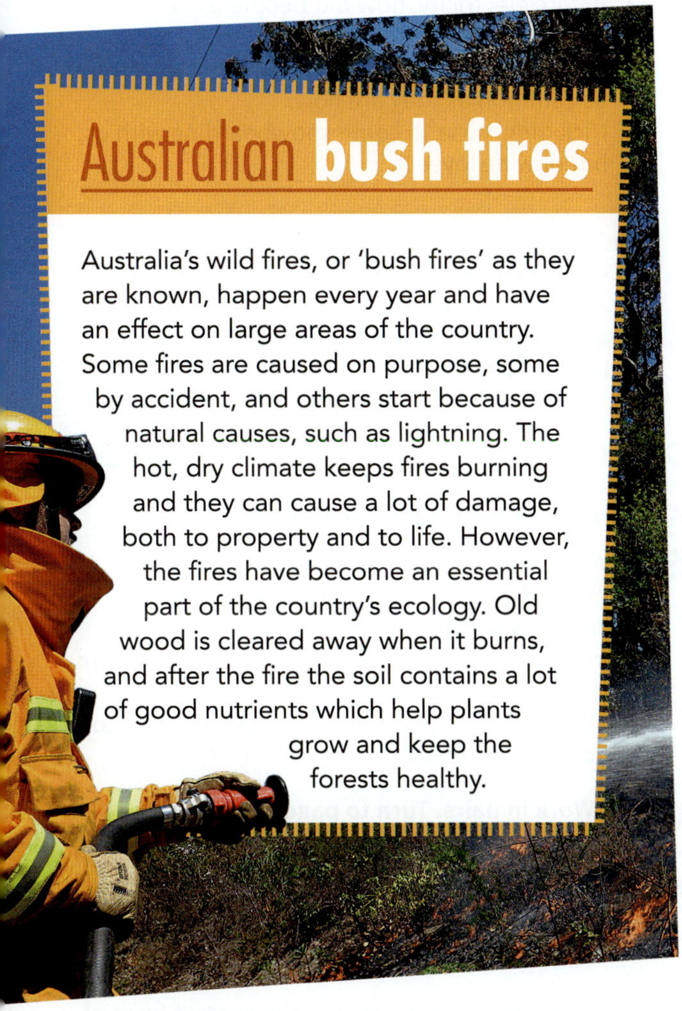

### Australian bush fires

Australia's wild fires, or 'bush fires' as they are known, happen every year and have an effect on large areas of the country. Some fires are caused on purpose, some by accident, and others start because of natural causes, such as lightning. The hot, dry climate keeps fires burning and they can cause a lot of damage, both to property and to life. However, the fires have become an essential part of the country's ecology. Old wood is cleared away when it burns, and after the fire the soil contains a lot of good nutrients which help plants grow and keep the forests healthy.

**2** **Read the article below quickly and decide on the best title (A–C). Don't worry about the spaces yet.**

**A** Firefighters in Australia take a break
**B** Canberra's hot weather is likely to continue
**C** Weather conditions create something unusual

## PREPARE FOR THE EXAM

### Reading Part 5

**3** **Look at the example space (0) at the bottom of the page and these possible answers. The correct answer is A. Why?**

**0** **A** number **B** sum **C** figure **D** total

**Complete sentences 1–3 with words B–D.**

1. The average rainfall for April is 70 mm but this year the ________ is much lower.
2. A huge ________ of money was needed to repair the damage caused by the storm.
3. The ________ number of bush fires in Australia last year was 50,000.

**4** **Read the article again and for each question, choose the correct answer.**

| | A | B | C | D |
|---|---|---|---|---|
| **1** | **A** handled | **B** created | **C** succeeded | **D** designed |
| **2** | **A** piece | **B** land | **C** area | **D** part |
| **3** | **A** reach | **B** get | **C** arrive | **D** travel |
| **4** | **A** improved | **B** raised | **C** lifted | **D** increased |
| **5** | **A** call | **B** tell | **C** describe | **D** believe |
| **6** | **A** action | **B** issue | **C** event | **D** challenge |

» PREPARE FOR THE EXAM PAGE 125

**5** **Read the article again and answer the questions.**

1. Why were so many houses destroyed?
2. Why couldn't the firefighters put out the fires?
3. What caused the fire tornado?

**6** **Match the highlighted words in the article to the meanings.**

1. the part of something which is furthest from the centre
2. happened at the same time as something
3. strong
4. very unusual or uncommon
5. damaged totally

### TALKING POINTS

When do people talk about the weather?
What problems do extreme weather conditions cause for people? Why?
Will people ever be able to control the weather? Why? / Why not?

13

In the past, summer fires were common in Australia. Now, because of climate change, there's an even higher [0] ________ than there used to be. And they're larger, too. Recently, one fire grew so **powerful** that it [1] ________ a tornado nearly 500 metres wide. It **destroyed** many homes in the capital city, Canberra. These unlucky houses were situated less than 100 metres from a large [2] ________ of pine trees on the **edge** of the city.

Several individual fires started burning and, because it was difficult for firefighters to [3] ________ them, they continued to burn. When the wind speed suddenly [4] ________ a few days later, the fires joined together. Scientists now [5] ________ this Australia's first 'fire tornado'. This was an extremely **rare** [6] ________ in Australia's history and was produced by storms which **accompanied** the fire.

## GRAMMAR Past simple

**1** **Match the examples to the rules.**

1 In the past, fires during the summer months **were** common in Australia.
2 It **destroyed** many homes in the capital city, Canberra.
3 Last summer, one fire **grew** so powerful that it **created** a tornado nearly 500 metres wide.

We use the past simple to talk about:
**a** a single completed past action or event.
**b** something that happened at a particular time in the past.
**c** things that happened regularly in the past.

**2** **Look at the past simple verbs in Exercise 1. What are their infinitive forms?**

**3** **Complete the text with the correct form of the verbs in brackets.**

### SURVIVAL ACADEMY
### The 24-Hour Family Course

Mum [0] *booked* Dad and me on this course as a surprise! I [1] ______ (not feel) nervous before we [2] ______ (get) there because I love surprises. It was great fun and we both [3] ______ (learn) so much. There were five other people about my age, and each [4] ______ (come) with one parent – mostly super-keen dads! The course [5] ______ (not begin) until midday on the Saturday and [6] ______ (include) one night outside under the stars. They [7] ______ (give) us our own backpack in which we [8] ______ (carry) all the things we [9] ______ (need). We [10] ______ (hike) through some difficult countryside and we even [11] ______ (cross) a river at one point. They [12] ______ (teach) us how to build and light a fire. We [13] ______ (dig) for food, [14] ______ (build) our own basic sleeping accommodation, and they [15] ______ (tell) us how to protect ourselves in extreme weather. [16] '______ (you sleep) well?' Dad asked me the next morning. I did, as I was exhausted! The next morning was all about 'self-rescue' – they [17] ______ (put) us in different groups and we [18] ______ (find) our way back to the main building. It was the best present ever!

## *used to*

**4** **Match the examples to the rules.**

1 My family **used to live** just outside Canberra.
2 As kids, we **used to spend** every August with our grandparents.
3 Before electricity, how **did** people **use to keep** warm during the long, cold winters?
4 Generally speaking, forest fires **didn't use to be** as common as they are now.
5 Nick **didn't use to come** snowboarding with us, but now he loves it.

We use *used to* to talk about:
**a** something that happened or didn't happen regularly in the past.
**b** a permanent situation in the past that is no longer the case.

» **GRAMMAR REFERENCE AND PRACTICE PAGE 150**

**5** **Correct the mistake in each sentence.**

1 When we were kids, we use to play together.
2 When you were younger, were you watching cartoons on TV?
3 In my country, it is used to rain more often than it does now.
4 The film is about a shop where people used to going in the 1980s.

**6** » **Work in pairs. Turn to page 135.**

## VOCABULARY Phrasal verbs

**1** EP **Complete the sentences with the correct form of the phrasal verbs in the box.**

| blow away | burn down | clear up |
|---|---|---|
| come out | fall down | put out |

1 The shop we used to go to for sweets ______ in a fire last month and they aren't going to rebuild it.
2 When we were camping, we didn't use to ______ our camp fire at night, but it was quite safe.
3 I left my essay on the wall outside for a minute and all the pages ______ in the wind!
4 It was pouring earlier today, but then the sun ______ again.
5 After a week of rain, the weather ______.
6 During the earthquake, many buildings on the high street ______.

**2** **Write sentences using each of the phrasal verbs from Exercise 1. Read your sentences to a partner.**

# LISTENING

1 What do you think you should do if you get lost in snow?

## PREPARE FOR THE EXAM

### Listening Part 4

2 (14) You will hear an interview with a teenage boy called Jake, who got lost on a snowy mountain in Oregon, USA. Read the six questions. Then listen and try to answer the questions, choosing A, B or C.

1 What happened to Jake's skis?
- **A** He carried them down the mountain.
- **B** He left them where they came off.
- **C** He hid them both in the deep snow.

2 Jake stopped walking down the mountain because
- **A** it was too dark for him to reach the bottom.
- **B** there was still a lot of snow falling.
- **C** he couldn't remember what to do from the TV shows.

3 What was good about Jake's snow cave?
- **A** It was built on flat ground.
- **B** It allowed him to remove his gloves.
- **C** It kept him completely out of the wind.

4 Who was out looking for Jake that evening?
- **A** a single helicopter
- **B** groups of people on foot
- **C** both of his parents

5 What part of Bear Grylls' advice did Jake follow in the woods?
- **A** search for tracks in the snow
- **B** look for lights to aim at
- **C** walk on your hands and knees

6 While Jake was missing, his mother
- **A** tried to contact him on her cellphone.
- **B** thought that not enough people were looking for him.
- **C** stayed positive by thinking about him.

(14) Compare your answers with a partner. Then listen again and check.

» PREPARE FOR THE EXAM PAGE 130

3 What would you do in Jake's situation?

# SPEAKING Talking about past experiences

1 (15) Read the questions. Then listen to Mariann's answers. What verb forms does she use to talk about her past experiences?

1 What was your favourite outdoor activity as a child?
2 How much time did you spend outdoors when you were younger?
3 Tell us about the things you did during good weather.

2 (15) Complete the text with the missing verbs. Then listen again and check.

Mariann [0]*used to live* in the mountains. She [1] ........ in the snow, and every winter, she [2] ........ a snowman with her friends. In the summer, she [3] ........ with her grandparents, who had a farm. When the weather was good, she [4] ........ in the river and [5] ........ flowers in the fields.

3 (15) Read the *Prepare to speak* box. Then listen to Mariann's answers again. Which phrases does she use?

## PREPARE TO SPEAK

### Answering questions (1)

**Asking, when you are not sure you have understood**
Do you mean ... ?

**Gaining time to think about your answer**

| | |
|---|---|
| Let me think. ... | Well, ... |
| Let me see. ... | Um ... |

**Adding more information**

| | |
|---|---|
| ... that kind of thing. | ..., actually. |

## PREPARE FOR THE EXAM

### Speaking Part 1

4 Ask and answer the questions in Exercise 1. Say as much as you can about your own past experiences. Use phrases from the *Prepare to speak* box.

# LIFE SKILLS COLLABORATION

## WORKING AS A TEAM

### LIFE SKILLS

**Working as a team**

Projects and other activities can be easier if we work with other people as a team. We can do tasks more quickly if we share the work and help each other. Different group members can combine their talents and work on tasks they enjoy, while teaching other people how to improve.

**1** **Ask and answer the questions with a partner.**

1. How often do you work in teams in your classes?
2. Do you do any team activities in your free time?
3. Do you like working in teams? Why? / Why not?

**2** **Read the text on the opposite page quickly. Why does Jenny enjoy team projects? What role does she like?**

**3** **Match the sentences with the introduction or tips 1–5 in the text.**

1. Some people may want to choose tasks they are good at doing.
2. Everyone has to be responsible and complete their own tasks.
3. If you don't understand the instructions, check with the teacher.
4. Think carefully about the best order for doing the different tasks.
5. When team members don't work well together, projects are more difficult.
6. It's more successful if team members each have a special part to play in the team.

**4** **Match the highlighted words in the text to the meanings.**

1. look carefully for something
2. making you feel nervous or worried
3. divide a thing into smaller parts
4. use something in a careless way
5. any time or always

A

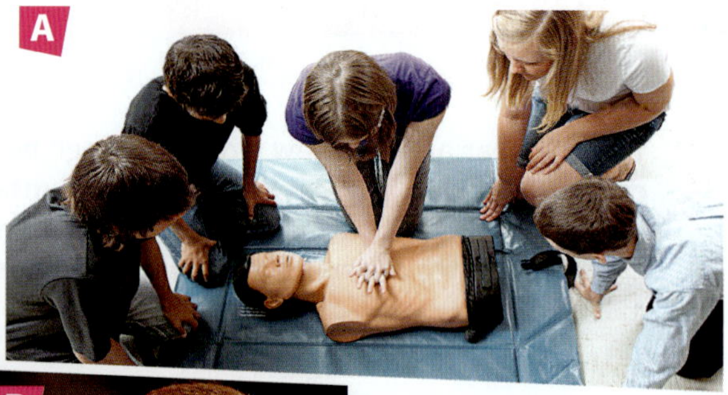

B

C

**5** **Look at photos A–C. What project topics could they represent?**

16 **6** **Listen to a conversation. Which topic from the photos does David like for the team project?**

16 **7** **Listen again and complete the sentences.**

1. Anna thinks they should do a project about …
2. David's mum thinks he should stay …
3. David's mum suggests that he asks his teacher …
4. David's first idea for the group project was …
5. Last year, David took a course about …

**8** **Read the *Useful language* phrases. Complete them with the words in the box.**

| about | could | know |
|---|---|---|
| sure | think | topic |

### USEFUL LANGUAGE

**Discussing ideas**

1. I ________ we should make a list.
2. I don't ________. Let me think.
3. What ________ collecting money?
4. I'm not ________. I can't decide.
5. How about a different ________?
6. That ________ be a good idea.

# TEAM WORK *tips*

**If you're like me, you do a lot of team projects at school. For example, last term, I did a school presentation about recycling with some classmates and it was much easier and faster than doing everything alone. I enjoy team projects because I'm a sociable person. I like sharing ideas with other people and I get bored when I work alone. Of course, team activities aren't always easy. In fact, they can be stressful if people don't know how to work well together. Here are some tips to make team work easier.**

By Jenny Larkins

## 1 Know the goals:

Make sure everyone understands the goal of the project. If you're doing a class project, you need to check the teacher's instructions carefully and ask questions whenever something isn't clear. There's a popular saying: 'If you don't know where you're going, you probably won't get there.'

## 2 Assign roles:

Teams work better when people have roles. For example, there should be a leader who helps everyone make decisions. There might also be a note-taker who writes down the team's ideas during meetings, and a time-keeper to make sure people don't waste time chatting. That was my role for the recycling project! Other roles might be fact-checker or group representative for speaking to the class.

## 3 Divide the work:

For large projects, we can divide the work into smaller tasks for particular people. Team members can choose tasks they do well or enjoy. I always volunteer to find information because I like to read and search for facts on the internet. Other people might be good at writing or making computer presentations. Of course, you shouldn't always do the same task. It's good to try new things, even if they're difficult!

## 4 Make a plan:

After you split up the work, write down a plan on paper. You can use a chart or a calendar to help you. List all the tasks and think about when each one must be finished. For example, I had to find the facts for my recycling project before my teammates could start the presentation. For that reason, it's important for everyone to follow the plan. And if you can't finish your part on time, tell the others as soon as possible.

## 5 Be respectful:

When you're working in a team, respect is essential. Listen when others are speaking and don't interrupt. Do your fair share, so other team members don't have to do your work for you. Finally, try to stay positive and enjoy yourself. Everything is easier when you're having fun!

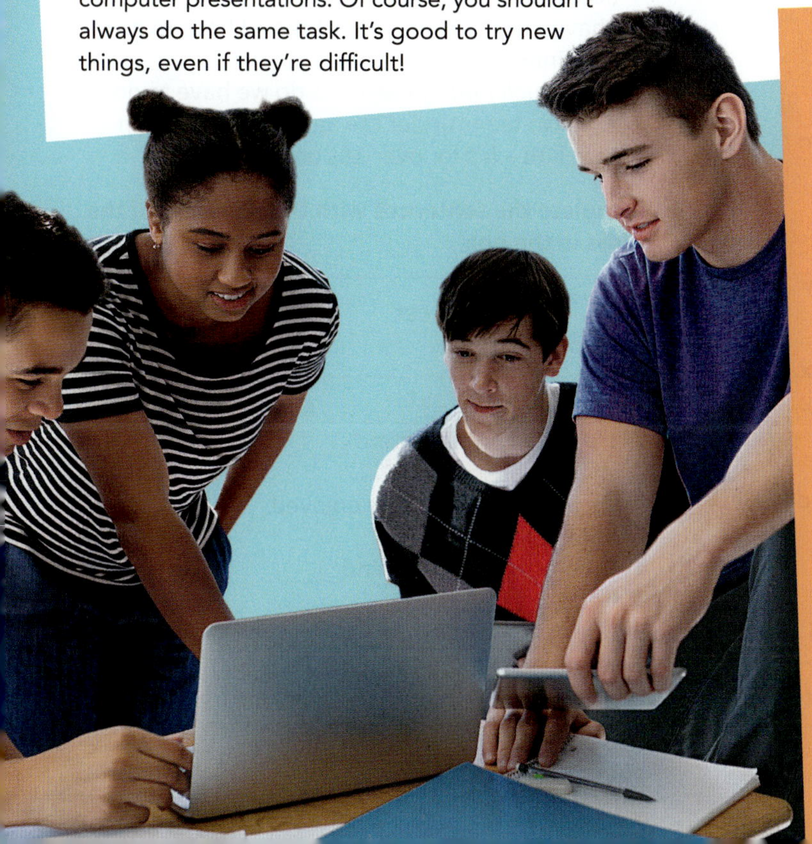

## PROJECT

***A team presentation***

**Work in a team of four to prepare a class presentation. Choose one of the ideas below or discuss other ideas with your teammates. Then use the checklist to help you work as a team.**

- Keeping a local park clean
- Staying safe when you do sports
- Collecting money for disaster victims
- Healthy eating

**1** What role will each person play in the team?
**2** How are you going to divide the topic and tasks?
**3** What task does each person want to do? Why?
**4** How long will each of the tasks take to complete?
**5** Which tasks need to be done first? And after that?
**6** How can you show respect for other team members?

**Present your work to the class.**

# REVIEW 1 UNITS 1–4

## VOCABULARY

**1 Match the sentence halves.**

1 The shop exchanged the item
2 We scored a goal in the last minute and
3 The young tennis player was confident
4 It poured with rain all night and I'm not surprised that
5 Mike is a talented canoeist
6 I didn't receive the letter in time, so

a and she won a medal.
b there were a lot of floods.
c I missed the opportunity to go on the trip.
d we beat the other team.
e because I had a receipt.
f and he's just entered an international competition.

**2 Complete each conversation with the correct form of one of the pairs of words in the box.**

| | |
|---|---|
| burn down / cruel | forecast / sensible |
| give /snowstorm | join / serve |
| miss / promotion | |

1 **A:** Did you see the ________ on TV last night?
**B:** Yes, it would be ________ to take an umbrella. It's going to rain.

2 **A:** Did you know the girl who ________ you in the shop?
**B:** Yes, she ________ the tennis club last week.

3 **A:** That's the house that ________ last week.
**B:** I know. I think someone did it deliberately. That's really ________!

4 **A:** That shop has ________ for students on Thursdays.
**B:** Well, we'd better go there. We don't want to ________ the opportunity of a bargain!

5 **A:** There was a heavy ________ on Sunday, wasn't there? We couldn't go anywhere!
**B:** Yes, but it ________ me the chance to do my homework.

**3 Complete the sentences with the words in the box.**

| | | | |
|---|---|---|---|
| lightning | refund | send back | sociable |

1 There was a really bad storm, with thunder and ________.
2 I took the item back to the store and got a ________.
3 We had to ________ the game because it didn't work on our computer.
4 Tess loves being with other people – she's very ________.

**4 Unscramble the words and complete the sentences.**

| | | |
|---|---|---|
| sineeivts | eols a mtcah | |
| eliltnetnig | lrliebae | iosdcutn |
| srie | uclkynu | lsdkeii |

1 If Mel says she'll do something, she will. She's very ________.
2 Angela always knows the answer – she's really ________.
3 Our team is the best – we didn't ________ last year!
4 You can't say anything to Michelle. She's very ________ and is easily upset.
5 This is an expensive bag, but the shop gave me a really big ________ on it.
6 It rained for days and we watched the water ________ and get closer to our house.
7 Some people think it's ________ to walk under ladders.
8 I ________ shopping and I hate shopping centres!

## GRAMMAR

**1 Choose the correct word to complete the sentences.**

1 Lucy didn't buy *any* / *much* shoes on Saturday.
2 Sophia wants to buy *some* / *any* new pens for school.
3 There are *plenty* / *many* of places that sell accessories for phones.
4 I haven't got *much* / *many* time – I have to go in 10 minutes.
5 How *much* / *many* exercises do we have to do?
6 *Any* / *No* teens under the age of 18 can watch that film – it's for over-18s only.

**2 Complete the sentences with the *-ing* form of the verbs in the box.**

| | | | |
|---|---|---|---|
| do | drive | eat | join |
| spend | study | | |

1 Jason considered ________ a football club.
2 My mum couldn't stand ________ sports when she was at school.
3 Jasmine and her mum enjoyed ________ time together.
4 My brother doesn't mind ________ me to your house.
5 She imagined herself ________ an ice cream.
6 ________ for exams can be really hard.

**3** **Complete the sentences with the correct form of the verbs. Use the present simple or present continuous.**

1 Mara ________ (enjoy) going for a run every morning.
2 Look! The weather ________ (get) worse.
3 I ________ (know) the answer to the question.
4 It's a really expensive bike. It ________ (cost) over $400.
5 She ________ (read) a book on her phone at the moment.
6 Marcia and Maisy ________ (meet) their friends at the shopping centre tonight.

**4** **Complete the article with the past simple form of the verbs in the box.**

| affect | be (x2) | burn | die | help |
|---|---|---|---|---|
| lose | post | take | work | |

**EVERY YEAR IN AUSTRALIA** there are a lot of bushfires. In 2013, there [1] ________ a particularly bad one that [2] ________ an area called the Blue Mountains, very close to Sydney. My friend Olivia lives there and her house was very close to the fire. She said that the fire [3] ________ for a long time and lots of people [4] ________ their houses.
Sadly, some animals [5] ________ too. But the fire services [6] ________ amazing and they [7] ________ long, hard hours to try to stop the fires. Olivia [8] ________ lots of photos during the fires and she [9] ________ them on her social media pages. She also [10] ________ to raise money to give to the people who lost their homes in the fire.

**5** **Choose the correct option.**

1 I used to spend *much* / *a lot of* money on clothes.
2 Many people are tired *in* / *of* spending so much time looking at screens.
3 Remember that we *meet* / *are meeting* at the shopping centre at 8 pm tonight.
4 Could you give us the same discount we *use* / *used* to get?

**6** **Correct the mistake in each sentence.**

1 Last night, I bought a shirt and a trousers online.
2 My best friend is very good in sailing.
3 I really like buy clothes online.
4 When we were younger, we use to visit my grandparents every weekend.

## PREPARE FOR THE EXAM

### Reading Part 5

**1** **For each question, choose the correct answer.**

#### Online shopping

Online shopping first **(1)** ________ available in the mid 1990s after the World Wide Web was created. Many people first began shopping on the internet to **(2)** ________ less expensive items like books, and they found the service extremely convenient. It **(3)** ________ people the chance to shop without leaving the comfort of their home.
Goods arrived quickly and people could **(4)** ________ items back if there was a problem. They received **(5)** ________ of their money quickly, and website security also improved. Soon, everyone was **(6)** ________ a go at shopping on the internet and the number of online shops quickly increased. Today, online shopping is more popular than ever and sites offer fantastic discounts which aren't always found in high street shops.

| | A | B | C | D |
|---|---|---|---|---|
| **1** | started | became | turned | grew |
| **2** | charge | spend | take | purchase |
| **3** | provided | served | gave | presented |
| **4** | change | send | return | put |
| **5** | refunds | prices | receipts | promotions |
| **6** | making | going | having | doing |

### Reading Part 6

**2** **For each question, write the correct answer. Write one word for each gap.**

#### Is competition a good thing in sport?

There can only be one answer to this question: yes! Of course, it feels great when you **(1)** ________ scoring goals or your team wins the match. But you don't have to be good **(2)** ________ sport to benefit from it. Competing against others teaches you **(3)** ________ lot of things about yourself and other people. It makes you try harder and become more sociable. It teaches you to win and lose well and no longer be afraid **(4)** ________ trying new things – nothing is ever as scary as it seems. When you work hard to achieve your aims, you feel more confident, whether you are successful **(5)** ________ not. Any negative feelings you used **(6)** ________ have about your ability to achieve whatever you want will disappear. Instead you'll start feeling proud of everything you've become.

# 5 YOU MADE IT!

## ABOUT YOU

**04 Watch the video and then answer the questions.**

Do you like making things? Why? / Why not?
Do you think it's important to learn manual skills?
What was the last handmade item you bought?

## VOCABULARY Verbs for making things

**1** **Look at the photos and describe what you can see. What is the object now and what was it before?**

18 **2** **Listen to three teens, Mark, Leah and Will. Match each speaker to one of the photos.**

18 **3** **Match the sentence halves. Then listen again and check.**

EP

Mark

**1** My brother Jake was **fixing** the bike
**2** When we **create** something new
**3** We all know it's important

**a** to **recycle**.
**b** a couple of years ago.
**c** from something old, it's really satisfying.

Leah

**4** One of the trainers had a hole in it,
**5** We had to **customise** them,
**6** First, we **designed** them on the computer and thought about
**7** I drew a cool pattern with coloured pens,

**d** how we wanted them to look.
**e** and I decided to **sew** some bits of material on, too.
**f** you know, make them our own.
**g** so I had to **mend** it first.

Will

**8** We decided
**9** Then, we thought it would be a great idea

**h** to **decorate** it.
**i** to **rebuild** it.

**4** **Match the words in Exercise 3 to the meanings.**

**1** make something look more attractive by putting things on it or around it
**2** make something
**3** repair clothes that are broken or torn
**4** use something again and not throw it away
**5** draw or plan something before making it
**6** change something to make it the way someone wants
**7** join things together with a needle and thread
**8** build something again
**9** repair something that isn't working correctly

**5** **Ask and answer the questions with a partner.**

**1** What was the last thing you created?
**2** Who generally fixes things in your home?
**3** Have you ever decorated or customised any of your possessions?
**4** Do you think it is important to recycle things? Why? / Why not?

## READING

**1** **Look at the title of the article and the photos. What do you think the article is about? Read the text quickly and check your ideas. Ignore the spaces.**

19

# From hobby TO JOB

**Twins Chet and Betts DeHart have achieved what many young people only dream of – they've made it in the fashion world. When they were just 15, they created the streetwear brand Lucid FC, which now sells worldwide.**

As kids, the boys loved trainers. [1] ________ Slowly, they built up a collection. Betts, the twin with the business brain, knew all about the trainers he wore, how many were sold and where they were being produced. [2] ________ He set up a YouTube channel, Sole Brothers, where he reviewed trainers in the twins' collection.

While they were still at school, the twins decided to make their own trainers. They sold their collection to raise money for their brand, communicated with manufacturers overseas and finally released a shoe. Unfortunately, it didn't sell well. [3] ________ The result of these conversations led to the production of a shoe decorated with a logo, which looked good and became popular.

After a couple of years, the boys decided to rename their brand Lucid FC and launch their first collection, which included items of clothing. While they were studying the fashion business at college, they looked for manufacturers who could make their products. [4] ________ The next challenge was to find stores to sell their products. The twins were shopping at the fashionable VFiles clothing shop when they were offered jobs and their manager later decided to stock the brand.

Celebrities were soon wearing it, too. One of their first customers, Rihanna, was wearing a Lucid FC jacket and cap at a basketball match in 2015 when someone took a photo of her. [5] ________ Today, the business continues to grow and the brothers have great plans for the future.

### PREPARE FOR THE EXAM

**Reading Part 4**

**2** **Five sentences have been removed from the text. For each question, choose the correct answer. There are three extra sentences which you do not need to use.**

**A** The boys refused to give up, however, and continued to talk to possible producers.
**B** It was immediately successful.
**C** They spent the money they earned in their part-time jobs on really good ones.
**D** Thanks to its publication, people noticed the brand.
**E** It wasn't the most attractive design that the twins produced.
**F** Meanwhile, Chet was the creative twin.
**G** He was pleased with the progress they were making.
**H** This wasn't easy, but they eventually found two.

**3** **Match the highlighted words in the article to the meanings.**

1 make a product or products available for the first time
2 gave his opinions about something
3 a type of product made by a particular company
4 increased, developed
5 companies which produce products in large numbers

### TALKING POINTS

Which of *your* hobbies could become a job in the future?
What are the advantages and disadvantages of having a job which is also your hobby?

## GRAMMAR Past simple and continuous

**1 Match the examples to the rules.**

1 One of their first customers, Rihanna, **was wearing** a Lucid FC jacket and cap at a basketball match in 2015 when someone **took** a photo of her.
2 While the boys **were studying** the fashion business at college, they looked for manufacturers …
3 Celebrities **were** soon **wearing** it, too.
4 Together, at the age of 15, they **created** the streetwear brand Lucid FC.

**a** We use the past simple to talk about completed actions and things that happened in the past.
**b** We use the past continuous to talk about actions and situations in progress at a certain time in the past.
**c** We can also use the past continuous to describe the background to a story.
**d** We can use the past continuous for an action in progress that is interrupted by a short action in the past simple.

» GRAMMAR REFERENCE AND PRACTICE PAGE 151

**2 Choose the correct verb form.**

1 When I *walked* / *was walking* near the river, I saw some beautiful flowers.
2 Freddie *spent* / *was spending* three months in Nepal last year.
3 My mum *fixed* / *was fixing* my computer for me last night. Now it works!
4 I'm sorry I didn't call you sooner but I *was studying* / *studied* all afternoon.
5 I *read* / *was reading* my text messages, when my doorbell rang.
6 They filmed us while we *are* / *were playing* in the garden.

**3 Complete the description with the correct form of the verbs in brackets.**

I [0] *found* (find) some interesting shells when I [1] ________ (walk) along the beach. I [2] ________ (pick) them up and [3] ________ (put) them in my pocket. Then I noticed that my dog [4] ________ (run) to me with a piece of wood in his mouth. When he got to me, he [5] ________ (drop) it and, of course, wanted me to throw it again. But while I [6] ________ (look) at it, I realised that it was a leg from an old chair. By the time I was ready to go home, I [7] ________ (have) quite a collection of things from the beach! While I [8] ________ (clean) them later, I [9] ________ (have) the idea of creating a piece of art with them. I [10] ________ (take) a photo of the finished piece and uploaded it to the internet.

## VOCABULARY Time adverbs

**1 Read the example. How many actions are there? Underline the adverbs that tell us when each action happened.**

She completed the fashion course, then she worked for a small company. Later, she started her own business.

**2 Choose the correct adverbs.**

I wanted to make a birthday card for a friend. [1]*First / Suddenly*, I went shopping and bought the card and other materials, and [2]*finally / then* I looked at some magazines and decided what I was going to do. [3]*Next / First*, I drew a picture of a cat because my friend loves them. I was doing this when [4]*finally / suddenly* there was a knock at the door. It was my friend! I had to hide everything quickly! I finished making her card [5]*later / next*, after she went home. [6]*Next / Finally*, I gave her the card on her birthday and she loved it!

**3 You are going to tell a partner about something interesting or exciting that happened to you. Prepare your ideas. Use the adverbs in the box and the ideas below, or your own ideas.**

EP

| finally | first | later | next |
|---|---|---|---|
| then | suddenly | | |

a visit to a city
a problem that you solved
a difficulty with a friend
a surprise from a friend
a trip to the cinema or a concert

**4 Tell your partner what happened to you. Use adverbs from Exercise 3.**

# WRITING A story (1)

**1** **Do you enjoy reading stories? What makes a story interesting?**

**2** **Read Evie's story quickly. How many people had the same sunglasses?**

## 'The same sunglasses' by Evie

My brother and I were planning a holiday to Spain and we wanted some good sunglasses. Last week we decided to go to the shopping mall. We were walking past our favourite shop, when I saw they had a sale! First, we tried on lots of pairs of designer label sunglasses. Next, we each picked out a pair. We both chose the same pair of really cool sunglasses. When we were leaving the shop, we saw our best friends, Poppy and Harvey. Suddenly, we started laughing at each other because we were all wearing the same pink and blue sunglasses! It was very funny!

**3** **Read the *Prepare to write* box. Then read sentences 1–3 below.**

**Do they come from the beginning, middle or end of Evie's story? Read the story again to check.**

**1** We were all wearing the same sunglasses.
**2** We each picked out a pair.
**3** We were planning a holiday to Spain.

### PREPARE TO WRITE

**A story (1)**

- At the beginning of a story, you can introduce the characters, say what they were doing, and describe the place or the weather.
- In the middle, you describe all the events that happened.
- At the end, you describe the final event. Often the final event solves a problem, or is surprising in some way. Say how the characters felt at the end.

**4** **Read Evie's story again. Find:**

**1** three verbs in the past simple
**2** three verbs in the past continuous
**3** three adverbs which say when things happened

### PREPARE FOR THE EXAM

**Writing Part 2 (A story)**

**5** **Read the task. Then plan your ideas and make some notes. Use the ideas below to help you.**

Your English teacher has asked you to write a story.
Your story must begin with this sentence:
*I decided to make a gift for my friend.*

- Who are the characters?
- What are the main events?
- What happens in the end?
- Why did you want to make the gift?

**6** **Compare your ideas with a partner. Can you improve your plan?**

**7** **Write your story.**

- Use the tips in the *Prepare to write* box.
- Write about 100 words.
- Remember to check your spelling and grammar.

» PREPARE FOR THE EXAM PAGE 127

# 6 TAKE CARE OF YOURSELF

## ABOUT YOU

Have you ever had to help someone who was hurt?
What did you do?
When did you last have a day off school because you were ill?

## VOCABULARY Health verbs

**1** **Look at the photos. What's wrong with the people?**

**2** **Read the quiz. Check the meaning of the words.**

EP

**1** If you **burn** your hand on a hot pan, you should …
**A** put some ice on your hand.
**B** put some butter on your hand.
**C** put your hand under cool water.

**2** If you **cut** your hand with a knife, you should …
**A** hold your hand in the air.
**B** put pressure on the area and then clean it with cold water.
**C** call a doctor.

**3** If your nose starts to **bleed**, you should …
**A** put your head back.
**B** hold the top of your nose firmly between your thumb and a finger.
**C** put your head forward and **blow your nose**.

**4** If you look at a screen for a long time, you must …
**A** **blink** regularly.
**B** turn off the lights in your room.
**C** wear glasses.

**5** You are at the cinema, and your friend starts **coughing**. You should …
**A** hit them on the back.
**B** offer them a sweet or a drink.
**C** give them a bar of chocolate.

**6** If you **injure** your foot while you are playing football, you should …
**A** change your shoes.
**B** continue kicking the ball.
**C** stop playing and rest for a few days until you **recover**.

**7** Your dad says his back **aches** after exercising. He should …
**A** always take an aspirin before going to bed.
**B** relax in a hot bath.
**C** go to the hospital.

**8** You're in class and you feel that you're going to **yawn**. You should …
**A** tell the teacher that you feel a bit bored.
**B** **breathe** in through your nose and out through your mouth.
**C** put your hand on your chest and feel your heart **beating**.

**3** **Do the quiz with your partner.**

20 **4** **Listen to a podcast and see how many answers in the quiz you got right.**

**5** **Complete the sentences with the correct form of words from the quiz.**

1. After an hour of running, my leg muscles really ________.
2. Be careful with that sharp knife or you might ________ yourself.
3. When I had something in my eye, my dad told me to ________ a few times.
4. My friend ________ her hand while she was ironing her clothes.
5. There was silence, the music started and then somebody ________. Very annoying!
6. When I was playing basketball, I fell over and ________ my foot.
7. Sometimes you ________ when you're tired or bored.
8. When we run or do exercise, we ________ more quickly.
9. Last year I had the flu and it took me ages to ________. I was off school for two weeks!
10. I was really excited and I could feel my heart ________.
11. The ball hit me hard in the face and my nose began to ________.
12. My mum had a really bad cold last month. She was sneezing and ________ all day.

## READING

1 How many hours sleep do you get most nights? How many hours do you think you should get?

2 Read the title of the article. Which of the topics do you think it will discuss? Read the article quickly to check your ideas.

- ☐ How to get to sleep
- ☐ How much sleep you need
- ☐ The true meaning of dreams
- ☐ Looking at your mobile phone
- ☐ Reading a book at bedtime

21

# SCREEN TIME at BEDTIME

**Do you find yourself yawning all day at school? You probably need more sleep – according to doctors, teenagers have to get at least nine hours' sleep a night. However, it's not just how much sleep you get that's important. What you do before you go to bed also has a huge effect on how you feel the next day. If you spend time chatting to someone on social media, or reading a book on your e-reader, you are not alone. However, you ought to reduce your screen time at night. Although scientists are only just beginning to understand the full effects, the main message is that using devices like phones or tablets before bedtime is not good for your health.**

**A** All devices' screens give out a large amount of blue light. That isn't a problem unless you want to go to sleep. This blue light affects the body's production of the sleep hormone, melatonin, which can change your sleep patterns, or circadian rhythms. So it isn't just getting to sleep that becomes hard, but the quality of your sleep also suffers. The result is that you can wake up several times during the night, and have difficulty getting up in the morning.

**B** Sleep is food for the brain, so not sleeping well can be a serious problem for anyone, but is especially bad for teenagers, because their brains are still developing. When you don't sleep well, it can be difficult to concentrate at school, which makes it harder to learn and get good grades. It can also affect your mood, making you feel sad or anxious.

**C** So, it's clear you shouldn't use your phone or tablet before you go to sleep. Why not leave your phone in another room? You mustn't worry about your friends. Nothing on social media is so important that it can't wait a few hours! You should rediscover paper books and enjoy feeling tired and sleepy before bedtime rather than wondering why your best friend hasn't liked your photo! How will you wake up? You don't have to use the alarm on your phone. Go and buy yourself an old-fashioned alarm clock!

**D** The negative effects that screen time is having on sleep has been in the news a lot recently, so manufacturers of smartphones and tablets have added a feature to their devices that can help reduce these. Most new phones have a night-time setting that changes the colour of the screen so that it gives out less blue light. So, if you really can't avoid going onto social media at bedtime, you ought to think about turning on this setting on your phone.

3 Match the titles to paragraphs A–D. There is one extra title that you don't need.

1 What are technology companies doing about this?
2 The dangers of not getting a good night's sleep
3 What you should eat before you go to bed
4 How to reduce your screen time
5 The science of sleep and technology use

4 Match the highlighted words in the article to the meanings.

1 an important part or characteristic of something
2 the way you feel
3 think about the thing you are doing and nothing else
4 pieces of electronic equipment, like phones or tablets
5 trying to understand the reason for something

### TALKING POINTS

What was the last thing you did before you went to sleep last night?
Do you have a routine before going to sleep?
Do you think you should change your bedtime routine? In what ways?

## GRAMMAR Modals: Obligation, necessity and advice (1)

**1** **Read the examples. Then complete the rules with the verbs in the examples.**

1 Teenagers **have to** get at least nine hours' sleep a night.
2 You **don't have to** use the alarm on your phone.
3 You **mustn't** worry about your friends.
4 You **ought to** reduce your screen time at night.
5 You **should** rediscover books.
6 It's clear you **shouldn't** use your phone or tablet before you go to sleep.

We can use modal verbs to express obligation, necessity and advice. We use:

**a** *should* and ________ to say that something is a good idea.
**b** ________ to say that something is a bad idea.
**c** ________ to say that something is necessary.
**d** ________ to say that something is not necessary.
**e** ________ to say it is very important not to do something.

» GRAMMAR REFERENCE AND PRACTICE PAGE 152

22 **2** **Listen. Choose the correct modal verbs.**

1 You *have to* / *shouldn't* protect your head in hot weather.
2 You *mustn't* / *should* park here.
3 You *don't have to* / *ought to* visit the sports shop.
4 You *don't have to* / *mustn't* run in the hospital.
5 You *ought to* / *don't have to* feed the dog.
6 You *have to* / *shouldn't* panic in this situation.

**3** **Choose the correct verbs.**

1 You *don't have to* / *must* buy food for me. I can do it myself!
2 In my opinion, all young people *have to* / *should* stay at school until they are 18.
3 I have a doctor's appointment before school tomorrow so I *must* / *have to* get up early.
4 I'm happy you like reading but you *don't have to* / *mustn't* sit down all day long. It's not good for you.
5 I must *to ask* / *ask* you one question.
6 You don't *must* / *have to* make lunch for me.
7 To keep fit, you *don't have to* / *shouldn't* take the bus every day.
8 Unfortunately, I will be late tomorrow because I *should* / *have to* visit the dentist.

## VOCABULARY Words with *some*, *any*, *every* and *no*

**1** **Choose the correct word to complete the examples.**

**Check your answer in the article on page 37.**

If you spend time chatting to *someone* / *no one* on social media, or reading a book on your e-reader, you are not alone.
*Nothing* / *Anything* on social media is so important that it can't wait a few hours!

**2** **Use words from each box to make new words.**

EP

any every no some

one thing where

| People | Things | Places |
|---|---|---|
| *anyone* | | |
| | | |
| | | |
| | | |

**3** **Choose the correct words.**

1 I think *someone* / *anyone* is trying to call you.
2 I spent the morning shopping, but I didn't buy *something* / *anything*.
3 I'd love to live *somewhere* / *everywhere* warm.
4 *No one* / *Everyone* is waiting to hear news about Jo. We're all ready.
5 I'm really hungry, but there's *nothing* / *anything* to eat!

**4** **Complete the email with words from Exercise 2.**

**To: auntiemay@teentroubles.com**

Dear Auntie May,

I want to tell you about [1] ________ in my class. He used to be really fun and easygoing, but I think that there is [2] ________ wrong with him. [3] ________ in my class thinks the same. We had to do a project together and he was annoyed all the time. He didn't seem to have [4] ________ to say and [5] ________ we could say made him feel any better. We don't know what to do. What should we do? Please help us!

Juan

# LISTENING

**1** **You are going to listen to some short extracts. Read the questions and look at the pictures. What can you see in each one?**

## PREPARE FOR THE EXAM

### Listening Part 1

**2** **Listen and for each question, choose the correct answer. Then listen again and check.**

23

1 Where did Lola leave her phone?

2 What's wrong with the boy at the moment?

3 What do they decide to eat for lunch?

4 What does the woman say many teenagers should do more of?

5 What does the doctor say the boy should do now?

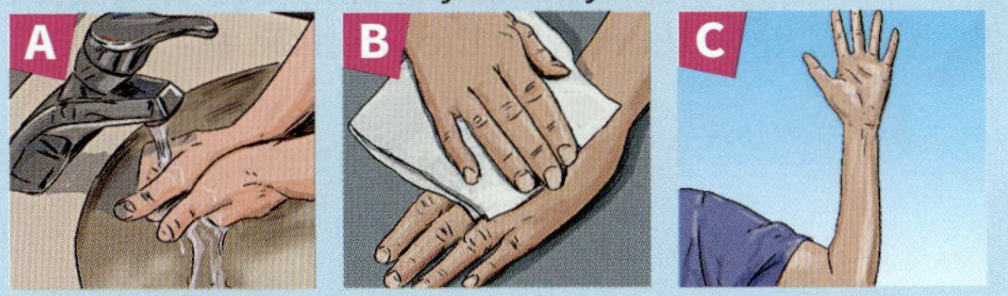

6 What does the girl hope to be able to do today?

7 What will the friends take John in hospital?

» PREPARE FOR THE EXAM PAGE 128

# SPEAKING Discussing options (1)

## PREPARE FOR THE EXAM

### Speaking Part 3

**1** **Read the instructions for the task below. Think about each idea and make notes. Compare your notes with a partner.**

A boy's sister is coming home from hospital. Here are some things they could do for her first day at home. Talk together about the **different** things they could do, and decide which one would be the **best**.

**2** **Discuss your ideas with your partner. Talk about all the ideas and agree on which is best. Use phrases from the *Prepare to speak* box.**

» PREPARE FOR THE EXAM PAGE 133

Things to do for sister's first day at home

## PREPARE TO SPEAK

### Expressing opinions

**Giving your opinion**

I think / don't think …

In my opinion …

In my view …

**Asking someone's opinion**

What do you think?

Do you agree?

# CULTURE

## SPORTS IN CANADA

### ABOUT YOU

What are the most popular sports in your country?
Can you name any typical sports from other countries?
What are the advantages of playing team sports?

**1** **Match the words in the box to the equipment (A–F) in the photos opposite.**

| bat | helmet | hoop | pads | puck | stick |
|---|---|---|---|---|---|

**2** **Read the article. For each sport, how many professional teams are there in Canada?**

**3** **Answer the questions with information from the texts.**

1 Where do many Canadians go skating for the first time?
2 What did Frederick Stanley do for Canadian ice hockey?
3 How are Canadian and American football different?
4 In what sport do athletes compete for the Grey Cup?
5 Why could softball be easier for children than baseball?
6 Which baseball team won the World Series in 1992?
7 Why can we say that basketball is a Canadian sport?

## LACROSSE

**4** **Match the highlighted words in the text to the meanings.**

1 free time
2 something that keeps you safe
3 started or created
4 at the present time
5 cold, solid and hard, like ice
6 not professional players

24 **5** **Listen to a presentation about lacrosse, another Canadian national sport. Number the topics in the order you hear them.**

a ...... the number of players
b ...... the people who invented it
c ...... the international federation
d ...... the stick that players use
e ...... how long the matches are
f ...... the national association
g ...... equipment for protection
h ...... the size of the lacrosse ball

24 **6** **Listen again. Are the sentences true or false?**

1 A French explorer invented lacrosse in 1637.
2 The national association was created in 1867.
3 Players pass the lacrosse ball with their hands.
4 There are two teams with ten players each.
5 Matches are two hours long with four periods.
6 The international federation has more than 50 member countries.

**7** **Read the *Useful language* phrases. Complete them with the words in the box.**

| equipment | hands | matches |
|---|---|---|
| players | scoring | team |

### USEFUL LANGUAGE

**Talking about sports**

1 Each ... has got (ten) players.
2 The ... have to (run) a lot.
3 They win by ... more points.
4 Players can/can't use their ...
5 They must use special ....
6 The ... are (one hour) long.

# TEAM SPORTS IN CANADA

**Many Canadians enjoy team sports. Some are amateurs who play in their free time, while others are professional athletes. Team sports also attract lots of spectators, especially when there is a national or international championship.**

## ICE HOCKEY

is Canada's official winter sport and the most popular sport on TV. In this cold, northern country, many people learn to skate as children, at public ice rinks or on frozen lakes. Many boys and girls sign up for junior hockey and continue playing as adults. Canada has seven professional teams that play in the National Hockey League. The NHL also includes 24 teams from the USA. Every year, these teams compete for the Stanley Cup, which is the oldest hockey award in North America. It's named after Lord Frederick Stanley, who established the competition in 1893.

## CANADIAN FOOTBALL

is another popular spectator sport in Canada. It's quite similar to American football because the players wear helmets, shoulder pads and other types of protection. However, Canadian teams have twelve players (instead of only eleven) and the playing field is larger. Many Canadian high schools and universities have football teams that compete in regional and national championships. There is also a Canadian Football League with eight professional teams. The most important CFL competition is the Grey Cup, which millions of fans watch on TV every year.

## BASKETBALL

isn't the most popular team sport in Canada, which is surprising because a Canadian teacher invented the game in 1891. James Naismith was working at a school in the USA when he had an idea for a new team sport. Nowadays, Canadian students often play basketball in PE class and it's also a typical after-school activity. At the moment, there is only one professional basketball team in Canada – the Toronto Raptors – which competes in the NBA. There are also Canadian players on other NBA teams.

## BASEBALL

is an iconic sport in the USA and many Canadians also enjoy playing and watching the game. Many young people play baseball in their leisure time and softball is also popular. Softball is similar to baseball, but the ball is softer and bigger, so it's easier to hit with a bat. At the professional level, Canada has one major league baseball team – the Toronto Blue Jays. They compete against teams in the USA and have won the World Series championship twice, in 1992 and in 1993. There used to be another Canadian team in Montreal, called the Expos, but they moved to Washington D.C. after the 2004 season.

## PROJECT *A presentation*

**Prepare a presentation about a national sport. Use the topics in Exercise 5 and the questions below to help you.**

1 Where is the sport popular? Who plays it?
2 How is the sport played?
3 What special equipment do players use?
4 Is the sport similar to any other sports?
5 What is the history of the sport?
6 What are the biggest competitions?

**Make your presentation to the class.**

05 NOW WATCH THE CULTURE VIDEO

# 7 SOUND CHECK

## ABOUT YOU

How important is music to you?
What's your favourite kind of music?
When and where do you listen to music?

## VOCABULARY Music

**1** **Look at the photos. Where do you think the people are? What are they doing?**

26 **2** **Listen and match the recordings to the photos.**

A

B

C

D

E

26 **3** **Complete the sentences with the words in the box. Listen again and check.**

EP

| celebrity | clip | concert hall | DJ | festival |
|---|---|---|---|---|
| gig | guitarist | live | lyrics | music channel |
| musicians | music video | production | | |
| sound technician | studio | | | |

1. I'm ______ Mike playing your favourite music.
2. And this morning, Gina is in the ______ with us.
3. I guess you could say I've been a ______ at home for about three years now.
4. But tonight is my first ______ in Europe.
5. The bass ______ is amazing, don't you think? He plays so well.
6. These ______ make no sense. They're awful.
7. And it's all recorded anyhow – not even ______!
8. They shouldn't call this event a live music ______!
9. We are live from the Sydney Opera House – a ______ that is familiar to our regular listeners.
10. And this is VVTV – the only ______ that plays *your* music.
11. Go to our website to watch a ______ of the band's recent show in Boston.
12. Let's take a look at boyband EE's latest ______.
13. Like me, you probably think the ______ record their music and that's it.
14. I've just come back from the London Sound Studio where I spoke to ______ Bob Jackson.
15. He has introduced me to a whole new world: the world of sound ______.

**4** **Ask and answer the questions.**

1. Have you ever been to a music festival? Would you like to go to one? Why? / Why not?
2. Do you watch music videos? How do you watch them?
3. Who are the most famous celebrities in your country?
4. Which musicians do you admire? Why?
5. Describe your favourite music video.

## READING

**1** Look at the photo. How do you think he became famous?

**2** These numbers are all about the life of the person in the photo. What do you think they represent?

**A** 2014 **B** 37 **C** 10.8 **D** 10,000

**3** Read the article and check your ideas.

# Shawn Mendes

***Our series of your favourite young celebrities continues. This week Rachel Mead writes about Canadian singer-songwriter Shawn Mendes.***

27

This is a true story of success. Shawn Mendes was like any other teenager who went to school and did sports activities like ice hockey and football. He also really loved music and he wanted to be able to play the guitar. So he taught himself from watching YouTube videos and practised every day. At the same time, he worked really hard on his singing. He's not only a great singer, he performs really well, too!

In 2014 he shot to fame, thanks to social media. The story began with the launch of the video sharing service Vine. Mendes added a short clip of himself singing a version of the Justin Bieber song *As Long as You Love Me.* When he checked his account the next day, he saw that he had 10,000 likes.

He soon moved to the bigger channel, YouTube, where he uploaded more and more clips, and his follower count grew. He interacted with his fans by asking them to tell him what to sing.

2014 was a big year for Mendes. He had 2.4 million followers on Vine, 10.8 million followers on Twitter and almost a million subscribers on YouTube. He signed up with a record company and his four-track debut EP reached number one on iTunes in 37 minutes! A year later, he was included in a list of the 25 most influential teenagers, and in 2016 he was in the Forbes' annual list of '30 under 30' – the 30 most important celebrities under 30 years old.

Mendes is young, but he's already achieved so much. He's opened for one of Taylor Swift's world tours, he's modelled for an agency and he's had an acting part in a TV show, *The 100*. He's received awards for his music and in 2015 he won the MTV Europe Music award.

I've just become a Mendes fan. But some of my friends have followed him from the beginning and still love him now. The special relationship with his fans has just grown and grown. On his website there is a section just for us, the fans – *Shawn Access*, and that's where you can get a ticket for the small gigs he holds. I'd love to attend a live show – it must be amazing!

**Next week:**

*If you would like to tell us about your favourite celebrity, just drop us an email to ed@prepareteen.co.uk*

**4** Read the article again and answer the questions.

1 How did Shawn learn the guitar?
 **A** He had lessons.
 **B** He watched some YouTube videos.
 **C** A friend taught him.

2 What did he first put on the video sharing site Vine?
 **A** his own song
 **B** guitar music
 **C** a well-known song

3 How did he increase his popularity on YouTube?
 **A** by uploading more clips of his songs
 **B** by telling fans to sing his songs
 **C** by setting up his own channel

4 Which area has he not worked in, according to the article?
 **A** fashion **B** sports **C** television

5 What can some fans enjoy?
 **A** He gives out extra tickets to his fans.
 **B** He spends the time posting about his fans.
 **C** He gives special concerts for a few fans.

**5** Match the highlighted words in the text to the meanings.

1 succeeded in doing something good, usually by working hard
2 entertains people by acting, dancing, singing, playing music
3 looked at
4 talked and did things with other people
5 officially joined

### TALKING POINTS

Have you ever uploaded a video to YouTube? Why? / Why not?

Why do people upload videos to YouTube?

In the future, do you think all stars will become famous through the power of social media?

## GRAMMAR Present perfect and past simple

**1 Match two examples to each rule.**

1 I've just become a Mendes fan.
2 The next day he checked his account.
3 Mendes is young, but he's already achieved so much.
4 He practised every day.

**a** We use the present perfect to talk about something in the past that has a link to the present.
**b** We use the past simple to talk about completed actions in the past. It only refers to the past.

**2 Complete the sentences with the past simple or present perfect of the verbs.**

1 Mike ________ (buy) his ticket for the music festival two months ago.
2 He ________ (pay) a lot of money for it.
3 He ________ (not / see) his favourite band live before and so he's excited.
4 Mike's mum wants to help, so she ________ (offer) to take him to the stadium.
5 Mike doesn't need a lift from his mum because he ________ (organise) a lift with a friend.
6 Mike ________ (call) his friend last night to make the final arrangements for their trip.

**3 We often use the adverbs *just*, *already* and *yet* with the present perfect. Read the examples and complete the rules with *just*, *already* or *yet*.**

1 Zara has just sent me a text.
2 We've already learned how to record a singer.
3 I haven't had time yet.
4 Have you started your school project yet?

With the present perfect, we use:
**a** ________ when something has happened at some time before now.
**b** ________ when something happened a short time ago.
**c** ________ in questions and negative sentences when something has (possibly) not happened.

» GRAMMAR REFERENCE AND PRACTICE PAGE 153

**4 Read the examples in Exercise 3 again. Which adverb is used at the end of a sentence? Where are the other adverbs used?**

**5 Correct the mistake in each sentence.**

1 I just seen your advertisement.
2 Yesterday I have bought a new album.
3 A new student, Maria Vaz have joined our class.
4 Did you already decide to buy the festival ticket?
5 I haven't seen the clip yesterday.
6 I didn't see the band play there yet.

**6 Complete the sentences with the present perfect form of the verbs. Put the adverbs in the correct place.**

1 I ________ an advertisement for *The X Factor* – I think I'll apply! (see / just)
2 Some of the singers ________ in front of a large audience. (sing / already)
3 They ________ who the judges are ________. (not announce / yet)
4 It's two hours to show time and the performers ________ their costumes on. (put / already)
5 Jake ________ in public ________. (not perform / yet)
6 Our town ________ its annual music festival. It was last week. (hold / just)

**7 Ask and answer these questions with a partner.**

1 Have you listened to an artist on social media recently? Who was it?
2 When did you last listen to music by your favourite artist? Did you listen to a track or the whole album?
3 How many artists have you seen live?

## VOCABULARY Word families

**1 Look at the words in the examples. What kind of word are they?**

1 I'd like David to help me to check it first.
2 He's really helpful.
3 If you need any help, give me a call.

**2 Complete the table.**

EP

| Noun | Verb | Adjective |
|---|---|---|
| music / musician | – | **1** |
| performance / performer | **2** | – |
| **3** | advertise | – |
| entertainment / entertainer | **4** | **5** |
| **6** | achieve | – |
| **7** | record | – |

**3 Talk about a musician you like for 30 seconds. Try to use at least one form of each of the words in Exercise 2.**

# WRITING An email (1)

**1** **Read part of an email that Sophia has received from her friend Jacob. Then read Sophia's reply. Does Sophia answer all Jacob's questions?**

> Last night, I went to an awesome concert in our town with my brother. It was amazing!
>
> Tell me about a concert you enjoyed. Where did it take place? What was it like? How did you feel?

> Dear Jacob,
>
> It was our school concert last week! And our band played!
>
> It took place in the school hall and there were loads of great performances from different year groups.
>
> I performed at the concert with my mates. When I first walked on stage, it was dark and scary – you can't imagine how nervous I felt! Then the lights came on and we played our music. It was awesome! We had such a cool time and I've never seen so many people clap – for us! We recorded it, so I'll send you a recording.
>
> Write soon,
> Sophia

**2** **Read the *Prepare to write* box. What phrases does Sophia use to begin and end her email?**

## PREPARE TO WRITE

### An email

In informal letters and emails:

- use an informal phrase to begin your letter: *Dear …, Hi …, Hello …*
- use an informal phrase to end your letter: *Write soon, Love, See you soon*
- use short forms: *I've, won't, we'll*
- use informal language: *amazing, great*

**3** **Find three short forms in Sophia's email.**

**4** **Rewrite the sentences using short forms.**

1 He has never been to a music festival.
2 We are going to give Amy a lift at 8 pm.
3 Do you know who is going to perform next?
4 I would really like to see a live classical music concert.
5 They have not bought their tickets yet.
6 Dan and Gemma could not find a place to park near the concert.

**5** **Match the highlighted informal words in Sophia's email to the meanings.**

1 lots
2 frightening
3 very good
4 friends
5 enjoyed

## PREPARE FOR THE EXAM

### Writing Part 1

**6** **Read this email from your English-speaking friend, Alex, and the notes you have made. Write your email to Alex, using ALL the notes. Use the tips in the *Prepare to write* box. Write about 100 words. Remember to check your spelling and grammar.**

> To:
> From: Alex
>
> Hi,
>
> I went to a music festival in the countryside at the weekend. We camped in a field for two days and went to lots of concerts. It was fun! — *Great!*
>
> Have you ever been to a music festival? — *Yes – say where you went*
>
> What did you enjoy most about it? — *Explain to Alex*
>
> I've never performed on a stage, have you? I'm too scared! — *No, but …*
>
> Write soon!
> Alex

» PREPARE FOR THE EXAM PAGE 127

# 8 AMAZING ARCHITECTURE

## ABOUT YOU

**06 Watch the video and then answer the questions.**

What is your favourite building?

Do you prefer old or modern buildings?

How important is it to have local facilities near your home?

## VOCABULARY Describing buildings

**1 Match the sentences to the houses in photos 1–3 on the opposite page.**

EP

**a** The solar panels and glass walls on this house make it look **brand new**. Its **original** shape is **spectacular** to look at. It's more contemporary than the other houses.

**b** This house is **unusual** because it's very narrow. Inside this home is very stylish thanks to its bright, **fresh** design.

**c** This house is a **classic** example of a **historic** tower. Its design is very **traditional** but it could be quite **cosy** inside. It's not as **modern** as the other houses.

**2 Complete the chart with the adjectives from Exercise 1.**

| Age | Opinion |
|---|---|
| *brand new* | *unusual* |

**3 Look at the photos again. Discuss the advantages and disadvantages of living in each building.**

28 **4 Listen to two people talking about the buildings in Exercise 1. Do they mention any of your ideas?**

**5 Discuss the questions.**

1 How much space do you need to live in? Why?
2 What sort of house would you like to live in?
3 Describe the most unusual building you have ever visited or read about.

## READING

### PREPARE FOR THE EXAM

#### Reading Part 2

**1 The five students below are learning about unusual homes around the world. Each student wants to find out more about one unusual home, which they will write about for an architecture project. Read the information about each student and underline the things they are interested in. The first one has been done for you.**

1 Marcelo loves all kinds of sport and wants to find out about a modern home that has been designed for a famous sportsperson. He loves buildings by the ocean, too.

2 Gloria is very interested in old buildings. She would like to write about one which is in the countryside, and has fantastic views of the landscape.

3 Harry wants to find out about a well-known architect who designed a building which the architect then lived in. He also has an interest in furniture.

4 Sofie is keen to learn about a building that is the smallest of its kind. She likes city buildings and wants to find one that is located in an interesting neighbourhood.

5 Kurt wants to learn about a modern home that is better for the environment than other buildings and has won competitions because of its original architecture.

**2 Read the descriptions of eight unusual homes (A–H) quickly. Which two are shown in the pictures on the opposite page? Decide which home would be the most suitable for each student (1–5) to write about.**

» PREPARE FOR THE EXAM PAGE 121

## TALKING POINTS

In what ways are some modern buildings better for the environment?

What makes a good family home, in your opinion?

Would you prefer to live in a city or the countryside? Why?

# UNUSUAL HOMES AROUND THE WORLD

## A Keret House

Keret House could be the world's narrowest home and is just 122 cm at its widest point! A Polish architect living in the country's capital walked past the space between a house and an apartment block one day and decided to build something there. The area around it is full of things to do and see.

## B Crossway

Located in the most beautiful part of England, this home was designed by architect Richard Hawkes to live in. Less than 20 years old, it is a 'passive' house: it uses little energy, the sun produces all its electricity, and it has a 'living' roof which reduces pollution. These unusual features have earned the house prizes.

## C House NA

The architects who built this house wanted to feel like they were living in the trees. This led to a modern house made of glass in a quiet part of Tokyo, Japan. The floors are at different levels, like branches, making it easier for the people who live there to move around – and it's good exercise for them, too!

## D Freston Tower

This historic tower in southern England has lasted for several centuries. There are six floors with a single small room on each one. The sitting room is right at the top of the building, and from here, you can see the beautiful river, where people go sailing, and the fields beyond.

## E Pas House

This unusual house near the beach in California, USA, is divided into three separate spaces, each ideal for skateboarding: the floor, walls and ceiling join together into one enormous tube. The idea came from a former world champion, who wanted somewhere exciting to live.

## F Old Light

Located off the coast of England, the Old Light is situated in one of the least busy areas of the country. The building was once a lighthouse, which warned ships at sea of nearby rocks. The house is now divided into two guest flats. The lighthouse is not as tall as some, but is in a beautiful position near the sea – perfect for swimming!

## G Gropius House

Other architects may be more famous, but the buildings Walter Gropius created are among the most important of the last century. He designed Gropius House in the USA as his family home which can now be visited. Inside there is a collection of chairs and other items which belonged to the family.

## H The Heliodrome

This recently built original house is situated in peaceful countryside in France. It was built so that its rooms, furniture and paintings are in the shade during summer. Even better than this is that in winter, the sun *does* enter through the windows, making the house warm without heating – and therefore cheaper to live in!

## GRAMMAR Comparative and superlative adjectives

**1** **Read the examples and write *C* for comparative or *S* for superlative.**

1. This is certainly not the world's **biggest** house! *S*
2. The floors are at different levels, like branches, making it **easier** for the people who live there to move around.
3. Kurt wants to learn about a modern home that is **better** for the environment than others.
4. It's only 122 cm at its **widest** point.
5. Located in **the most beautiful** part of England …
6. The Old Light is situated in one of **the least busy** areas of the country.
7. Other architects may be **more famous**.
8. … making the house warm without heating – and therefore **cheaper** to live in!
9. Most houses without views are **less expensive** than those with views.
10. Keret House is **as narrow as** a car.
11. We've just read about a house that is **narrower** than any other.

» GRAMMAR REFERENCE AND PRACTICE PAGE 154

**2** **Read Exercise 1 again and answer these questions.**

1. Which adjective is irregular?
2. What do we add to regular adjectives with one syllable?
3. What happens to adjectives like *big*?
4. What happens if a one-syllable or two-syllable adjective ends in *-y*?
5. How do we form positive and negative comparatives and superlatives for most adjectives with more than one syllable?
6. What do we use when we want to say that two things are the same?

**3** **Complete the sentences with the correct form of the adjective in brackets.**

1. I picked this house because it's ______ than the houses in the city centre. (quiet)
2. My parents would be ______ in the countryside than in the busy town. (happy)
3. I think my town will be ______ in 20 years' time. (big)
4. In Spain, one of ______ festivals is in January. It's Día de los Reyes Magos. (popular)
5. Henry is ______ person in our class. (intelligent)
6. My cousins live ______ from my grandparents than me. (far)
7. I think this is ______ advice I can give you. (good)
8. This mirror is ______ than that one. I think I'll take both! (cheap)

**4** **Rewrite the sentences so that they have the same meaning. Use the words in brackets.**

1. My house is bigger than Maggie's. (not as)
2. The design wasn't as traditional as I thought. (less)
3. Homes with sea views are more expensive than all others. (most)
4. Both films were entertaining but I preferred the first. (more)
5. Our new house is closer to shops than our old house. (far)
6. My old bike wasn't as good as my new one. (better)

**5** **Answer the questions about your town or city. Talk to your partner. Do you have the same ideas?**

1. Which is the biggest building?
2. Which is the oldest building?
3. Which is the most unusual building?
4. Which is the most beautiful building? Why?
5. Which is the least attractive building? Why?

## VOCABULARY Strong adjectives and adverbs

**1** **Look at the photos and the captions. Which adjective has a stronger meaning?**

a big house

an enormous house

**2** **Put the adjectives in the correct column to make pairs.**

EP

~~ancient~~ brand new bad big
cold enormous exhausted
freezing good new ~~old~~
spectacular terrible tired

| Normal adjectives | Strong adjectives |
| --- | --- |
| *old* | *ancient* |

**3** **Read the examples and complete the rules.**

The house was **absolutely** spectacular.
It had **incredibly** big windows.
The family was **very** happy with their new house.
It was **extremely** difficult to find the house.

With normal adjectives we use the adverbs ______, ______, *incredibly*, *really*.
With strong adjectives we use the adverbs ______, *really*.

**4** » **Work in pairs. Turn to page 135.**

# LISTENING

## PREPARE FOR THE EXAM

### Listening Part 2

**1** 30 **Read question 1 and look at the underlined words. Can you think of words with a similar meaning? Listen to the first part of the recording, which is about people who are moving to a new place. Choose A, B or C.**

1 You will hear a boy talking to his friend about her move. How does the girl feel about moving to a city?
- **A** sad that she won't see her friends any more
- **B** excited about living in a more interesting place
- **C** glad it isn't too far from where she's living now

**2** 31 **Now listen to the rest of the conversations about people who are moving to a new place. For each question, choose the correct answer.**

2 You will hear a boy talking to his friend about his new school. What does he like about it?
- **A** how good the facilities are
- **B** how much space there is
- **C** how modern it is

3 You will hear a boy and a girl talking about making friends. What does the girl say about making friends in her new village?
- **A** She doesn't think she will be very good at it.
- **B** She expects people will be friendly towards her.
- **C** She has met some interesting people her age.

4 You will hear two friends talking about the boy's new family home. What does he like most about it?
- **A** It is in a peaceful location.
- **B** It looks similar to his old home.
- **C** He will have his own bedroom.

5 You will hear a girl telling her friend about the town she is going to live in. How does she feel about the move?
- **A** excited to have the chance to attend a sports event
- **B** keen to do a new activity in the town
- **C** pleased to continue with an old hobby

6 You will hear two friends talking about moving to the countryside. They agree that
- **A** it will be a good place to practise their hobby.
- **B** it will be hard to find interesting things to do.
- **C** it will be nice to live a less busy life.

» PREPARE FOR THE EXAM PAGE 129

# SPEAKING Describing a picture (1)

**1 Look at the photo of skateboarders inside Pas House on page 136. How would you describe it?**

32 **2 Listen to Julia. Does she mention any of your ideas from Exercise 1?**

32 **3 Which adjectives in the box does Julia use? Listen again and check.**

awesome big comfortable
large lovely normal perfect
soft strange unusual

**4 Read the 'order of adjectives' table below. Then put the adjectives in the correct order in the phrases below.**

1 a ________ sofa (leather / brand new / gorgeous)
2 some ________ bowls (little / beautiful / glass)
3 a ________ table (square / big)
4 some ________ chairs (red / comfortable / large)

32 **5 Read the *Prepare to speak* box. Which phrases does Julia use? Listen again and complete the sentences below.**

1 I can see a room in what ________ a house.
2 It's got designer lights and ________.
3 A guy is sitting on ________ seat.
4 Not pillows exactly, but ________ pillows?
5 It ________ to be made out of skateboards.
6 This place looks ________ a skate park than a house.

## PREPARE TO SPEAK

### When you don't know the right word

It looks (a bit) like …
It looks more like …
It seems to be …
that kind of thing
something like that
some kind of

## PREPARE FOR THE EXAM

### Speaking Part 2

**6** » **Work in pairs. Turn to page 136.**

Order of adjectives

| QUALITY | SIZE | SHAPE | AGE | COLOUR | NATIONALITY | MATERIAL |
|---|---|---|---|---|---|---|
| *awesome* | *large* | *square* | *old* | *black* | *Polish* | *leather* |

# LIFE SKILLS CREATIVITY AND INNOVATION

## CREATIVE WRITING

### LIFE SKILLS

**Creative writing**

Many young people enjoy writing in their free time. It can be fun and it also helps people develop their creativity and imagination. For these reasons, students should also do creative writing tasks at school. With practice, they become easier, even for people who don't write as a hobby.

**1 Ask and answer the questions with a partner.**

1 What do you enjoy reading in your free time?
2 What was the last book or story that you read?
3 Do you ever write or imagine your own stories?

**2 Read the article on the opposite page about how to plan a story. Do you use a similar process for writing stories? Complete the sentences in the article with the words in the box.**

| main | middle | person | time | true |
|---|---|---|---|---|

**3 Complete the sentences about the article with two or three words.**

1 There are ways ........ the creative writing process.
2 The villain is someone who ........ for other characters.
3 Sometimes the narrator knows what a character ........ .
4 The setting includes facts about the ........ of the story.
5 Most writers revise and ........ many times before they are happy.

**4 Match the highlighted words in the text to the meanings.**

1 unusual or unknown
2 well-known and easy to recognise
3 work to find an answer
4 the feeling of a situation
5 working in the best way
6 think or believe that something will happen

33 **5 Listen to Sam and Kate. How does Sam describe the genre of his story for English class?**

33 **6 Listen again and answer the questions.**

1 Why hasn't Sam finished writing his story yet?
2 What location is Sam thinking about for his story?
3 Who are Sam's four main characters going to be?
4 What happens when they go down to the basement?
5 Why can't the characters call the police for help?
6 What type of ending is Sam planning for his story?

**7 Complete the list of narrative connectors in the *Useful language* with connectors from the box which have a similar meaning.**

| All of a sudden | A while later | First of all |
|---|---|---|
| In the end | Luckily | Next |

### USEFUL LANGUAGE

**Narrative connectors**

1 At first / …
2 Then / …
3 After a while / …
4 Suddenly / …
5 Fortunately / …
6 Finally / …

# WRITING A STORY

## How to plan a story

**Have you ever written a story for school or for fun? Did you find it hard to get started? Creative writing can be hard, but there are ways to plan the process so it's more efficient.**

**1 Choose a genre.** The genre is the type of story you want to write. There are fictional stories that writers imagine and [1] ________ stories about events that really happened. Fiction includes specific genres, such as mystery, fantasy, science fiction, romance and suspense. Try a genre that you enjoy reading so it will be familiar to you.

**2 Think about characters.** Most stories have one or two [2] ________ characters. They are the most important people, but they aren't always good characters, or heroes. They can also be villains who make problems for other people. Some genres also have typical characters that readers expect to find in the story. For instance, in mysteries there are generally criminals and detectives, while science fiction has robots, spaceships or aliens from other worlds.

**3 Who's the narrator?** The narrator is the [3] ________ who tells the story. It might be a character who describes his or her experiences by saying something like, 'I was walking in the woods when I heard a strange noise.' The narrator can also be an observer who reports events but doesn't play a role. In that case, the narrator could say, 'Laura was walking in the woods when she heard a strange noise.' In some stories the narrator also knows what characters are thinking.

**4 Choose a setting.** Most stories take place in a particular place and [4] ________, or setting. It can be very simple, such as 'a rainy day in the countryside' if the events are more important than the setting. In other cases, the setting can be very specific, with facts about the location, historical period and weather. The narrator can also describe how the setting feels, with words like *cold*, *dark* and *sad*. This helps to create a mood for the story.

**5 What's the plot?** The plot is the sequence of events in a story, from beginning to end. In the [5] ________, there is often a problem that the characters have to solve. This problem grows and develops until the most important moment of the story, called the climax. In a mystery, this is when the detective solves the crime. After the climax, the story comes to an end, which can be happy … or maybe not. That depends on the writer, of course!

**Once you've finished planning, you're ready to start writing your story. But remember, most writers revise and change their work many times before they are happy with the result. Good luck, and happy writing!**

## PROJECT *A story*

**Plan a short story. Then work with a partner to compare ideas. Use the story ideas and the questions below to help you. Share your plan with a partner. Give each other ideas to make the stories better.**

- A mystery story in a strange town
- A romantic story in an exciting city
- A science fiction story in outer space
- A fantasy story in a magical forest
- A suspense story in an old castle

1. Who are the main characters of the story?
2. What is the general setting of the story?
3. What happens at the beginning?
4. What problems do the characters have?
5. What is the most important moment?
6. What type of ending will the story have?

**Write a first draft of your story. Then revise the draft, making corrections and any changes that are necessary. Read your story to the class.**

# REVIEW 2 UNITS 5–8

## VOCABULARY

**1 Complete the sentences with the words in the box.**

create customise design
rebuild recycle repair sew

1 Jake offered to ______ my bike because it wasn't working properly.
2 The button on my coat fell off. I'll have to ______ it back on again.
3 I think it's really important to ______ rubbish, to help the environment.
4 For a school project, I have to ______ an original cover for a mobile phone.
5 I love to ______ new things from stuff I don't use any more.
6 When their house burned down, they had to ______ their whole life.
7 Lots of people like to ______ their things so that they are a little bit different.

**2 Match the sentence halves.**

1 I usually cough a lot
2 When you look at the computer all day,
3 My legs ached so much
4 When we feel very tired,
5 It took me a long time to recover
6 Be careful! That pan is hot

a after all the running we did yesterday.
b we yawn.
c when I have a cold.
d it's important to blink.
e and you could burn yourself.
f from the illness.

**3 Match the words in the box to the meanings.**

celebrity clip festival live
lyrics musician soundtrack studio

1 someone who is famous, especially in the entertainment business
2 a series of special events and performances that takes place over several days
3 someone who plays a musical instrument, often as their job
4 a room where TV or radio programmes are made
5 the words of a song
6 this describes a TV or radio programme that is seen or heard as it happens
7 a short video or audio recording
8 the music that accompanies a film

**4 Complete the adjectives in the conversation.**

**Anna:** Do you know the [1] h______c town of Samport?
**Fred:** I think so. It's a [2] t______l English town, isn't it?
**Anna:** Yes. Most of the buildings are in an old, [3] c______c design but there are some quite [4] m______n buildings too.
**Fred:** There's a [5] b______d n______w art gallery there, isn't there? I think it opened last month.
**Anna:** That's right. There's a [6] s______r exhibition on at the moment that includes lots of different art forms. Everyone says it's amazing!
**Fred:** Oh, yes, I read about it. It includes things like ballet and paintings. It sounds really [7] o______l and different. I'd like to see it!

## GRAMMAR

**1 Complete the sentences with the correct form of the verbs. Use the past simple or past continuous.**

1 The weather was awful at the festival – it ______ (rain), and I ______ (not have) my umbrella.
2 Justine ______ (watch) TV when she ______ (receive) a text message.
3 At the park last week, Magdalena ______ (text) while I ______ (read) my book.
4 Yesterday Alex ______ (miss) the bus and ______ (forget) his homework.
5 Hannah's mum ______ (decorate) her birthday cake in secret, but Hannah ______ (see) it in the cupboard.
6 Jack ______ (listen) to music when his mum ______ (call) him for dinner.

**2 Complete the sentences with the modal verbs in the box.**

don't have to have to
mustn't ought should

1 I think you ______ study tonight – you have a test tomorrow.
2 When you are in class, you ______ use your mobile phone – it's against the rules.
3 You ______ do the shopping – I'll do it later.
4 That doesn't look good – you ______ to go to the hospital and see a doctor.
5 I ______ be at home for dinner tonight – my aunt is coming.

## 3 Choose the correct form of the verbs.

1 Sophia *visited* / *has visited* England last year.
2 Mark *ate* / *has eaten* sushi before. It isn't his first time!
3 I *just bought* / *'ve just bought* a ticket for a concert next month. I'm so excited!
4 Mr Johnson *didn't give* / *hasn't given* us our biology homework back yet.
5 My cousin *has added* / *added* me to his Instagram account yesterday.

## 4 Complete the sentences with the correct comparative or superlative form of the adjectives in the box.

| enjoyable | fresh | good | narrow |
|---|---|---|---|
| reliable | stylish | thick | tired |

1 It's a really small shop, and it's in ________ street I've ever seen!
2 Jessica is ________ than Emma. You can always trust her to arrive on time.
3 The water at the top of the stream is ________ than the water at the bottom. It's safer to drink.
4 I'm ________ at sports than Jo.
5 It's so cold that I am wearing ________ jumper I have!
6 You can't be ________ I am: I had to get up at 3 am!
7 The inside of the house is ________ than the outside. It's disappointing. We would have to decorate it before we moved in.
8 That was ________ gig I've ever been to. Never again!

## 5 Choose the correct option.

1 When I *walked* / *was walking* by the river, I saw a little dog jump into it.
2 I *musn't* / *ought to* forget to bring my school bag.
3 She was the *most lovely* / *loveliest* person I've ever known.
4 We have not received the materials for this project *yet* / *already*.

## 6 Correct the mistake in each sentence.

1 I have just buy a new phone.
2 The fresh air of the countryside is most important thing for me.
3 I have gone to Spain on holiday last year.
4 I love my town and the better thing is the new shopping centre.

# PREPARE FOR THE EXAM

## Reading Part 5

**1 For each question, choose the correct answer.**

### Blogs: today's diaries

Throughout history, people have written about **(1)** ________ events in their lives. In the past, people kept diaries, and these documents are **(2)** ________ helpful to experts, who are able to understand important events in history.

These days, people keep a record of their lives by **(3)** ________ a blog instead. There are differences between blogs and **(4)** ________ diaries, however. Diaries require only a pen and paper while blogs require a computer, access to the internet and something entertaining to write about. This could be something you've **(5)** ________ done or something you did a while ago. Diaries of the past were often **(6)** ________ with drawings, while blogs often include photos, videos and links. Whatever their differences, though, both diaries and blogs are important records of life which will be interesting for the people to read in the future.

| | | | | |
|---|---|---|---|---|
| **1** | **A** brand new | **B** recent | **C** modern | **D** fresh |
| **2** | **A** absolutely | **B** exactly | **C** totally | **D** extremely |
| **3** | **A** creating | **B** customising | **C** mending | **D** inventing |
| **4** | **A** classical | **B** original | **C** traditional | **D** historical |
| **5** | **A** yet | **B** still | **C** just | **D** only |
| **6** | **A** fixed | **B** decorated | **C** painted | **D** made |

## Reading Part 6

**2 For each question, write the correct answer. Write one word for each gap.**

### Why you should eat more chocolate

You're enjoying a nice bar of chocolate and you hear a voice in your head: 'Chocolate's bad for you!' Too late, you think. You **(1)** ________ almost finished it – all that fat and sugar! It's true that some chocolate contains a lot of the bad stuff. However, research shows that although you ought **(2)** ________ to eat too much chocolate, you don't **(3)** ________ to stop eating it altogether.

Chocolate makes us feel good and there's **(4)** ________ wrong with that. But some kinds are definitely better for us **(5)** ________ others. A small amount of dark chocolate is good for your heart and brain – it's even good for your skin! Unfortunately, milk chocolate isn't as good for you **(6)** ________ dark chocolate because it contains less cocoa: the ingredient which provides all the benefits.

# 9 THE FUTURE IS NOW

## ABOUT YOU

Which electronic devices do you use every day?
What do you use them for?
Which is the most important to you?

## VOCABULARY Technology

**1** Look at the photos. What can you see?

**2** What do you know about driverless or 'self-driving' cars? Do the quiz and find out!

### QUIZTIME

**This week's quiz is about driverless cars. Can you answer these questions in less than one minute? Ready, steady, go!**

**1 When did engineers begin to think about self-driving cars?**
- **A** in the 1920s
- **B** in the 1930s
- **C** in the 1980s

**2 What does *autonomous* mean?**
- **A** The car will choose your music.
- **B** You only need to tell the car when to turn.
- **C** The car drives itself.

**3 The licence you'll need for a driverless car**
- **A** will be the same as for any other car.
- **B** won't exist – you won't need one.
- **C** will be a special licence.

**4 These cars will run on**
- **A** electricity – just like your phone.
- **B** petrol.
- **C** a fuel made from vegetables.

**5 Which feature does not appear in some driverless cars?**
- **A** a computer
- **B** a display
- **C** an internet connection

35 **3** Listen to a clip from a podcast. Check your answers.

35 **4** Complete the sentences with the words in the box. Then listen to the podcast again and check.

EP

| charge | connection | display |
|---|---|---|
| experiments | fuel | invention |
| plug in | power | pump | satellite |

1. You can get a self-driving car. What exactly is this ______?
2. Does it mean no more stops at the petrol ______ on a long journey?
3. You will of course have to stop for some kind of ______, and for these cars it's electricity.
4. Like an electric car, you ______ it ______ to ______ the battery so that it gets the ______ it needs to continue.
5. Just like the map app on your phone, it will get directions from GPS ______ signals and that will show up on the ______ in the car.
6. But many autonomous cars will not have a ______ to the internet because of safety concerns.
7. At the moment, companies are carrying out a lot of safety tests and ______ on these cars.

**5** Discuss the questions.

1. Do you think everyone will have driverless cars in the future?
2. How do *you* feel about driverless cars?
3. Do inventions interest you? Why? / Why not?

## READING

1 Look at the title of the article. How do you think a car could use social media for fuel?

2 Read the article quickly to check your ideas.

36

# ELECTRIC CAR USES SOCIAL MEDIA FOR FUEL

**High school students in Kansas City in the United States are going to experience a very special journey next week, thanks to an organisation called Minddrive. The charity, set up by director Steve Rees, helps kids to get ahead in their education by involving them in creative car design outside of school. The idea is that they will be encouraged to think about their future goals and how they would like to give something back to society.**

With this in mind, one carefully chosen group of teenagers has worked on a 1967 Volkswagen, replacing the original petrol engine with a lithium-ion battery and adding twenty-first century electronic technology. This is a completely new subject area for them. Rees says, 'We want them to say, when it's all over, "I can't believe we actually did something like this!" It gives them the sense of being able to go back to school and do anything.'

Twenty-one students will be driving their car across the USA to its capital city, Washington DC, where they're meeting politicians and talking to journalists about the need for a different kind of education – one that is 'hands-on', like their car-building experience, which would give them useful life skills. To make sure their idea gets noticed, they've programmed the car's computer to control the amount of electricity used for fuel. The car will only move forward if it gets enough interest on social media. In other words, it'll be using Twitter power for fuel!

The project provides an important lesson for the students: if you want people to care about what you're doing, you have to make sure they know about it. To reach their destination, they'll need a total of 71,040 'social watts', gaining five watts for every new Twitter follower. The car's computer will recognise the hashtag #MINDDRIVE, and posts on Facebook and other social networking sites. Rees thinks collecting this 'social fuel' won't be a problem. He's going to watch their progress carefully, and he is actually expecting huge public support along the route.

## PREPARE FOR THE EXAM

### Reading Part 3

3 **Read the article more carefully and for each question, choose the correct answer.**

1 What is the writer explaining in the text?
- **A** how important social media is for teenagers
- **B** how to make better progress at school
- **C** how an after-school project was carried out
- **D** how valuable it can be to repair old vehicles

2 Paragraph 2 mentions that the purpose of the Minddrive project is
- **A** to encourage particular students to feel more confident.
- **B** to persuade talented students to attend Minddrive courses.
- **C** to teach some students about petrol-driven cars.
- **D** to give students a qualification in engineering.

3 According to paragraph 3, the kind of education that the students want would
- **A** pay attention to students' individual skills.
- **B** provide them with experience of real situations.
- **C** include the use of more advanced technology.
- **D** avoid teaching traditional subjects.

4 According to paragraph 4, the 'lesson' that students will learn from the project is
- **A** recognising the value of achieving goals.
- **B** asking others for advice when necessary.
- **C** being willing to accept other people's help.
- **D** achieving something by getting enough public support.

5 What would someone taking part in this Minddrive project say?
- **A** I haven't really enjoyed the experience, as it's exactly how we're taught in school. The drive to Washington will be fun, though.
- **B** The project's amazing! We're going to tell people in Washington that the lessons we get in school aren't right for everyone.
- **C** I'm studying electronic technology and social media at school, so I'm learning more about both at the moment.
- **D** It's been cool turning the Volkswagen into an electric car. Steve Rees is going to employ me full time now I've left school.

## TALKING POINTS

What do you think the students involved in the Minddrive project enjoyed about it?

Would you like to take part in a project like Minddrive? Why? / Why not?

## GRAMMAR Future forms

**1** **Read the examples. Then complete the rules with *will, be going to* or *the present continuous*.**

1 In Washington DC, they**'re meeting** politicians.
2 Listen to my podcast and I**'ll tell** you how driverless cars work.
3 Rees thinks collecting this 'social fuel' **won't be** a problem.
4 He**'s going to watch** their progress carefully.

We use:
**a** ________ for a general prediction about the future.
**b** ________ for a definite future arrangement.
**c** ________ for an offer or promise relating to the future.
**d** ________ for a personal plan or intention for the future.

### Future continuous

**2** **Look at the examples of the future continuous. Choose the correct words to complete the rules.**

1 Twenty-one students **will be driving** their car across the USA.
2 It**'ll be using** Twitter power for fuel.

**a** We form the future continuous with *will* + *be* + *-ing* / *past participle*
**b** We use the future continuous to talk about something that is *certain* / *unlikely* to happen at a particular time in the future.

» GRAMMAR REFERENCE AND PRACTICE PAGE 155

**3** **Complete the sentences with the future continuous form of the verbs in the box. There are two extra verbs that you don't need.**

| break | drive | hold | make |
|---|---|---|---|
| not see | study | take | wait |

1 I ________ for you outside the station tonight.
2 From next week, the class ________ American history.
3 We ________ a party on New Year's Eve, as usual.
4 My brother ________ his university exams in a month's time.
5 Julia ________ her friends on Friday.
6 Within ten years, everyone in this city ________ electric cars.

**4** **Choose the correct verb form.**

1 Tomorrow I *will go* / *am going* to buy a new DVD with my money.
2 I think that I *go* / *am going* to visit my cousins.
3 I*'ll be working* / *'ll work* on Saturday, unfortunately.
4 It's great to hear that you *will* / *are going to* visit my country.
5 I'm sure you *like* / *will like* it.
6 Don't worry, we*'ll collect* / *'re collecting* your suitcase from the hotel.

**5** **Complete the sentences with your own ideas.**

1 For my next birthday, …
2 At seven o'clock this evening, …
3 When I'm old enough, …

## VOCABULARY *enough, too, very, not … enough*

**1** **Read the examples. Then write *(not) enough, too* or *very* next to meanings a–d.**

EP

1 It will be a **very** special journey.
2 The car will only move forward if it gets **enough** interest on social media.
3 Some computer systems are **too** complicated.
4 Driverless cars are**n't** safe **enough** to be on the roads at the moment.

**a** as much as necessary ________
**b** more than is wanted or necessary ________
**c** used to make an adjective or adverb stronger ________
**d** less than necessary ________

**2** **Choose the correct option in sentences 1 and 2. Then choose the correct option to complete rules a and b.**

1 There is *enough petrol* / *petrol enough* in the car.
2 This car isn't *big enough* / *enough big* for a family of 6!

**a** *Enough* comes *before* / *after* nouns.
**b** *Enough* comes *before* / *after* adjectives.

**3** **Complete the sentences with *enough*, *too* or *very*. Use each word twice.**

1 This invention makes dirty water clean ________ to drink.
2 My parents wanted to buy an electric car, but it was ________ expensive.
3 You have to be ________ careful when driving in heavy rain.
4 Have we got ________ time to get something to eat before the film starts?
5 Some people think that driverless cars are ________ dangerous to be on the roads.
6 Computer programming is a ________ useful skill to have nowadays.

**4** » **Work in pairs.** **Turn to page 135.**

## WRITING An article (1)

**1** **Look at the photo of a smartphone. What can it do?**

**2** **Read the task and the sample answer. Which point in the task is not covered in the answer?**

**Articles wanted!**
**Phones of the future**
What do you think is the best thing about mobile phones?
What do you think mobile phones will be able to do in the future?
Do you think mobile phones will become even more popular?
Tell us what you think!

**Write about 100 words.**

The best thing about mobile phones is that you can do so many different things with them. For example, you can text or chat to friends, post updates on social media, play games, take photos and download music to listen to on them.

In the future, the range of apps will continue to increase and the graphics will get better and better. Phones will also be faster to use and the batteries will last longer.

**3** **Add a sentence to the article to answer the final point in the task.**

**4** **Read the *Prepare to write* box. What kinds of mistake do you usually make in your writing?**

### PREPARE TO WRITE
**Checking your writing**

Check your writing carefully for:

- spelling
- punctuation
- word order
- agreement – does the verb match its subject?
- pronouns – have you used the right ones?
- grammar – is the verb form correct?
- vocabulary – does the word fit?

**5** **Correct the underlined mistakes in the sentences. Then match the mistakes to the types of mistake in the *Prepare to write* box.**

1. The <u>batterys'</u> too old.
2. The internet connection isn't <u>enough fast</u>.
3. I dropped my phone and <u>he</u> stopped working.
4. I'd like a smartphone with a <u>fatter</u> screen.
5. What are the most popular <u>Canadien</u> phones?
6. One of the best phones <u>are</u> made by an American company.

**6** **Find and correct seven mistakes in the student's piece of writing.**

I like my phone but I want a new one becous I have an old one but he is broken. Is so important for me. For me, the most important things in a phone is the size of the screen and the number of memory. I enjoy to take photos.

### PREPARE FOR THE EXAM
**Writing Part 2 (An article)**

**7** **Read the task below and plan your ideas. Make sure you cover all the points in the task.**

You see this notice on an English-language website.

**Articles wanted!**

**Great games for mobile phones**

*What makes a good mobile phone game?*
*Why do people enjoy playing games on their phones?*
*What kinds of games will be available for phones ten years from now?*

**Write an article answering these questions and we'll post the best ones on our website!**

**8** **Write your article in about 100 words.**

- Use the tips in the *Prepare to write* box.
- Remember to add some extra information and use a range of tenses.

» PREPARE FOR THE EXAM PAGE 127

# 10 ANIMALS IN DANGER

A

## ABOUT YOU

**07 Watch the video and then answer the questions.**

How important are animals to you?
Do you have any favourite animals?
Which animals in your country are in danger? Why?

## VOCABULARY Nature and wildlife

**1** **Look at the photos. Why do you think each animal is in danger? Which do you think is most in danger? Give your reasons.**

B

C

D

37 **2** **Listen to three teenagers talking about three of the animals. What problems does each person mention?**

37 **3** **Complete the sentences with the words in the box. Then listen again and check.** EP

| | | |
|---|---|---|
| creatures | crops | endangered |
| environment | habitat | humans |
| hunting | jungle | landscape |
| population | rainforest | |

1 This problem is as serious as saving the ______.
2 The ______ of honey bees today is far lower than it used to be.
3 Bees and other insects help our ______ to grow in the fields.
4 Some people say that the bluefin tuna is one of the tastiest living ______ in the sea.
5 Well, this large fish is also ______, probably more so.
6 The balance of the ocean ______ will be damaged forever.
7 This is all due to the actions of ______.
8 Besides ______, tigers are facing another challenge.
9 The ______ where they live is changing, as more and more trees are cut down.
10 The areas of ______ are getting smaller.
11 Their ______ is decreasing all the time.

**4** **Work in groups. Decide which animal in the photos is the most important to humans. Can you all agree?**

**5** **Discuss the questions.**

1 How important is it to protect animals in the wild?
2 What could you do to help?
3 Is enough being done to save the rainforest in your opinion?

## READING

**1** **The photo shows the Sumatran orangutan. Read the *fact file* and answer the questions.**

1 Where do Sumatran orangutans live and who with?
2 Do orangutans feed at the same time as each other?
3 Are the orangutans likely to become extinct in the future?

## PREPARE FOR THE EXAM

### Reading Part 5

**2** **Read the text about the Sumatran orangutan. For each question, choose the correct answer.**

| | A | B | C | D |
|---|---|---|---|---|
| 1 | A injured | B cut | C damaged | D hurt |
| 2 | A limited | B closed | C stopped | D controlled |
| 3 | A leaving | B decreasing | C removing | D losing |
| 4 | A stay | B hold | C save | D keep |
| 5 | A discover | B realise | C look | D recognise |
| 6 | A change | B transfer | C travel | D pass |

**3** **Match the highlighted words and phrases in the texts to the meanings.**

1 the natural environment in which an animal usually lives
2 continue to live
3 for a long time
4 from or in the hottest parts of the world
5 a natural environment where there are no humans

FACT FILE

## THE SUMATRAN ORANGUTAN

**Where do they live?**
High up in the trees. Female orangutans almost never touch the ground, and males rarely do. They used to live on the island of Java, too, but have now disappeared from the area. Male orangutans usually live on their own, while females live with their young.

**What do they eat?**
Sumatran orangutans have a healthy diet, consisting of fruit, leaves and insects. They often eat together in groups where the main food sources are.

**How many species are there?**
Nine, but only seven are likely to survive in the long term. Only three species have more than 1,000 orangutans left.

SAVE THE

# SUMATRAN ORANGUTAN!

At one time, orangutans lived in tropical rainforests across the whole island of Sumatra. Unfortunately, because humans have [1] ________ much of this forest, the orangutan population is now [2] ________ to the north of the island. Besides the fact that their habitat is disappearing, their numbers are quickly [3] ________ too. Unless we do more to help them, the 7,000 which are left will disappear completely.

People are not allowed to [4] ________ orangutans as pets in Indonesia, and if wildlife experts ever [5] ________ them in people's homes, they take them to a rescue centre. When the animals are healthy enough, the experts [6] ________ them to a safe area in a national park, and eventually put them back into the wild.

**If we protect orangutans now, they will have a future. If we do nothing, they may not.**

38

### TALKING POINTS

What effect does our lifestyle have on animals in the wild?
Does it matter if certain animals disappear forever? Why? / Why not?

## GRAMMAR Conditional sentences

**1** **Look at the examples. Which tenses are used in each pair? Match each example to rule a or b.**

1 If wildlife experts ever **discover** them in people's homes, they **take** them to a rescue centre.
2 **When** the animals **are** healthy enough, the experts **transfer** them to a safe area in a national park.
3 **If** we **protect** orangutans now, they **will have** a future.
4 They **won't have** a future **if** we **do** nothing.

a We use the zero conditional for events or situations that actually happen. We use: *If / When* + present simple + present simple.
b We use the first conditional to imagine what is likely to happen. We use: *If* + present simple + *will / won't*.

**2** **Match the sentence halves. Which sentences use the first conditional?**

1 If there is better protection for tigers,
2 When people clear an area of jungle,
3 If the area of Arctic ice gets smaller,
4 If an animal has a bad injury,
5 When there is more tourism in an area,

a they often use the land for farming.
b it has many benefits for local people.
c their numbers will probably increase.
d there won't be many polar bears left.
e it isn't able to hunt for food.

**3** **Complete the second example in each pair of sentences so that it means the same as the first. What do the examples tell you about the meaning of *unless*?**

1 **Unless** we do more to help orangutans, they will disappear completely.
If we ………… more to help orangutans, they will disappear completely.
2 **Unless** we protect the rainforests, many species will lose their habitat.
If we ………… the rainforests, many species will lose their habitat.

**4** **Complete the sentences with *if* or *unless*.**

1 Polar bears won't find enough to eat ………… we do more to protect their environment.
2 ………… we don't protect these animals now, they will die out.
3 Many birds will suffer ………… sea levels continue to rise.
4 ………… we control whale fishing, there'll be no whales left soon.
5 Elephant numbers will continue to fall ………… governments do more to protect them.

### Second conditional

**5** **Read the examples and the rule. Which example uses the second conditional?**

1 If bees **disappear** completely, we **will** all **suffer**.
2 If bees **disappeared** completely, we **would** all **suffer**.

We use the second conditional to talk about something that is unlikely to happen or is imaginary. We use:
*If* + past simple + *would*.

» GRAMMAR REFERENCE AND PRACTICE PAGE 156

**6** **Choose the correct verb form to complete the sentences.**

1 If *you'll go / you go* on holiday with your parents, it'll be fun!
2 If I were you, I *will / would* go with my friends.
3 If *you would go / you went* to the beach with your parents, you'd be bored.
4 If *you'll agree / you agree*, we can visit you on Monday.
5 If I had to move, I *will / would* move to the USA.
6 If *I have / I'll have* enough money, I'll go shopping with you.
7 I think that if *we meet / we'll meet* at 8 pm there's enough time before the film starts.

**7** **Complete the sentences so they are true for you.**

1 If I had the chance to see any animal in the wild, …
2 When I read about animals in danger, I …
3 If I saw an injured animal on the road, I …

## VOCABULARY Phrases with *at*

**1** **Read the examples and match the phrases to the meanings.**

1 **At least** 95% of wild tigers have disappeared.
2 Things are happening **at long last** to protect tigers.
3 **At first**, I thought she wasn't friendly, but actually she's just shy.
4 I loved this trip because we saw nature **at its best**.
5 Many wild animals are **at risk** of extinction.
6 The animals appeared **at once**.
7 **At present**, she's working as a wildlife reporter overseas.

a finally
b not less than
c now
d in danger
e as good as it can be
f in the beginning
g immediately

**2** **Complete the sentences with the phrases in the box.**

EP

| | | |
|---|---|---|
| at first | at its best | at least |
| at long last | at once | |
| at present | at risk | |

1 The amazing filming of wildlife in the Pantanal Wetlands is documentary-making ________.
2 When the horse suddenly stopped, I knew ________ that something was wrong.
3 It's very dry here ________, but rain is forecast for next week.
4 ________ I didn't recognise her because she looked so different.
5 ________ 70% of the Earth's surface is covered with water.
6 Zoos often breed animals that are ________ in the wild.
7 ________, the wild giant panda population is starting to grow.

**3** » **Work in pairs. Turn to page 135.**

## LISTENING

39 **1** **You will hear a video call between two teenagers, Lola and Pete. What do they have to do for their homework?**

39 **2** **Listen again and answer the questions.**

1 Why is the first animal they talk about endangered?
2 Why doesn't Lola think they should include tigers in their presentation?
3 What are marine animals? Why does Pete think they should talk about them?
4 What do they decide to do at the beginning of their presentation?
5 What three animals do they decide to include in their presentation?

## SPEAKING Discussing a topic (1)

**1** **Read the advice for taking part in discussions. Choose the five pieces of advice which are true. Can you add more advice?**

1 Don't be afraid to ask what something means.
2 Say as much as possible, even if the other person wants to speak.
3 Try to develop your ideas.
4 Make sure you give the other person enough opportunities to join in.
5 Apologise if you interrupt someone, and allow them time to speak.
6 Make links to what you or the other person has said.
7 Talk loudly if another person is trying to speak.

39 **2** **Read the *Prepare to speak* box. Listen to the conversation again to hear some of the phrases in the box. Match the phrases in the box to the functions below. Some phrases match the same function.**

### PREPARE TO SPEAK

**Taking part in a discussion**

1 I missed that. Can you repeat that, please?
2 Sorry, I don't understand.
3 Going back to …
4 Sorry, what were you going to say?
5 Do you mean … ?
6 Like I said before, …
7 On a completely different subject …

**a** asking for further explanation if you don't understand something
**b** encouraging someone to continue after you have interrupted them
**c** changing the topic
**d** referring back to an earlier topic
**e** asking someone to say something again if you didn't hear it

### PREPARE FOR THE EXAM

**Speaking Part 4**

**3** **Work in pairs. Discuss the questions, using phrases from the *Prepare to speak* box.**

Do you learn about endangered species at school? Which?
Have you ever seen an endangered animal species? Which?
Would you like to work with animals? Why? / Why not?
Have you ever visited a wildlife park? What did you see?
How could you help to protect local wildlife species?

» PREPARE FOR THE EXAM PAGE 134

# CULTURE

## ANIMALS AS NATIONAL SYMBOLS

**1** **Match the photos to the names of the animals. Which two aren't real?**

| | | |
|---|---|---|
| beaver | bison | dragon |
| eagle | emu | horse |
| kangaroo | kiwi | lion |
| tuatara | unicorn | |

**2** **Read the article. Find the names of the animals from Exercise 1. In which countries are they important?**

40

## Animals *and* countries

**Some animals are well-known symbols that make people think of certain countries. They may be national animals that appear on flags, coins or stamps because they have a special meaning. They might also be animals that only live in that country or imaginary animals from traditional folk tales.**

When people think of the United States, there's one animal that comes to mind – the bald eagle. It's the national bird and has been a symbol of the USA for more than 200 years. It represents the qualities of independence and freedom. Another symbol of the USA is the bison, which became the national mammal in 2016. The bison is the largest land animal in North America and it symbolises strength and power.

Canada has got two national animals – the beaver and the Canadian horse. Both animals were important to the first Europeans who came to Canada. They hunted beavers and used their fur to make warm coats and hats. Beavers are also hard-working animals, which makes them a positive symbol. In a similar way, Canadian horses were very useful to early farmers because of their strength and good nature.

The United Kingdom hasn't got a national animal, but its different countries have got traditional animal symbols. England is represented by the lion – a strong, brave animal that is often a symbol for kings. Scotland's animal symbol is the unicorn – a mythical white horse with a long, magical horn on its head. Similarly, Wales is represented by a red dragon with wings. This symbol appears on the Welsh national flag.

One of Australia's national animals is the red kangaroo, which isn't surprising. After all, kangaroos are unique to Australia. They don't appear anywhere else in the world. The same is true for the emu, which is Australia's enormous national bird. It can be up to two metres tall and weigh up to 60 kilograms. Many places and companies in Australia are named after kangaroos and emus because they're so typically Australian.

The kiwi is a small, brown flightless bird that only lives in New Zealand. It's such a famous national symbol that the word 'kiwi' has become a nickname for New Zealanders. Another unique animal from New Zealand is the tuatara. It's a reptile that looks like a lizard that only lives on 32 small islands. The tuatara's closest relatives died about sixty million years ago, so many people call them 'little dinosaurs' or 'living fossils'.

**3** **Are the sentences true or false? Correct the false sentences.**

1 The bison is a typical symbol of independence.
2 Beavers and Canadian horses were useful in the past.
3 Canadian horses were strong but difficult to manage.
4 The national animals of Scotland and Wales aren't real.
5 Emus are found in Australia and some other countries.
6 Tuataras live in most of the areas of New Zealand.

**4** **Match the highlighted words in the text to the meanings.**

1 imaginary or not real
2 an animal's coat of hair
3 small pieces of metal that we use as money
4 not able to fly
5 the quality of being strong
6 not afraid of anything

41 **5** **Listen to Sonia giving a presentation to her class. Tick (✓) the topics that she talks about.**

1 when the eagle became a national symbol
2 where the bald eagle lives in winter
3 how Sonia feels about the bald eagle
4 why bald eagles became endangered
5 some other animals that people suggested
6 how a famous man felt about the bald eagle
7 how the bald eagle usually gets its food

41 **6** **Listen again. Answer the questions.**

1 When did the bald eagle become a national symbol?
2 Why does Sonia think the eagle is a symbol of freedom?
3 When was the bald eagle more common: now or in the eighteenth century?
4 What mistake can you find on some old ten-dollar coins?
5 Why didn't Benjamin Franklin want the bald eagle as a national symbol?
6 How does Sonia feel about the bald eagle and what it symbolises?

**7** **Read the *Useful language* phrases. Complete them with the words in the box.**

| appears | independence | national |
|---|---|---|
| represents | symbol | unusual |

## USEFUL LANGUAGE

**Describing animals as national symbols**

1 It's the country's ____ animal.
2 It has been a ____ of our country for 200 years.
3 It's quite an ____ animal.
4 It ____ on coins and stamps.
5 It ____ the quality of freedom.
6 It's a symbol of ____.

## PROJECT

***A presentation about a national animal***

**Prepare a presentation about a country's iconic animals. Use the following questions to help you.**

1 Are the animals official national symbols?
2 What specific types of animal are they?
3 What is special about those animals?
4 Are they important to the country's history?
5 Do the animals symbolise any qualities?

**Give your presentation to the class.**

# 11 OFF TO SCHOOL

## ABOUT YOU

09 **Watch the video and then answer the questions.**
How many hours a week do you spend at school?
How long does it take you to get to school each day?
What do you think is important to have in a classroom?

## VOCABULARY School

**1** **Look at the photos of difficult journeys to school. Which journey do you think is the most difficult? Why?**

42 **2** **Listen to a photographer talking about the photos. In what order does she talk about them?**

42 **3** **Complete the sentences with the words in the boxes. Listen again and check.**

EP

| primary | qualifications | secondary | Year |
|---|---|---|---|

1 The children are very young and go to the ________ school in the village.
2 I'm not sure where they will go to school when they are ________ school age.
3 I think he was in ________ 1, so age six.
4 I wonder what ________ these children will end up getting.

| attend | boarding school | degree | do well |
|---|---|---|---|

5 The children ________ a school which is on the other side of the mountain.
6 Fortunately, the children can live at the ________.
7 The children and their parents want them to ________.
8 They want them to go on to university and get a ________.

| broke up | done badly | education | undergraduates |
|---|---|---|---|

9 We had been ________ together at the University of Cambridge.
10 The children had two more weeks before they ________ for the holidays.
11 One young teen I spoke to afterwards thought he had ________ in his exams.
12 It seems that ________ is a priority for this community.

**4** **Group the words in the boxes in Exercise 3 into verbs and nouns. What are the infinitives of the verbs?**

**5** **Read the sentences about school. Do you agree?**

1 All children should attend school up to the age of 18.
2 Only excellent students should go to university and get a degree.
3 Schools should break up for holidays every four weeks.
4 Children who do badly should never have to repeat a year.
5 Children should start primary school when they are aged 4, and secondary school when they are aged 12.
6 It's really important to do well at school.
7 Education should be free and available to everyone in the world.
8 Experience in life is more important than qualifications.
9 All children should start learning another language in Year 1.
10 Undergraduates shouldn't have to pay to attend university.

## READING

**1** What things do you like about your classroom? What things do you dislike?

**2** Read the three texts quickly. Which classroom (A, B or C) is the most traditional? Which is the most unusual? 43

# CLASSROOMS AROUND THE WORLD

**Last month on TeacherWeb, we asked you to tell us about the most interesting classrooms you've ever taught in. We received hundreds of replies from teachers around the world. Here is a selection of our favourite stories.**

**A**

**Jack** When I was looking for somewhere to teach English as a foreign language, I decided to apply for a school that was far away. However, this place was definitely further than I had imagined, and I never thought that a school classroom could be in a cave! It was a really unusual place to have a school. The families of a Chinese village had built the school, known as Middle Cave Elementary School, in the cave about 50 years before. They had transported the materials for the school furniture up the mountain. It took days, and then they made the tables and chairs by hand. Children come from many different places around the area and walk up a stone path to reach the school every day. I arrived at the school in early April to teach English conversation, and I helped the music teacher. There were always two teachers, which I enjoyed. Having these lessons in a cave was incredible because of the sound produced inside caves. The classroom made music by itself!

**B**

**Katie** I wasn't sure what to do in the summer after I left school and before I went university. Then I found out by accident about a teaching programme in Samoa for three months. I had never worked with children before, so I was a bit nervous. But when I walked into the classroom, the children were so welcoming! Our classroom was fairly ordinary, with desks and a blackboard. There were hardly any computers, but the walls were covered with colourful pictures and writing, mostly in English. I had an amazing time at the school, helping the class teacher, and teaching some classes myself. The teacher had the most beautiful wooden chair that her grandfather had made for her by hand to celebrate her first job. It was a very different school to the one that I had attended back home. I thought that the children all worked really hard and they mostly did well in their exams.

**C**

**Georgie** I had a very special experience when I went to this school in Cuba a few years ago. Three years earlier, the parents and teachers had built several outdoor classrooms for the summer terms. They had spent a lot of time talking about the design of the classrooms, and eventually they decided to have lots of different 'classroom areas'. There was a classroom in the vegetable garden, there was another one surrounded by trees and there was even a classroom in a rose garden, although there were a couple of sunflowers that someone had planted by mistake! The parents had put a lot of effort into making their children's learning a good experience. I think the children enjoyed it because they didn't feel as if they were in a classroom. However, I was teaching maths and I found I missed having a whiteboard!

**3** Read the texts again. Which classroom …

1 had the children's work on the walls?
2 was built by local people about half a century ago?
3 was inside a garden?
4 did the students like?
5 had very few computers?
6 was good for music?
7 was challenging for the teacher?
8 had a gift made by the teacher's relative in it?

**4** Match the highlighted words and phrases in the text to the meanings.

1 with things all around a place
2 energy that you use to do something
3 not special
4 do something enjoyable because it is a special day
5 request something officially

### TALKING POINTS

Which of the three classrooms would you most like to have?
What would your ideal classroom be like?

# GRAMMAR Past perfect

**1** **Read the example and look at the verbs. Answer the questions.**

I **went** to this school a few years ago. Three years earlier, the parents and teachers **had built** several outdoor classrooms.

1 Which action happened first?
   a the writer went to the school
   b the parents and teachers had built the classrooms
2 Which verb is in the past simple? Which is in the past perfect?

**2** **Choose the correct words to complete the rules.**

a We use the past perfect to talk about an action that happened *before* / *after* another action in the past.
b We form the past perfect with *had + past participle* / *had + -ing form*.

» **GRAMMAR REFERENCE AND PRACTICE PAGE 157**

**3** **Read the sentences and look at the verb forms. Which action came first, a or b?**

0 When Jake got home, Mark had left the house.
   a Jake got home.
   (b) Mark left the house.
1 I'd gone to bed when Harriet got home.
   a Harriet got home.
   b I went to bed.
2 Martin didn't go to the cinema because he'd seen the film before.
   a Martin didn't go to the cinema.
   b Martin saw the film.
3 Juliana wasn't hungry because she'd had lunch at school.
   a Juliana had lunch at school.
   b Juliana wasn't hungry.
4 Paul called me when he had finished his homework.
   a Paul called me.
   b Paul finished his homework.

**4** **Choose the correct form of the verbs.**

1 I was really surprised when I read the email: I *had won* / *won* the lottery!
2 I decided to call my brother and say that I *changed* / *had changed* my mind.
3 Yesterday, when the crime *had happened* / *happened*, I was at home.
4 I *had been* / *went* to Malaysia for my summer vacation last year.
5 I told him about the new restaurant that *opened* / *had opened* in my town the week before.
6 Waterskiing was cool. I *never did* / *had never done* anything like it before!

**5** **Read about a school in Norway and complete the text with the correct form of the verbs.**

Before I [1] ________ (go) to Norway, I [2] ________ (work) all over the world and I [3] ________ (see) many different classrooms. But this [4] ________ (be) definitely more impressive than anything I [5] ________ (experience) before. I [6] ________ (not / work) with a class before in which every child had their own computer. But I also [7] ________ (not / go) to a school before where children had to leave the island when they [8] ________ (reach) the age of 16, to continue their education on the mainland.

# VOCABULARY Compound nouns

**1** **Read the examples and look at the compound nouns.**

**What kind of words do we join together to make compound nouns?**

1 Our **classroom** was fairly ordinary.
2 I missed having a **whiteboard**!
3 I meet up with my friends at the **bus stop**.

**2** **Choose a word from each box to make compound nouns. Write the words next to the meanings.**

| black | break | head | home |
|---|---|---|---|
| lunch | school | text | time |

| board | book | bus | table |
|---|---|---|---|
| time | teacher | time | work |

1 the person in charge of a school
2 study and exercises that you do out of school
3 this is when you eat in the middle of the day
4 teachers write on this with a white material called chalk
5 *Prepare!* Level 5 is your …
6 a list that tells you when and where you have your classes
7 a vehicle that takes children to and from school
8 a short period of rest during the school day

**3** **You have two minutes. How many compound nouns can you make from the words?**

WORK HOME HOUSE BUS JOURNEY LUNCH SCHOOL TICKET BREAK TIME TRAIN

**4** » **Turn to page 136.**

# WRITING A story (2)

**1** **Have you read any stories that take place in school? What happened?**

**2** **Read Alex's story. Choose the best first sentence.**

**a** It was a really bad day at school.
**b** It was the first day back at school after the summer holidays.
**c** I was looking forward to the summer holidays.

........ I was sitting quietly in the classroom and feeling very nervous. Before the holidays the teacher had asked us to do some simple homework. I hadn't done it because I'd forgotten all about it. I was really worried that the teacher would be angry. Then the teacher came into the classroom. She took the register, but she didn't mention the homework. She carried on with the class as usual. Finally, at the end of the class she said quickly, 'Don't forget to bring your homework tomorrow.' How lucky! I handed in my completed homework the next day – and I got a good mark!

**3** **Read the *Prepare to write* box. Read Alex's story again and find examples of verbs in the past simple, past continuous and past perfect.**

## PREPARE TO WRITE

### A story (2)

When you write a story:

- use a range of verb forms.
- use adverbs to describe verbs:
  *I was sitting **quietly** in the classroom.*
- use adjectives to describe nouns:
  *I handed in my **completed** homework the next day.*
- check that your story has a beginning, a middle and an end.

**4** **Look at the highlighted adjectives and adverbs in Alex's story. How do adjectives and adverbs improve the story?**

**5** **Add a suitable adjective to the sentences. Use your own ideas.**

**1** A ........ man walked into the room.
**2** The teacher gave us some ........ homework.
**3** We had a ........ day!
**4** The lessons take place in a ........ classroom.

**6** **Add an adverb to each sentence. Use the adverbs in the box or your own ideas. Compare your sentences with a partner.**

| angrily | cheerfully | easily | immediately |
|---|---|---|---|
| quickly | quietly | slowly | well |

**0** He shouted at me.
*He shouted at me angrily.*
**1** She walked out of the room.
**2** I finished my homework.
**3** We ate our lunch.
**4** He smiled at me.
**5** The teacher answered her questions.

## PREPARE FOR THE EXAM

### Writing Part 2 (A story)

**7** **Read the task below and plan your ideas, then compare your ideas with a partner. Can you improve your plan?**

Your English teacher has asked you to write a story.
Your story must begin with this sentence:
*I had to set off for school a little earlier than usual that morning.*

**8** **Write your story.**

- Use the tips in the *Prepare to write* box.
- Write about 100 words.
- Remember to check your spelling and grammar.

# 12 GETTING AROUND

## ABOUT YOU

Which is the most exciting form of transport you have been on? Why was it exciting?
Which forms of transport have you travelled on alone?

## VOCABULARY Travel

**1** **Look at the photos. What forms of transport do they show? What are the different reasons for using them? What other forms of transport can you think of?**

44 **2** **Listen to four people talking. Match them to the photos.**

44 **3** **Listen again. Complete the sentences with the correct form of the words in the box.**

EP

| abroad | be held up | check in | go away | |
|---|---|---|---|---|
| land | reach | sail | set off | tour | unpack |

**Speaker 1**
1 They'd never been ________ before, so they flew to Venice.
2 They ________ and found their ship waiting in the harbour.
3 They ________ down the Adriatic Sea.
4 They ________ Dubrovnik, in Croatia, on the Monday morning.

**Speaker 2**
5 He ________ from home at 7 am every morning,
6 He ________ about an hour later and gets a taxi to his office.

**Speaker 3**
7 We ________ in the summer. Mum plans amazing road trips for us.
8 If we're in a city, we usually go on a ________ with a guide.
9 But as we're travelling so much, we don't really ever ________.

**Speaker 4**
10 If the train ________, the rail company gives him a refund.

**4** **Complete the sentences with the correct form of the words from Exercise 3.**

1 Josie's plane ________ at 7.28. We should leave now to meet her at the airport.
2 You can ________ across the water from one island to another.
3 Some students go ________ for a year to a different country.
4 We're ________ at 5.30 tomorrow morning, so make sure you set your alarm!
5 We want to ________ for a few weeks this summer.
6 Nowadays, you can ________ online using the airline's website or app.
7 It was late at night by the time we ________ the hotel.
8 Mum ________ in traffic – she'll be here in about 30 minutes.
9 I can't come over now – I have to ________ after my holiday and put everything away.
10 When we go to new cities, we always go on a ________.

**5** **Discuss the questions.**

1 Which forms of transport do you really enjoy using? Why?
2 Have you ever been abroad? Where and how did you go?
3 Why do some people always go away to the same place for their holiday?

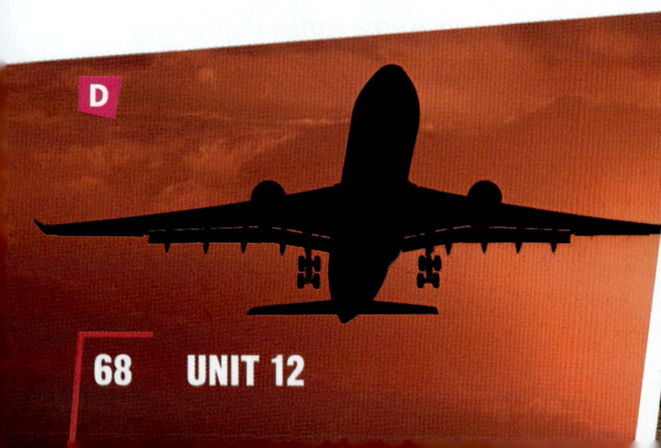

## READING

**1** **What things do you have to do before you go on holiday? Make a list. Read the web page and compare your ideas.**

**2** **Match these headings to the paragraphs.**

Contacting home Flying What documents to take
Where to stay What to pack

45

# Travelling WITHOUT your parents

Do you go on school trips abroad? Are you planning a summer holiday with your besties and without your parents? If your parents let you go away without them, you should do some of the research and planning yourself. Alice Maddison gives you some top tips.

**1** ..............

If you want to go abroad, you have to take a form of ID with you. This could be a passport, or a national ID card, and it has to have your photo on it. You should also check out the rules for under 18s travelling on their own on the website of the embassy of the country you are going to. For example, for some countries, you need to have a letter from your parents giving permission for you to travel alone. If you don't have that, you might find that you are not allowed into the country! You should also buy travel insurance in case anything happens, for example, if you lose your luggage or if you have a medical emergency.

**2** ..............

The rules here depend on the different airlines. For most airlines, if you're over 15 years old, you can travel alone. Remember that it's easy to book a flight, but it's also easy to miss it! You should make sure you get to the airport on time. For most flights you should get to the airport at least two hours before your flight. Although, if you are travelling to the United States, it's three hours. The airline staff will make you show them your ID again – it's normal, so don't worry about that!

**3** ..............

For accommodation, you should book a youth hostel because it's cheaper and also you'll be able to sleep in the same room as your friends. You shouldn't choose somewhere that closes its doors at 8 pm. Many cheaper flights arrive after dinner and you don't want to be left out on the street.

**4** ..............

The only person who is going to carry your stuff is you, so you should think carefully about what you need to take with you. You needn't take lots of clothes because most youth hostels have washing machines you can use. You need to check the weather so that you know what clothes to take. If you have a good rain coat, you don't have to take an umbrella!

**5** ..............

While you're enjoying your holiday with your friends, it's easy to forget about everything else. Use social media to post pictures and videos of all the fun you are having. This will also let your friends and family know that you are safe and having a good time. And, of course, don't forget to call or text your parents every day so that they don't worry!

**3** **Read the blog post and answer these questions according to the text.**

1. What do you always need to take when you travel to another country?
2. Why might you need a letter from your parents?
3. How long before your flight should you arrive at the airport?
4. What important point does Alice make about the times that accommodation closes?
5. What advice does Alice give about packing?
6. Why do you need to post things on social media?

**4** **Match the highlighted words in the article to the meanings.**

1. a cheap, simple hotel, especially for young people
2. studying something to find out more information about it
3. an official document that shows or proves who you are
4. a company that takes people and things to places in planes
5. an informal word for best friends
6. an informal word for objects or things

### TALKING POINTS

Have you ever travelled alone? If so, did you enjoy it? If not, why not?

At what age do you think children should be allowed to travel alone? Why?

What are the advantages of travelling alone, rather than with your family?

## GRAMMAR Modals: Obligation, necessity and advice (2)

**1** **Read the examples. Then complete the rules with the verbs in the examples.**

1 If you want to go abroad, you **have to** take a form of ID with you.
2 You **should** also buy travel insurance in case anything happens.
3 If you have a good rain coat, you **don't have to** take an umbrella!
4 You **shouldn't** choose somewhere that closes its doors at 8 pm.
5 You **need to** buy a good guidebook.
6 You **needn't take** lots of clothes because most youth hostels have washing machines you can use.

We use:
**a** ______ and ______ to give advice to someone.
**b** ______ to say that something is necessary because of a rule or law.
**c** ______ to say that something is important, but not a rule or law.
**d** ______, ______ or *don't need to* to say that something is not necessary.

Notice the different patterns with *need*:
You **need to** buy a good guidebook.
You **don't need to** take lots of clothes.
You **needn't** take lots of clothes.

**2** **Complete the sentences with the correct verb from Exercise 1.**

1 You ______ sit at a computer all day. It's bad for you.
2 You ______ show your passport if an official wants to see it.
3 You ______ check the weather before you pack your clothes.
4 If you are travelling alone, you ______ be scared – the airline will look after you.
5 We ______ make sure we catch the last train.
6 You ______ worry, Mum. I'll be fine!

### *let* and *make*

**3** **Read the sentences. Match the verbs to the meanings below.**

1 My parents **made** me go on the school trip to the History Museum. It was so boring!
2 My parents **let** me go on holiday to Italy with my friends.

**a** giving permission to do something
**b** forcing you to do something (that you probably don't want to do)

» GRAMMAR REFERENCE AND PRACTICE PAGE 158

**4** **Choose the correct option.**

1 The airline *let / made* us switch off our phones for take-off and landing.
2 My parents *let / made* me travel alone for the first time when I was 15.
3 When you go through the security control at the airport, they sometimes *make / let* you take your shoes off.
4 My friends went on holiday together last year, but my parents didn't *make / let* me go.
5 The driver won't *let / make* you get on the bus without showing your ticket.
6 Airport staff *make / let* you show your boarding card at the gate.

**5** **Complete the sentences with your own ideas.**

1 My parents tell me I should …
2 When I stay with my grandparents, I don't have to …
3 Right now I need to …
4 My teachers never let me …
5 Last week, my parents made me …

## VOCABULARY Phrases with *on*

**1** **Read the example. What other phrases do you know with *on*?**

He sets out at 7 am and he's **on board** by 8.20 am.

**2** EP **Complete the sentences with the phrases in the box.**

| on board | on display | on foot |
|---|---|---|
| on purpose | on sale | on time |
| on my/your/her own | | |

1 There were lots of posters ______ on the walls at the train station.
2 We have to get to the airport ______ so that we don't miss our flight.
3 We went from the domestic terminal to the international terminal ______ because it wasn't far.
4 My favourite author's latest book was ______ at the airport shop.
5 As soon as you get ______, the airline staff want you to fasten your seat belt.
6 'I didn't do it ______! It was an accident,' said the driver.
7 My older sister is very adventurous. Last year she travelled around South America ______.

**3** » **Work in pairs. Turn to page 136.**

# LISTENING

**1** **Look at the photos. What might an announcement say in these places?**

**Compare your ideas with your partner.**

## PREPARE FOR THE EXAM

### Listening Part 3

**2** **Look at the notes. What kind of information is missing? Share your ideas with your partner.**

**FLIGHT INFORMATION**

Languages spoken by cabin crew: English, Chinese and **(1)** ..........

Arrival time at destination: **(2)** ..........

**VIDEO ENTERTAINMENT**

New channel: will show **(3)** .......... programmes

**MEAL SERVICE**

Vegetarian dish: **(4)** ..........

Choice of desserts

**ON-BOARD SALES**

Special offer on **(5)** ..........

Name of magazine for children: **(6)** ..........

**3** 46 **You will hear an announcement on board a plane. For each question, write the correct answer in the gap. Write one or two words or a number or a date or a time.**

# SPEAKING Talking about travel

47 **1** **Read the questions in Exercise 4. Listen to Luca and Kasia answering some of the questions. Which ones do they answer?**

47 **2** **It's important to add more information when you answer questions. Match sentences 1–6 with a–f from the recordings. Then listen again and check.**

**1** Actually, I like all kinds of transport but above all I love travelling by train.
**2** I guess it would be a helicopter because they look exciting.
**3** I usually stay at home with my family and do fun things.
**4** Yes, I'm going to visit my cousin in London for a few days.
**5** I want to go to Mexico to see the Mayan ruins.
**6** Last year, we went to Spain to visit my grandparents.

**a** I'd never been abroad before and we spent a lot of time at the beach – it was really hot!
**b** For example, we go to the pool and go on bike rides and stuff like that.
**c** I've never been before and I can't wait to see all the famous stuff in the city, like Big Ben and Trafalgar Square.
**d** They're ancient and look really interesting, and the coast is supposed to be gorgeous, too.
**e** You can see loads out of the windows and walk around.
**f** I'd love to go on one in New York and fly between the buildings!

**3** **Read the *Prepare to speak* box, then look at the sentences in Exercise 2 again. Find examples of the phrases and the range of tenses that Luca and Kasia use.**

## PREPARE TO SPEAK

### Answering questions (2)

| Adding extra information | Using a range of tenses |
|---|---|
| For example … | I usually (stay) … |
| Actually, … | I want to (go to) … |
| because … | I'm going to (visit) … |
| above all … | Last year, we (went to) … |

## PREPARE FOR THE EXAM

### Speaking Part 1

**4** **Ask and answer the questions with a partner. Use phrases from the *Prepare to speak* box.**

**1** Which kind of transport do you use most often?
**2** What's your favourite / least favourite kind of transport? What do you like / dislike about it?
**3** What kind of transport would you like to try? Why?
**4** What's been your most interesting journey? Why?
**5** Where do you go on holiday?
**6** Are you going on holiday this year? Where are you going?
**7** Which country would you most like to visit? Why?
**8** What's been your best holiday? What did you do?

# LIFE SKILLS DECISION-MAKING

## EVALUATING OPTIONS

**LIFE SKILLS**

**Evaluating options**

We make decisions every day of our lives. In some cases, we decide about little things, like what to do at the weekend. In other cases, we must make decisions about more important things like school studies, job choices and personal relationships. For those big decisions, it's good to evaluate our options carefully in order to make the best choice possible.

**1** **Ask and answer the questions with a partner.**

1. Do you find it hard to make decisions? Why? / Why not?
2. Who do you ask for advice about important decisions?
3. Do you sometimes change your mind after you decide?

**2** **Read the forum posts. Who mentions the following topics?**

1. Using exercise to relax
2. Reading articles online
3. Chatting with close friends or relatives
4. Taking language classes

## TEEN-WORLD Forum

Profile

Log out

**TOPIC:** Life decisions

**QUESTION:** How do you make decisions? What advice can you give other people?

**JENNA** 2:46 pm

When I'm having trouble with a decision, I usually write things down because it helps me organise my thoughts. Sometimes I make a table with two columns, for advantages and disadvantages. I did that when I was trying to choose between Spanish and German classes after school. In the end, I chose Spanish, because it's similar to French, which I already speak. And more people speak Spanish, so it might be more useful. When I'm having a hard time making a choice, I also talk to myself out loud. I know that sounds a bit strange, but it actually helps!

**BRYAN** 5:53 pm

Sometimes I think too much when I have to make a decision. I think and think again, and when I've finally made a choice, I start to worry that I might be wrong! When that happens to me, I often go for a walk or I do some exercise to relax and take my mind off the problem. After a while, I can think calmly, without feeling so worried and stressed. The time of day is also important for me. I have a hard time making decisions in the morning or in the late evening when I'm tired.

**MICHAEL** 11:24 am

I hate making decisions quickly because I prefer to think carefully about all the options. For example, I had to choose a topic for a history presentation about Ancient Rome, and I spent four days reading lots of articles online. After all that, I decided that Roman architecture would be a good topic because there was a lot of information, and I found some great photos that I could use. That's how I often make decisions. I take time to think and explore different ideas, and then after a while the best choice usually becomes obvious.

**EMILY** 3:19 pm

When I need to make a decision, I always talk to people that I trust. Sometimes it's enough to chat about the problem and hear what other people have to say. Other times, I ask for practical advice and suggestions. I usually ask my friends or close relatives, but there's also a guidance counsellor at our school. She's really patient and she always has time to listen. I had an appointment last week to talk about my options for university and she's given me some things to read before our next meeting. Choosing a career isn't easy!

48

**3** **Read the forum posts again and answer the questions.**

1. How does Jenna organise her ideas more clearly?
2. What unusual thing does Jenna do sometimes?
3. Why was Michael looking for photos online?
4. Why does Michael need time to make decisions?
5. Why does Bryan get stressed about decisions?
6. Who is helping Emily think about her studies?
7. Which person is similar to you? Why?

49 **4** **Listen to Molly and Patrick. Who makes decisions quickly? Who needs more time? Why?**

## Summer Camps

*Are you going to be here in July? Sign up for one of our summer camps!*

**Monday–Friday 9:00 am to 2:00 pm**

### Outdoor Adventures

This camp offers a variety of outdoor sports and physical activities, such as football, cycling, hiking, swimming and rockclimbing. If you aren't in good shape, you will be!

### French Culture

This camp combines French language practice with fun cultural studies, including music, film, art and literature. Participants must have an intermediate level of French.

### Art and Design

This camp is ideal for anyone who enjoys art and creative expression. It includes activities like drawing, painting, sculpture and graphic design using computers.

### Science 4 Fun

This camp offers fun, practical experiments for exploring sciences like biology, chemistry and physics. Classes will be in the science lab at Kingsway Secondary School.

49 **5** **Listen again. Are the sentences true or false?**

1. Molly wants to be outdoors because she loves camping.
2. Patrick doesn't mind being indoors for summer camp.
3. Molly wants to know who is going to teach the art camp.
4. Patrick suggests they sign up for the French camp together.
5. Patrick suggests they ask for more information about the summer camps.
6. Molly wants to talk to her friends before she makes a decision.

**6** **Read the *Useful language* phrases. Change the words in brackets. Use your own ideas.**

## USEFUL LANGUAGE

**Discussing options**

1. I prefer to be (outdoors) in summer.
2. I think I'd rather (go hiking) in July.
3. The (French) camp sounds boring to me.
4. The (science) camp might be interesting.
5. I'm not sure about the (adventure) camp.
6. I'd probably choose the (art) camp.

## PROJECT

***Evaluating options for summer camp***

**Imagine you are going to choose one of the summer camps above. How would you evaluate the options? Use the questions below to help you. Discuss the options with a partner and try to make a decision.**

1. Do you usually think a lot about your choices?
2. Would you make a list or table of the options?
3. What additional information would you need?
4. How long might you need to make a decision?
5. Who would you ask for advice before deciding?

**Tell the class which summer programme you would prefer, explaining your reasons and how you evaluated the options.**

# REVIEW 3 UNITS 9–12

## VOCABULARY

**1** **Complete the sentences with the words in the box.**

| display | fuel | invention |
|---|---|---|
| plug in | power | pump |

1 Do you ______ your phone to charge it overnight?
2 Some people think that the wheel is the greatest ______ ever.
3 After the flood, we used a ______ to get the water out of our house.
4 My calculator doesn't need batteries – it gets its ______ from sunlight.
5 I can't see the ______ on my phone when the sun is shining.
6 Cars that have a bigger ______ tank can travel further without stopping.

**2** **Rewrite the second sentence with *enough*, *too* or *not … enough*, adding any other words necessary.**

1 The river was too cold to swim in.
The river ______ to swim in.
2 There wasn't enough information about the trip.
There was ______ little information about the trip.
3 Brian hasn't got enough qualifications to go deep-sea diving.
Brian has got ______ few qualifications to go deep-sea diving.
4 This online game isn't simple enough to learn in an afternoon.
This online game is ______ to learn in an afternoon.

**3** **Complete the sentences with compound nouns formed from one word in each box.**

| black | break | head | text | time |
|---|---|---|---|---|

| board | books | table | teacher | time |
|---|---|---|---|---|

1 Our teacher wrote the answers on the ______.
2 If students are late for school more than once, they are sent to the ______.
3 In my school, we write in our notebooks and not in our ______.
4 On the first day of the school year, they give me my new ______.
5 My best friend and I are in different classes, but we always meet up at ______.

**4** **Match the two parts of the phrases.**

| | | | |
|---|---|---|---|
| **1** | do | **a** | primary school |
| **2** | attend | **b** | for the school holidays |
| **3** | set off | **c** | badly in an exam |
| **4** | be held up | **d** | abroad |
| **5** | break up | **e** | in traffic |
| **6** | go | **f** | on a journey |

**5** **Read the definitions and write the words in the puzzle. What is the missing word going down?**

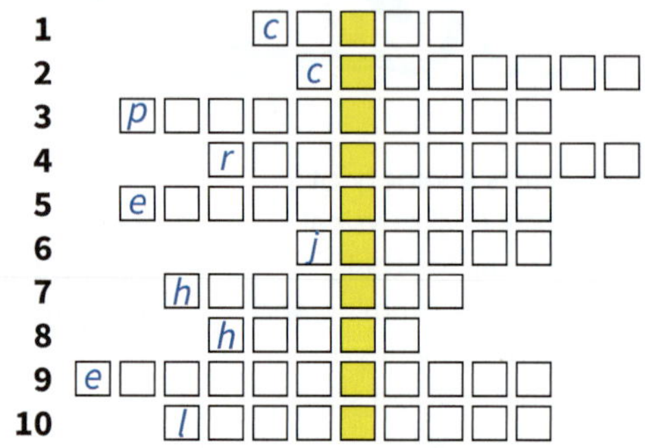


1 plants such as vegetables that are grown in large amounts by farmers
2 something that is living but is not a plant
3 the number of people or animals living in a particular area
4 a forest with tall trees where it rains a lot
5 when a type of animal gets fewer and fewer in number we say it is …
6 a tropical forest with large trees growing close together
7 the natural environment in which an animal or plant usually lives
8 a man, woman or child
9 the air, land, and water where people, animals, and plants live
10 the appearance of an area of land, especially in the countryside

## GRAMMAR

**1** **Complete the sentences with the correct form of the verbs. Use the past simple and past perfect.**

1 The strong wind the day before ______ (blow) all the leaves off the trees and they ______ (look) very ugly.
2 Although I ______ (hear) the news earlier, I still ______ (not believe) it.
3 A man was standing at the school gates for ages, but when I ______ (look) again, he ______ (disappear).
4 My younger sister ______ (never visit) the mall before, so I ______ (take) her there last Saturday.
5 I ______ (decide) not to go on the evening river cruise, as I ______ (not feel) well all day.

**2** **Complete the sentences with the future continuous form of the verbs in the box.**

| enjoy | happen | study |
|---|---|---|
| travel | wait | |

1 This time next week we ________ the sun in the south of Spain.
2 Next week, our class ________ the fruit fly in biology.
3 Lots of free events ________ when the music festival is on.
4 My dad ________ for us outside the stadium.
5 Looking at the timetable for our trip, we ________ mostly at night.

**3** **Rewrite the sentences to give advice. Use *don't have to*, *should* or *shouldn't*.**

1 Make sure you get plenty of sleep. You …
2 It isn't necessary to book a tour in advance. You …
3 If I were you, I wouldn't spend so much money on sweets. You …
4 It isn't necessary to bring anything to eat. You …
5 It isn't sensible to walk home on your own at night. You …

**4** **Complete the conditional sentences with the correct form of the verbs.**

1 If we ________ (catch) the early bus, we'd get to school by 8.00.
2 If Sam ________ (have) enough time, he'll bring that video game round later.
3 If Tom doesn't see anyone at the weekend, he always ________ (get) really bored.
4 I'd make a cake if I ________ (know) everyone was coming later.
5 We'll meet at the zoo tomorrow, unless you ________ (suggest) somewhere else.

**5** **Correct the mistake in each sentence.**

1 I came home and saw my sister made a cake, so I had a slice.
2 My parents made me to tidy my room last weekend.
3 You haven't to bring any drinks, but you must bring some snacks.
4 Yesterday evening, when the crime had happened, I was at home having dinner with friends.

## PREPARE FOR THE EXAM

### Reading Part 5

**1** **For each question, choose the correct answer.**

#### Water clocks

Ancient engineers developed many complicated clocks using flowing water to show time passing. Some of these involved building clock towers which were at **(1)** ________ nine metres high. Similar clocks were in use right up until the last century in some parts of the world.

Twenty-first century scientists have **(2)** ________ how to create smaller, yet still environmentally friendly methods for keeping time. This has led to the **(3)** ________ of the Eco-friendly Water-powered Clock, which uses tap water to create power for a simple battery. This means it doesn't need to be **(4)** ________ in, and the water in the clock doesn't need to be replaced for six months, either. The clock has a digital **(5)** ________ and because it is cheap to produce, this **(6)** ________ it easier to sell at a reasonable price, too.

| | A | B | C | D |
|---|---|---|---|---|
| **1** | **A** minimum | **B** less | **C** least | **D** minus |
| **2** | **A** researched | **B** looked | **C** requested | **D** controlled |
| **3** | **A** experiment | **B** technology | **C** connection | **D** invention |
| **4** | **A** moved | **B** plugged | **C** put | **D** joined |
| **5** | **A** presentation | **B** picture | **C** display | **D** show |
| **6** | **A** lets | **B** allows | **C** helps | **D** makes |

### Reading Part 6

**2** **For each question, write the correct answer. Write one word for each gap.**

#### A very unusual school

Imagine if you went to a school with no books. Well, that's exactly what happens at the West Philadelphia School of the Future, where students do all their work on computers. They learn Maths on an app and the teachers use smart boards. This is all done **(1)** ________ purpose, in order to improve students' technology skills.

The school wasn't very successful **(2)** ________ first: some of the students didn't know enough **(3)** ________ technology to use some of the devices. Now, the school is much better. Its students **(4)** ________ doing well and getting high scores for their work. Many parents want their children to go there because employers need **(5)** ________ find people with the skills which the School of the Future provides them with. It's expected that students from this school **(6)** ________ get jobs easily when they graduate.

# 13 #NOFILTER

## ABOUT YOU

**10 Watch the video and then answer the questions.**

Where and when do you take selfies?

Describe your favourite selfie.

Which photo apps do you use?

Have you ever used #NoFilter with one of your photos? What does the hashtag mean?

## VOCABULARY Social media

**1** **Look at these 'before and after' pictures, where digital changes were made to the original photos. What changes do you notice in each one?**

50 **2** **Listen to a teenager. Which 'after' picture does she describe, A2 or B2?**

50 **3** **Listen again and complete the text with the words in the box.**

EP

| block | commented | follow | liked |
|---|---|---|---|
| posted | shared | tagged | take down |

So here I am on the red carpet with Hollywood actress Pippa Cox! Straight away, I [1] ______ it on social media and [2] ______ Pippa, of course! Loads of my friends [3] ______ it and they then started to [4] ______ her. I think someone must have [5] ______ it and then there were people who [6] ______ on it, asking me to [7] ______ it ______ because it wasn't real. Well, of course not … duh! I [8] ______ people like that. I mean, it was just a bit of fun!

**4** **Match the words you added in Exercise 3 to the meanings.**

1. put something on a website or social media page
2. stop someone from seeing your social media page
3. wrote something, for example, your opinion
4. remove something so that it can't be seen any more
5. choose to see everything that someone posts on social media
6. included someone using @ or their name
7. showed that you had read, and that you approved of a message
8. put someone else's message on your social media page, or a friend's social media page

**5** **Discuss the questions.**

1. How often do you post on social media? Why? / Why not?
2. When might you block someone?
3. What is the most number of 'likes' you have ever received for a post? What was the post?
4. How do you feel when you get lots of likes for your posts?

## READING

**1** **Look at the photo. Do you think the woman looks like this in real life? What message does this give to readers?**

# Don't airbrush me!

51

**AIRBRUSHING** is when photos are changed by using computer software to make people look even better in them. In the beginning, it was used to 'tidy up' small problems in photos: a hair standing up on someone's head was removed, or a spot on their skin was hidden. These days, digital technology and editing are more advanced, and it's difficult to find a photo of a model or celebrity in a magazine which hasn't been 'improved' by airbrushing.

'You see these women with legs like sticks and perfect skin and you know they aren't real,' says 15-year-old Shelly. 'But when you're reading an article about a celebrity you admire, you forget that, and just want to look like them.' Corey, also 15, says, 'People think it's just girls that are upset by this stuff but it's boys, too. We're supposed to have big muscles, like sportspeople, but that's impossible to achieve if it isn't your natural body shape.' Research has shown that seeing pictures of 'perfect' models in magazines leads readers to feel less confident about the way they look. This also leads to negative body image.

Mobile phone apps aren't helping the situation. They allow us to change photos of ourselves until we feel happy enough with the way we look to post them online. And although stricter rules are now in place for adverts, unfortunately, there is still a long way to go in changing the media industry's attitudes towards what is thought beautiful.

Fortunately, there are plenty of people campaigning to change things. Former actress Meghan Markle and singer Paloma Faith have both spoken out about not liking magazines to airbrush their photos. Politicians have fought for even stricter rules on how airbrushing can be used. On a smaller scale, the Girl Guides (a UK Scouts organisation for young women) have already approached the government to get labels put on airbrushed photos (with no positive result so far). They've also introduced the 'Free being me' badge, which members can achieve by showing they can recognise airbrushed pictures and by spreading messages in their local community about how positive it is to have a natural look. These are small steps, but if people keep taking them, perhaps one day we'll find that the natural look is considered beautiful again.

## PREPARE FOR THE EXAM

### Reading Part 3

**2** **For each question, choose the correct answer.**

**1** In the first paragraph, the writer says that
**A** airbrushing did not provide good results at first.
**B** celebrities prefer their photos to be airbrushed.
**C** almost all pictures in magazines are airbrushed.
**D** it is easier to access airbrushing equipment than it used to be.

**2** What is the purpose of the second paragraph?
**A** to provide examples of how airbrushing is done
**B** to explain the effect that airbrushed photos have on people
**C** to warn young people against believing what they see in photos
**D** to advise readers to choose what magazines they read carefully

**3** In the third paragraph, the writer shows that she is feeling
**A** surprised that some adverts were never shown.
**B** pleased that some mobile phone apps help people feel better.
**C** unhappy that the media is ignoring airbrushing rules.
**D** disappointed that things are not changing more quickly.

**4** In the final paragraph, the writer says that
**A** famous people are more likely to change people's opinions.
**B** there is hope people will have different ideas in future.
**C** new laws will stop airbrushing being allowed in photos.
**D** not enough people are trying to give out positive messages.

**5** What might a Girl Guide write in her diary?
**A** The work we're doing is already helping me to accept my body the way it is.
**B** The 'Free being me' badge is great – we're learning how to look better through exercise and food.
**C** We've just had an interesting session about making airbrushed photos look more natural.
**D** It isn't necessary to label airbrushed photos because it's our responsibility to understand what's been done to them.

### TALKING POINTS

Should there be limits on how photos are changed in advertising? Why? / Why not?

Why do companies use models, celebrities or sportspeople to advertise their products?

## GRAMMAR The passive

**1** **Underline the passive forms in the example. Which are present simple passive and which are past simple passive?**

Airbrushing is when photos are changed by using computer software to make people look even better in them. In the beginning, it was used to 'tidy up' small problems in photos.

**2** **Complete the rules with the correct words.**

| be | by | past | present | subject |
|---|---|---|---|---|

**a** We form the passive with the verb ________ + past participle.
**b** For the ________ simple passive, we use *is* or *are* + past participle.
**c** For the ________ simple passive, we use *was* or *were* + past participle.
**d** We use the passive when:
- we want the object of a sentence to become the ________
- we don't know or it isn't important who does the action

**e** To say who does the action in a passive sentence (the agent), we use ________ + agent.

### Modal passives

**3** **Read the examples and complete the rules.**

1 It's amazing what **can be done** on a computer.
2 The images didn't show the true results that **could be achieved**.
3 The Advertising Standards Authority decided the adverts **couldn't be shown** any longer.

Modal verbs are often used in passive structures.
We use: modal verb + ________ + ________.

» GRAMMAR REFERENCE AND PRACTICE PAGE 159

**4** **Complete the sentences with the correct modal passive forms.**

1 A lot of time ________ (can / spend) on preparing adverts.
2 Mobile phones ________ (must not / use) during performances at the theatre.
3 A visa ________ (may / require) for certain countries.
4 When ________ the photos ________ (must / send) to the company?
5 People arriving late for the concert ________ (may not / allow) to enter.
6 You ________ (might / give) a free ticket for the exhibition.

**5** **Choose the correct option.**

1 A filter *must* / *can* be chosen to make the picture look better.
2 This game can be *play* / *played* online.
3 Then the vegetables must *mix* / *be mixed* together with the eggs and cream.
4 The assistant told me that all the equipment could be *hire* / *hired*.
5 The ceremony will *open* / *be opened by* our headteacher.

## VOCABULARY Phrases with *in*

**1** **Read the examples and match the phrases to the meanings a–g.**

EP

1 They couldn't consider the digital effects **in detail**.
2 **In fact**, most people say they prefer photos without airbrushing.
3 **In general**, photos in adverts are airbrushed.
4 **In future**, can you ask me before posting photos of me?
5 If you're going to be late, please let me know **in advance**.
6 Are you looking for anything **in particular**?
7 I was going to make a comment on the post but, **in the end**, I decided not to.

**a** usually, or in most situations
**b** giving more information, which is often surprising
**c** finally, after a lot of thought or discussion
**d** before a particular time or before doing something
**e** considering all the information about something or every part of something
**f** special
**g** beginning from now

**2** **Complete the text with phrases from Exercise 1.**

When I saw the advert, I couldn't believe my eyes – my favourite band was going to play in our town! There was a problem, though, because it was on a school night. [1] ________, my parents don't let me stay out late during the week, but I had to persuade them this was special. So I told them about the concert two months [2] ________ and after a huge amount of 'discussion', [3] ________ they agreed I could go! Dad was great and offered to drive me there with a friend and pick us up afterwards. [4] ________, he even wanted to get a ticket for himself, but Mum persuaded him not to be so embarrassing! Anyway, it was a great concert and we liked all the songs – the new ones [5] ________. I'll never forget it.

**3** » **Work in pairs. Turn to page 136.**

## WRITING An online review

**1** **What do you think these things can do? Which one would you like to try?**

**2** **Read the online review. Which product (A–C) is it describing? Does the review recommend the product?**

### THIS PRODUCT IS AWESOME!

It's a ball that you throw up in the air and it takes amazing photos. People will be really impressed with your photos. Another advantage is that it's small enough to fit in your pocket. You can achieve a huge amount with this tiny piece of electronic equipment! For a start, it can take amazing photos that your phone can't, and the outdoor photos it takes are very impressive, in particular. Plus it's really fun! The only disadvantage is that you need a special app to edit and post your photos online. Annoyingly, the app goes really slow on my phone and it can be quite complicated to use. Overall, it's definitely worth saving up for!

REVIEWED BY **GUSTAVO2006**

**REVIEWER RATING** ★★★★☆

**3** **Read the *Prepare to write* box. Then complete the table with the highlighted words and phrases from the review.**

### PREPARE TO WRITE

**An online review**

In an online review:

- write in an informal style.
- use adjectives and adverbs to show how positive or negative you feel about the product.
- use phrases to join your ideas.
- end the review by saying whether or not you recommend the product.

**Words and phrases for positive reviews**

| Positive adjectives | Adverbs | Linking phrases |
|---|---|---|
| awesome | really | another advantage is that |

**4** **Complete the sentences with the words and phrases for negative reviews.**

Besides this problem　limited　One disadvantage　really disappointing　too expensive

1 It's ______ for most people to buy.
2 ______ is its size – it can't be put in a pocket.
3 The choice of games is ______ to very simple ones.
4 ______, there are bugs in the software.
5 In fact, this product is ______ overall!

**5** **Tick (✓) the sentences that make a recommendation and put a cross (✗) beside ones that advise against a product.**

1 If you can only buy one game this year, choose this!
2 This camera is just not worth the money.
3 Definitely something to put on your wish list!
4 You can't afford to miss this opportunity.
5 Don't even consider it!

**6** **You are going to write an online review. Choose a product you know and plan your review. Go online to find out more facts about the product if necessary.**

**7** **Write your review.**

- Use the tips in the *Prepare to write* box.
- Write about 100 words.
- Remember to check your spelling and grammar.

# 14 LET'S COOK!

## ABOUT YOU

Do you ever cook for yourself, or does someone else always do it for you?
Describe your favourite meal. How is it made?

## VOCABULARY Verbs for cooking

**1** Look at the dishes. What ingredients do you recognise in each one? Do you know how to cook any of them?

52 **2** Listen to three young chefs, Adam, Melissa and Ravi, talking about the dishes in Exercise 1. Match each chef to a dish.

52 EP **3** Read the descriptions of how to make the dishes and match them to the three chefs. Then listen again and check.

1 **Barbecue** the chicken pieces, or **roast** them in a hot oven for 40 minutes. Then **bite** into them. They're spicy and delicious! You can **freeze** this dish.

2 **Fry** the onion and garlic – but don't let them **burn**! … **Grill** the aubergines first. **Stir** the stew occasionally with a wooden spoon.

3 Cook this really slowly on the stove – don't **boil** it. **Taste** it regularly and add salt and pepper. **Bake** some bread and **steam** some rice to serve with this dish.

**4** Match the verbs from Exercise 3 to the pictures below.

52 **5** Work in groups of three. Each group takes one dish. Listen to the chefs again and each write down as many ingredients as possible for your group's dish.

**6** Tell the class as much as you can remember about your chef's dish.

**7** What dishes can you cook? Write a recipe for something tasty!

## READING

**1** Look at the texts below. What kind of texts are they (e.g. note, email, label)?

**2** Read the texts quickly. Who could the writer and the reader be in each case?

**1** 53

From: Emilio
To: Donna
Reply Forward

The new chef is starting work tomorrow. He's the one who we interviewed last month – Jack Smith. Could you show him round the kitchen when he arrives, please?

**2**

Mum
Are you roasting that chicken in the fridge for dinner? Text me – I can pick up some vegetables from my friend's farm on the way home. I'll tell you about school while you cook.
Dan

**3**

Jim, whose sister is in my class, is having a barbecue at the weekend. He said I can bring someone. Do you want to go? Let me know by Thursday because he's got to buy the food.

**4**

Please keep this area clear for orders which are ready to serve only.

**5**

Guess what? Pico's Café, where we used to go after football practice, is closing! I suppose they didn't have enough customers. Shall we go one last time for a grilled sandwich? Joe

## PREPARE FOR THE EXAM

### Reading Part 1

**3** Look at the texts again. For each question, choose the correct answer.

**1** Emilio is emailing Donna to ask her to
**A** come to work earlier tomorrow.
**B** help a new employee.
**C** interview a chef.

**2** **A** Dan's mum needs to make a decision.
**B** Dan's mum is going shopping later.
**C** Dan and his mum will cook together.

**3** **A** Jim only wants his classmates to attend his barbecue.
**B** Jim has invited his friends to a barbecue on Thursday.
**C** Jim needs to know who is coming to his barbecue before the end of Thursday.

**4** The sign is telling restaurant staff to
**A** make meals only in this area.
**B** only put meals for customers here.
**C** clean dishes only in this area.

**5** **A** Joe wants to go to the restaurant again before it closes.
**B** Joe is sorry that the restaurant is no longer open.
**C** Joe is confused about why the restaurant is closing.

» PREPARE FOR THE EXAM PAGE 120

**4** Match the highlighted words in the texts and questions to the meanings.

1 go to an event
2 think that something is likely to be true
3 not covered or blocked by anything
4 someone who is paid to work for a person or company
5 a choice that you make

### TALKING POINTS

Why might working in a restaurant be stressful?
What are the benefits of cooking your own food?
Why do people like going out somewhere to eat?

## GRAMMAR Defining relative clauses

**1** **Read the examples and look at the underlined relative clauses. Complete the rules with the words in the box.**

1 He's the man who we interviewed last month.
2 Shall I roast the chicken that I bought this evening?
3 My friend only eats food which is vegetarian.
4 That's the restaurant where the famous chef works.
5 She's the chef that became famous on a TV cooking competition.

| who | where | which | that (x2) |
|---|---|---|---|

We use a defining relative clause to give essential information about the thing, place or person we are talking about. This information cannot be omitted.

We use the pronoun:
**a** ________ or ________ to define a person.
**b** ________ or ________ to define an object, or thing.
**c** ________ to define a place.

### Non-defining relative clauses

**2** **Read the examples. Then complete the rules with *who, which* and *whose*.**

1 Ella, who is in my tennis club, has won a national cookery competition.
2 Pico's Café, which is near the football ground, is closing down.
3 Jim, whose sister is in my class, is having a barbecue at the weekend.

We use a non-defining relative clause to give more information about the person or thing we are talking about.

We put commas around the clause because it contains extra information, which could be deleted.

We use the pronoun:
**a** ________ to introduce more information about things.
**b** ________ to introduce more information about people.
**c** ________ to introduce something that belongs to a person, thing or place.

» GRAMMAR REFERENCE AND PRACTICE PAGE 160

**3** **Read the examples. Which has a defining relative clause? Which has a non-defining relative clause? Match the examples to the meanings.**

1 The recipes, which teenagers have created, will be posted on our website.
2 The recipes which teenagers have created will be posted on our website.

**a** There are recipes from people of all ages, but only the ones from teenagers will be posted.
**b** The recipes are all by teenagers and they will all be posted.

**4** **Correct the mistake in each sentence.**

1 The film was about a man lost his way in the desert.
2 It's a quiet place that you can study.
3 I must look after my brother, which is a baby.
4 We met a girl which my friend Jill knows.

**5** **Rewrite the information in single sentences. Use non-defining relative clauses.**

0 Thai food can be quite hot. (it contains chillies and other spices) *Thai food, which contains chillies and other spices, can be quite hot.*
1 The waiter is very friendly. (he comes from Barcelona)
2 My mum's soup is delicious. (it is made from beans, garlic and tomatoes)
3 Kim will order my birthday cake. (her uncle is a baker)
4 This dessert is very rich. (it has 300g of chocolate in it)

## VOCABULARY Transitive and intransitive verbs

**1** **Look at these sentences. Underline the objects. Two sentences don't have one.**

EP

1 **Boil** the carrots for five minutes.
2 The soup **boiled** for an hour.
3 Can I **taste** your food?
4 This ice cream **tastes** great!

**2** **Read these definitions and complete the rule.**

Some verbs can be both transitive and intransitive. For example *boil* and *taste*. In Exercise 1, the verbs in sentences ____ and ____ are transitive.

**3** **Put the words in the correct order. Then decide which sentences include a transitive verb.**

1 the / for /minutes / We / roasted / vegetables / 10.
2 roasted / vegetables / The / hour / an / for.
3 an / fried / I /egg / for / breakfast.
4 The / pan / frying / is / egg / in / the.

**4** » Turn to page 136.

# LISTENING

**1** Look at the pictures in 1–7 below. What can you see in each one?

## PREPARE FOR THE EXAM

### Listening Part 1

**2** For each question, choose the correct answer.

54

**1** Where do the friends decide to eat?

**2** Which ingredients would the girl prefer to use in her cooking?

**3** Which product do the students select for their art project?

**4** What will they have for dinner?

**5** Which cake does the man decide to bake?

**6** Where is the new café?

**7** What will they give players after the football match?

# SPEAKING Discussing options (2)

**1** Imagine you want to choose what food to cook for some friends. Which of these things would be the most important to consider? Why?

- cost of ingredients
- time needed to prepare the food
- OK for everyone, e.g. vegetarians?
- easy to eat inside/outside

55 **2** Look at the pictures and listen to Laura and Ben making arrangements for a party outdoors. Which food do they decide would be best?

55 **3** Read the *Prepare to speak* box. Then listen again. Which phrases do Ben and Laura use?

## PREPARE TO SPEAK

### Suggestions and decisions

**Making suggestions**

Let's try your first idea.
How about …?
So, why not … then?

**Considering options**

If we … , it would be … .
… might be a better choice?
What if we …?

**Making a decision**

It's time to decide!
Are you OK with that?
We'll go for that one, then.
That sounds good to me.

## PREPARE FOR THE EXAM

### Speaking Part 3

**4** » Turn to page 137.

# CULTURE

## SOCIAL MEDIA

### ABOUT YOU

Answer the questions in *My life online* and compare with a partner.

### MY LIFE ONLINE

1. How many social media sites or apps do you use?
2. How many times a day do you check your profiles?
3. How many posts do you write on a typical day?
4. How many times a week do you post selfies?
5. How many followers would you like to have?

**1** **Read the article on the opposite page. Which of these sentences is the best summary?**

1. The internet is causing a lot of problems for teenagers.
2. Social media has negative as well as positive effects.
3. Online popularity is very important for young people.

**2** **Complete the sentences with ideas from the article.**

1. Parents and other adults don't use ______
2. The teenagers in the CNN study wrote ______
3. More than 60% of the teens wanted to know ______
4. Some people take lots of selfies because ______
5. Students get poor grades if ______
6. In the past, young people ______

**3** **Match the highlighted words in the text to the meanings.**

1. not very nice or friendly to people
2. do something to help another person
3. think and worry about someone that is important to you
4. when lots of people know and like you
5. very surprising, often in a negative way

56 **4** **Listen to four people talking about their social media habits. Complete the sentences with the person's name.**

1. ______ uses social media to keep up with what friends are doing.
2. ______ is more interested in spending time with friends offline.
3. ______ likes making videos to share opinions with other people.
4. ______ is too busy to spend a lot on time on social media.

56 **5** **Listen again. Answer the questions.**

1. What do Greg's friends think about his online habits?
2. When does social media become a problem for Greg?
3. How does Zoe's friend Vanessa make her laugh?
4. Does Zoe use social media for serious activities?
5. For the most part, what does Marta do online?
6. How does Marta deal with negative people?
7. Why don't nasty messages bother Tyler?
8. How does Tyler keep in touch with friends?

**6** **Read the *Useful language* phrases. Complete them with the words in the box.**

general meeting tend think update usually

### USEFUL LANGUAGE

**Making generalisations**

1. I ______ to go online quite a lot.
2. I don't ______ use Facebook.
3. In ______, I don't post videos.
4. I generally ______ my profiles every week.
5. For the most part, I like ______ in person.
6. Overall, I ______ social media is a good thing.

## LIVING ONLINE

# TEENS AND SOCIAL MEDIA

Teenagers today have grown up using the internet and they use social media much more than their parents and other adults. However, young people may not be using this technology in a way that's effective or healthy. In a recent study, the CNN news agency followed a group of 200 North American teenagers for a period of six months to see how they were using social media. The results were quite shocking, especially for parents who thought they knew what their children were doing online.

57

During the experiment, scientists recorded 150,000 posts and messages, which means approximately 125 messages a month for each person, although some teens wrote more messages than others. However, the most suprising fact was how often some teens were checking their social media profiles. Some people looked at them up to 100 times a day, even at school or when they were hanging out with other friends. But why were they checking their profile so often? When the scientists asked, they discovered that:

**21%** of teens wanted to know if people had written about them. They looked forward to positive posts, but they also worried about negative ones and how they should respond to rude comments.

**36%** FOMO wanted to know what other people were doing and they worried about not being part of an online group. This 'fear of missing out' (FOMO) can be quite stressful for many teens.

**61%** were checking their profiles for new 'likes', followers and comments on their posts. All of these things are extremely important in the world of social media.

In fact, a lot of what teens do on social media is related to self-image and popularity. Some people always want to look perfect, so they take hundreds of selfies and then post only the very best one. Other people upload photos of all the great places they visit, the fun things they do, and all of the amazing people they meet and know. This competition can be terrible, especially for people who aren't very cool or popular. It can also have a negative effect on schoolwork. The CNN study found that people who spent the most time on social media often had lower grades.

On the positive side, social media seems to create stronger connections between young people and their friends. Some people might write nasty posts, but many teens use social media in a good way, to support their friends and show how much they care. They send messages to each other, tell jokes and celebrate special occasions. Young people could never share information about their lives in this way in the past. The world might be changing, but fortunately young people are changing along with it.

## PROJECT

**A presentation about social media habits**

**Prepare a presentation about your online and social media habits. Use the following topics to help you.**

1. the amount of time you spend online
2. the social media sites and apps you use
3. the types of things that you post online
4. how often you update your profiles
5. the way you communicate with friends
6. the general opinion you have of social media

**Give your presentation to the class.**

# 15 CITY OR COUNTRY?

## ABOUT YOU

Do you live in a city, a town or the countryside? Would you like to live somewhere different? Where? Why?

## VOCABULARY Artificial and natural world

EP **1** What type of person are you? Do the quiz and find out!

### City or country

**1 What is your perfect Saturday in summer?**

- **a** waking up early to the sound of the **wildlife**, ready for an active day walking up the hill and down into the **valley**!
- **b** spending the morning with your friends at the shopping centre – there's **air conditioning**!
- **c** going to visit some **historic buildings** and learning something new
- **d** inviting your friends round to play video games and then ordering a pizza

**2 Which would you like to do in your holidays?**

- **a** look at historic monuments and **ruins** – all your history lessons come alive!
- **b** visit relatives who live in a small village. It's so quiet, and you can read your book!
- **c** go on a camping trip away from all the **pollution** and **street lights**
- **d** admire **modern architecture** (probably a shopping centre!) and bright city lights

**3 Which is important to you in the place where you live?**

- **a** peace and quiet, and **open spaces**
- **b** interesting things to see and do
- **c** people and shopping!
- **d** **facilities** such as sports centres, cinemas and **health centres**

**4 Which is your favourite season?**

- **a** I love all the **seasons** – I like seeing the differences in nature.
- **b** I love winter – winter clothes are so stylish!
- **c** I don't really like summer – too many **bugs**.
- **d** If the air conditioning or the central heating is working, it's all the same to me.

**2** Turn to page 137 and add up your scores. Do you agree with the description of you?

**3** Look at the words in the quiz. Decide if they are from the man-made world or the natural world.

| artificial world | natural world |
|---|---|
| *air conditioning* | *wildlife* |

58 **4** Listen to three teenagers talking about where they live. Match each speaker to a picture (A, B or C). What do they like about the place where they live?

**5** Choose the correct option.

1. Although it is an old town, there is quite a lot of *modern architecture / historic buildings*.
2. The levels of *pollution / air conditioning* in our city have increased a lot because more people have cars.
3. I love the countryside because of the *valley / wildlife* like small birds and animals.
4. With all the *ruins / street lights* on at night, it's hard to see the stars.
5. With the temperature going up to 40°C today, I'm glad we have *air conditioning / pollution*.
6. Our city has excellent *seasons / facilities* where you can find most things you want.

**6** Discuss the questions.

1. What facilities would you like to have closer to your home? Why?
2. How important is it to look after historic buildings? Why?
3. Why do some people move to the countryside?

## READING

**1** What do you think life in Australia is like? How do you think it's different from life where you live?

**2** You are going to read about two Australian teens. Read the texts quickly. Where do they live? Do they like living there? Why? / Why not?

# TEENTALK ... DOWN UNDER

**What is living in Australia really like? Can life in the outback be fun? We caught up with two Aussies who have very different experiences of life down under.**

59

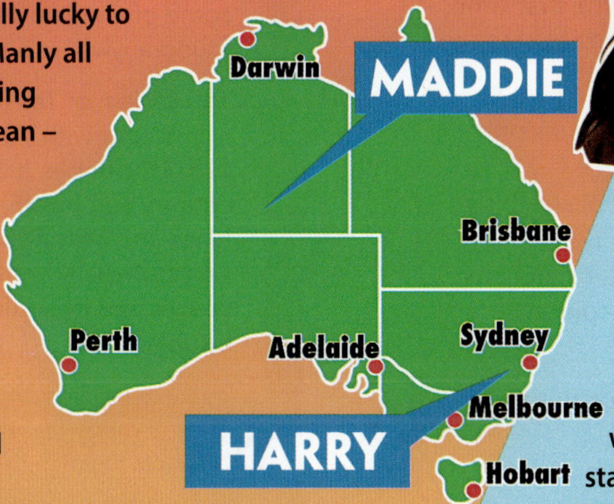


I live in a part of Sydney called Manly. It's incredibly beautiful and I'm really lucky to live here. In fact, tourists visit Manly all year round because of its amazing beaches. It's situated by the ocean – well, I guess most of Sydney is! In summer, there are almost more visitors than people who live here, and I don't like that. I catch a ferry and then a bus to my school, which is near the city centre. One of my friends lives in the Blue Mountains and he visited me during the last summer holidays. I showed him around and we did loads of interesting things, including a trip to the zoo, and hanging out in my favourite mall. We hardly stayed in at all! But the best part was our surfing lessons on Bondi Beach! I think that being free in the ocean and seeing the tall buildings of the city at the same time is the best thing in the world. After all, it's the best of both worlds.

I was born in the outback on a cattle station – that's a big farm with a lot of cows! It's about 7,000 km², so there are plenty of open spaces to be in! It's great when it gets dark, you can look up at a million stars – there are no street lights, no pollution, no noise except all the amazing sounds from the wildlife. I do loads of exciting things with my brothers – fishing, hiking, horse riding, quad biking and all that kind of thing. And when it gets really hot, we jump in a creek! I don't think that there is as much stress as in the city, although we have to be careful we don't step on a snake by accident! For me, country living is certainly healthier living. Something else that is different – I didn't actually go to a school until I was 12. The nearest school was a six-hour drive away, so I attended the School of the Air. That meant I had classes at home and did school work over the internet. Most terms there was a camp where we all joined in loads of different activities. It was great fun and I met all my friends. Now I go to a boarding school in a city and I definitely miss the open spaces and my animals.

**3** Read the texts again and answer the questions. Write *M* (Maddie), *H* (Harry) or *B* (both). Who …

1. mentions doing fun activities with a family member?
2. mentions visiting interesting places?
3. likes to cool down in water?
4. mentions that they used the internet a lot for school?
5. uses public transport daily?
6. is living away from home at the moment?
7. suggests that there are many things to do nearby?
8. loves seeing nature and modern things together?

**4** Match the highlighted words in the text to the meanings.

1. riding a vehicle similar to a motorcycle with four wheels
2. a stream or narrow river
3. an informal word for Australian people
4. the areas of Australia that are far away from towns and cities
5. in or to Australia or New Zealand

### TALKING POINTS

Would you prefer to live where Harry lives or where Maddie lives?

Why do most young people prefer to live in cities?

What things make a place enjoyable to live in?

## GRAMMAR Articles: *a/an*, *the* and zero article

**1 Match the examples to the rules.**

1 What is living in Australia really like?
2 I didn't actually go to a school until I was 12. The nearest school was a six-hour drive away.
3 It is the best thing in the world.
4 One of my friends lives in the Blue Mountains.
5 You can hear all the sounds from the wildlife.
6 Mum's a writer.
7 In fact, tourists visit my suburb all year round.

We use *a / an*
**a** when we mention something for the first time.
**b** to describe a person's job or what they do.

We use *the*
**c** when we mention something for the second time.
**d** when we talk about particular people or things.
**e** when there is only one of something.
**f** in the names of groups of mountains, oceans, and states, and countries that are plural.

We use the *zero article*
**g** to talk about plural or uncountable nouns when we are talking in general.
**h** with the names of towns, countries and continents, and individual lakes and mountains.

» GRAMMAR REFERENCE AND PRACTICE PAGE 161

**2 Choose the correct option.**

1 Yesterday I went to – / *the* cinema with my friend, Bianca.
2 My parents' first house was near – / *the* city park.
3 My best friend and I have *a* / *the* same hobbies.
4 If you have – / *a* problem, please call me.
5 My grandparents have always lived in *a* / *the* countryside.
6 My aunt is – / *a* doctor.
7 Let's have – / *a* party tomorrow!

**3 Complete the sentences with *a / an*, *the* or zero article.**

1 ________ population of Australia is 24 million.
2 ________ Mount Kosciuszko is the highest mountain in Australia.
3 ________ Lake Eyre is often empty unless there is a lot of rain.
4 ________ capital of ________ Australia is ________ Canberra.
5 ________ Australia is ________ island and ________ continent.
6 ________ Great Barrier Reef is made up of over 2,900 individual reefs and 900 islands.

## PREPARE FOR THE EXAM

### Reading Part 6

**4 For each question, write the correct answer. Write one word for each gap.**

### TASMANIA, AUSTRALIA

Tasmania is an island situated 240 km south of Australia. It is the country's largest island and is surrounded by **(1)** ________ Indian and Pacific Oceans. The island attracts a lot of visitors because of its mountains, rainforests and beaches. **(2)** ________ wildlife is interesting, too, because some of the animals which live in Tasmania are not found anywhere else in **(3)** ________ world.

The capital of Tasmania is Hobart. Hobart is quite a small city with **(4)** ________ population of around 225,000 people. It is the second oldest city in the country and has **(5)** ________ old centre, with narrow lanes and historic buildings. **(6)** ________ climate isn't especially hot but Tasmania has lots of open spaces and beautiful scenery, and there is plenty for people to do.

» PREPARE FOR THE EXAM PAGE 126

## VOCABULARY Phrasal verbs

**1 Read the examples. Underline the phrasal verbs.**

I showed him around.
Some people think we stay in all the time.

**2 Complete the sentences with the correct form of the phrasal verbs in the box.**

| catch up with | end up | move in |
|---|---|---|
| move out | show someone around | stay in |

1 My sister ________ last year to go to college.
2 If it's raining, we usually ________ and watch a movie.
3 When my friends came to visit, I took them to London and ________ them ________.
4 My cousin went on a train journey across Europe and ________ in Turkey.
5 I can't talk now – let's ________ each other later.
6 Our new neighbours ________ about three weeks ago – they're still unpacking.

**3** » **Work in pairs. Turn to page 138.**

## WRITING An email (2)

**1** **Where do you and your friends usually meet up? Compare your answers with your partner.**

**2** **Read the task and Inês's email. Does she use all the notes in the task?**

Read this email from your English-speaking friend, Jon, and the notes you have made. Write your email to Jon, using all the notes.

Hi!

I'm doing a project at school about where people live and I need some information about where you live. Can you help me? — *Yes!*

Where do young people meet where you live? Is there plenty for them to do? — *Tell Jon*

What activities would you recommend for teenagers visiting your city? — *Suggest ...*

I'm hoping to come and visit you soon. Let me know when is a good time for you. — *Great! Say when*

Jon

Hi Jon,

Yes, of course I can help you!

The city where I live is really lively, despite it being small. I usually meet my friends in a café on Saturday afternoons. The food's amazing. However, it can get crowded in summer. There are loads of other things to do, though – there's a skateboard park, shopping and cinemas.

I'd recommend visiting the famous City Museum. It's not like other museums! The art's cool and they show interesting films. Lots of students go there – you can get snacks and eat in the museum garden. Actually, I'm going there next week.

Finally, I've got some great news – I got the highest mark in class for maths last term! Woo hoo!

Write soon!
Inês

**3** **Read the *Prepare to write* box. Then look at the highlighted linking words in Inês's email. Match them to their meanings 1–4.**

1 used to give additional information that is interesting or surprising
2 used to introduce a contrast, or an opposite point
3 used to introduce the last point you want to make
4 used when something is true, although something makes it unlikely

### PREPARE TO WRITE
**An email**

In emails:

- use linking words to link your ideas.
- use adjectives to make your writing interesting.
- remember to use informal language and short forms.

**4** **Complete the sentences with the highlighted words in Inês's email.**

1 I still went to Jamie's house after school, ________ having lots of homework.
2 We wanted to play some online games. ________, the internet wasn't working properly.
3 Amsterdam is a lovely city. ________, my cousin lives there.
4 ________, I got home at about 7 pm after a six-hour journey!

**5** **What adjectives does Inês use to describe these things? What other adjectives could you use?**

1 the city
2 the food in the café
3 the museum
4 the art and films in the museum

### PREPARE FOR THE EXAM
**Writing Part 1**

**6** **You are going to write your reply to Jon's email about where you live.**

**Read the task in Exercise 2 again and plan your ideas. Remember to use all the notes.**

**7** **Write your email to Jon.**

- Use the tips in the *Prepare to write* box.
- Remember to begin and end your email correctly.
- Write about 100 words.
- Remember to check your spelling and grammar.

# 16 LIGHTS, CAMERA, ACTION!

## ABOUT YOU

**12 Watch the video and then answer the questions.**

What's the last film you saw? What was it about?

Do you watch videos on YouTube? Why is it so popular?

Have you ever made a video and put it on YouTube?

## VOCABULARY Film

**1** **Look at the photos. Which of the films have you seen? Which would you like to see?**

**2** **Match three of the sentences to photos A–C.**

EP
1 A lot of new films **come out** at special times of the year; for example, **animated** films are often around during school holidays.
2 Daisy Ridley's **performance** in *Star Wars Episode 8* was fantastic.
3 Eddie Redmayne has the lead **role** in *Fantastic Beasts and Where to Find Them.* Katherine Waterston and Samantha Morton also **appear** in the film.
4 Sam Mendes is a very well-known film **director**. He's **directed** many of the James Bond films.
5 The film of *The Lion King* has a great **soundtrack**, with songs written by Elton John. Did you know it has been made into a **musical** which you can see live at the theatre? You can also buy the original **recording** of the performance as an MP3 download.

**3** **Match the words to the meanings.**

1 with drawings, computer images or models that seem to move
2 sounds or moving pictures that have been recorded
3 perform (in a play or film)
4 an actor's part in a film or play
5 the person who tells the actors in a film or play what to do
6 acting, singing, dancing or playing music to entertain people
7 the music used in a film or a TV show
8 told the actors in a film or play what to do
9 become available for people to see or buy
10 a film or play with singing and dancing

**4** **Choose the correct option.**

1 I'd love to *come out* / *appear* in a film.
2 My friend and I want to see a new film that *comes out* / *directs* in December.
3 The *recording* / *role* of most films takes place in Hollywood in Los Angeles.
4 The *director* / *performance* controls the creative aspects of a film.
5 I loved the main actor's *performance* / *director* in the film we saw last week.

60 **5** **Listen. Match each speaker to the type of film that they want to see.**

a an interesting animated film
b a film starring an actor who won a TV show contest
c a new film by a well-known director

60 **6** **Listen again. Which film would you like to see? Why?**

**7** **Complete the sentences with your own ideas. Then compare with a partner.**

1 The most famous film director in my country is …
2 My favourite animated film is …
3 I loved …'s performance in the film …
4 I love the soundtrack of the film ….. because ….
5 The role of … in … was amazing because …
6 If I could appear in one film, it would be …

C

# MEET EVAN HARA: WRITER, DIRECTOR, FILMMAKER

61

Evan Hara was just 16 and still at school when he produced his first full-length feature film. At the film's premiere there was a red carpet, paparazzi and movie posters. Did it take place in Hollywood? No, in Plano, Texas. I've seen the film and it's great! It's called *The Boundary* and tells the story of astronauts who travel to the edge of the universe. I caught up with Evan to find out more about this exciting young filmmaker.

**A** Evan has always enjoyed all things related to film. He has won a local filmmaking competition, has run the school news channel, which he also created, and has written a series for TV. But his adventures began behind the camera when he was much younger, when he used to make films of his toy cars using his dad's video camera. There is, of course, a huge difference between the camera he used then and the DSLR camera that he had to use when he joined the Dallas Young Actors Studio. Evan also has his own YouTube channel. You can see some examples of his work there, ranging from comedy skits to short films.

**B** As if this were not enough, at just 14 years old, Evan took the lead role in the film *Round of your Life*. When asked about the experience of acting, he said 'I loved it. There really is no other experience like it – it was amazing to get to know what it feels like on the other end of the camera.'

**C** At such a young age, we wondered how he managed to fit everything in; after all, he is still at school! 'I basically have zero free time!' he explained. He attends acting classes and film classes and does the school news channel on YouTube. Despite all that, he says he's still able to do his homework, although it's sometimes difficult.

**D** Evan wants to be one of the youngest directors of a feature film. When asked how he intends to make this a reality, he said, 'I intend to fulfil my goal by submitting my films to film festivals around the country, getting feedback, and then fine-tuning my editing and directing skills.' However, he admits that he has competition from other young filmmakers like Ed Burns and Richard Linklater.

Well, I've seen him on the red carpet in Plano, and I hope that I'll see him on the red carpet in Hollywood soon. Good luck, Evan!

## READING

**1** **Read the interview quickly and match the questions to the paragraphs.**

1 How does he find the time for everything?
2 How did he become interested in film?
3 What does he hope to achieve in the future?
4 What else has he done?

### TALKING POINTS

Which would you prefer to do – direct a film or act in one? Why?
Would you like to produce a film? Why? / Why not?

**2** **Read the interview again and answer the questions.**

1 In what ways was the premiere of Evan's film *The Boundary* similar to a Hollywood premiere?
2 How did Evan start making films?
3 What was Evan's first experience as an actor?
4 How did he feel about his experience as an actor?
5 What training is he receiving at the moment?
6 What are his hopes for the future?

## GRAMMAR Reported speech

**1 Match the examples of direct speech a–d to the reported speech 1–4.**

**a** I basically **have** zero free time!

**b** It **was** amazing to get to know what it **feels** like on the other end of the camera.

**c** I **hope** that I'**ll see** him on the red carpet in Hollywood soon.

**d** I'**ve seen** the film and it'**s** great!

1 The interviewer said she'**d seen** the film and it **was** great.
2 Evan said it **had been** amazing to get to know what it **felt** like on the other end of the camera.
3 Evan said he basically **had** zero free time.
4 The interviewer said she **hoped** that she **would see** him on the red carpet in Hollywood soon.

**2 Choose the correct words to complete the rules.**

We use reported speech to report what someone said in the past.
**a** We usually *change* / *keep* the verb tense.
**b** We generally move the verb one tense *back into the past* / *forward into the future*.
**c** We sometimes need to change the *pronouns* / *adjectives* in the sentence.
**d** In reported speech, *will* becomes *was* / *would* and *can* becomes *could*.

» **GRAMMAR REFERENCE AND PRACTICE PAGE 162**

**3 Complete the reported speech with the missing verbs.**

1 'I like making films.' → He said he ________ making films.
2 'I'm making a film.' → He said he ________ a film.
3 'I've made a film.' → He said he ________ a film.
4 'I made a film.' → He said he ________ a film.
5 'I'll make another film.' → He said he ________ another film.
6 'I can make good films.' → He said he ________ make good films.

**4 Rewrite the sentences using reported speech.**

1 'I really enjoyed the performance,' my dad said.
2 'I'm making your favourite dinner,' said Anna's mum.
3 'My parents haven't visited England,' said Maria.
4 'It was my first trip on a plane,' said Paul.
5 'I'll do my homework after dinner,' Tom said.
6 'I can ride my bike with no hands,' Jason told his friends.

**5 Correct the mistake in each sentence.**

1 I told him that my brother isn't at home.
2 He asked me if I want to go to the cinema with him.
3 My mother said that I have to buy some flowers for my aunt's birthday, which was the next day.
4 They asked us if we are going to the cinema.
5 My step-mum told me she will help pay for my university course.

**6 Tell your partner about one of the things below. Listen and make notes while your partner talks.**

- Your favourite film
- Your favourite app
- Your favourite food
- Your weekend activities

**7 Report what your partner said to the class.**

## VOCABULARY Reporting verbs

**1 Read the examples and notice how the reporting verbs are used.**

1 She **said** she was terrified.
2 I **told** him that I hadn't done it before.
3 He **announced** that the instructor was going to be late.
4 He **insisted** that she did the course.
5 They **suggested** that I saw *The Boundary*.
6 The teacher **demanded** that the students stopped talking.

**Complete the rule about *insist*, *suggest* and *demand*.**

In the past we use: *suggested* / *insisted* / *demanded* + *that* + subject + ________.

**2 Choose the correct reporting verb.**

EP

~~announce~~ demand explain insist suggest

0 The train will arrive at 5.30 pm. *announce*
1 First you have to press this button and then you can choose the channel you want.
2 Give me that letter back!
3 Why don't we visit the exhibition together?
4 I really need you to help me with my homework.

**3 Complete the sentences with the correct form of *suggest*, *insist* or *demand* and the verb in brackets.**

0 My mum *suggested* that I *bought* the cinema tickets online as they are cheaper. (buy)
1 Our teacher ________ that we ________ the project before the end of the month. (finish)
2 Sue ________ that I ________ her the letter back. (give)
3 She ________ that we ________ the exhibition together. (see)
4 He ________ that I ________ him with his homework. (help)

**4** » **Work in pairs. Student A, turn to page 138. Student B, turn to page 140.**

# LISTENING

**1** **Have you ever read a book and then seen a film of the same story? Which did you prefer? Why?**

## PREPARE FOR THE EXAM

### Listening Part 2

**2** **For each question, choose the correct answer.**

62

**1** You will hear two friends talking about a film they have both seen. How does the boy feel about it?
**A** surprised by the choice of actor
**B** disappointed with the music
**C** annoyed about the ending

**2** You will hear two friends talking about a film club they both attend. What does the girl think about it?
**A** They ought to show a greater range of films.
**B** It starts too early in the evening for her.
**C** She doesn't find the seats very comfortable.

**3** You will hear a girl talking to her friend about film locations. She says that seeing particular locations in a film
**A** makes her want to go and visit the place.
**B** makes her feel more involved in the story.
**C** makes her understand the characters better.

**4** You will hear a boy talking to his friend about the main character in a film he has seen. What did he think about the character?
**A** She was quite realistic.
**B** She was exactly as he had expected.
**C** She was too similar to a character in another film.

**5** You hear two friends talking about film directors. They both agree that directors
**A** should have experience of what they are filming.
**B** should not try to control their actors too much.
**C** should be careful about which films they choose to direct.

**6** You hear two friends talking about making short films. The girl advises the boy to
**A** make a film about something he knows well.
**B** avoid worrying too much about what people think.
**C** consider what the film tells the audience.

**3** **Listen again and check your answers.**

# SPEAKING Describing a picture (2)

**1** **Look at the photo. What can you say about it? Note down your ideas.**

63 **2** **Listen to Marcus talking about the photo. Did he have the same ideas as you?**

63 **3** **Read the *Prepare to speak* box. Then listen again. Which phrases do you hear?**

## PREPARE TO SPEAK

### Describing a picture

**Describing what you can see**
I can see …
In the background there is / are …
On the left / right there is / are …
In the middle is …

**Making guesses**
It looks like they are …
It might be …
I think the …

**When you don't know the word**
I don't know what it's called.

## PREPARE FOR THE EXAM

### Speaking Part 2

**4** **» Work in pairs. Turn to page 138. Follow the instructions.**

**5** **Work with a partner. Talk together about the different forms of entertainment that you like and those that you don't like. Ask your questions, and the questions below.**

**1** Why do people like going to the cinema?
**2** Why are programmes like *The Voice* and *The X Factor* so popular?
**3** Many people nowadays want to be stars. Is this a good thing? Why? / Why not?

# LIFE SKILLS COMMUNICATION

## GIVING PRESENTATIONS

### LIFE SKILLS

**Giving presentations**

Presentation skills are important at school and in other areas of life. Some people don't like giving presentations because they don't know what to say or because they get nervous about public speaking. However, there are tips anyone can use to make presentations easier and more enjoyable.

**1 Ask and answer the questions with a partner.**

1 When was the last presentation you gave?
2 What was the presentation about? Did you do it alone or in a group?
3 How do you feel when you have to speak in public?

**2 Read the text about presentations on the opposite page and complete the sentences.**

1 You should have three or four main ........ .
2 Don't show people too much ........ at once.
3 Use small ........ to help you remember.
4 Always ........ the audience when you finish.

**3 Read the article again and answer the questions.**

1 Why would someone start a presentation with photos?
2 What are two advantages of using visual materials?
3 How can too many visual materials be a problem?
4 What changes might people make after practising their presentation?
5 Why is it important to watch the audience carefully?
6 What can happen if the speaker sounds tired?

64 **4 Listen to Sarah and her dad talking about her presentation. Tick (✓) the topics that they discuss.**

| | | | |
|---|---|---|---|
| 1 | ..... weather | 5 | ..... animals |
| 2 | ..... holiday photos | 6 | ..... the audience |
| 3 | ..... outdoor sports | 7 | ..... videos |
| 4 | ..... a lake | 8 | ..... transportation |

64 **5 Listen again. Are the sentences true or false? Correct the false sentences.**

1 Dad said that Sarah hadn't practised her presentation enough.
2 Sarah said she was feeling nervous about her presentation.
3 The teacher said that students needed to include lots of facts.
4 Dad told Sarah that she had spoken too quickly at times.
5 Sarah said that she wanted to make a documentary film.
6 Dad said that Sarah had looked at her notes too much.

**6 Read the *Useful language* phrases. Complete them with the words in the box.**

| for | instance | like | such | well |
|---|---|---|---|---|

### USEFUL LANGUAGE

**Giving examples**

1 There are lots of natural sights, ........ **as** mountains and lakes.
2 I hope to see some wild animals, ........ bears and foxes.
3 The weather will be cold, and it may be snowy **as** ........ .
4 ........ **example**, there are lots of trees and wild flowers.
5 **For** ........, I'd like to go hiking or canoeing.

*Perfect*

# Presentations

## Five essential steps for public speaking

65

## 1 Get organised

The best presentations are well planned and clearly organised. You can brainstorm lots of ideas and write them down, but then choose the most important ones. Consider the amount of time you have, and don't include too many topics. In most cases, three or four main ideas will be fine. For example, if you're making a presentation about a film, you can talk about the characters, story, music and special effects. The beginning of your presentation should also be interesting. Show some photos or a video clip, or tell a short, amusing story to make people laugh.

## 2 Use visual materials

Many people find it difficult to stand up in front of an audience without any materials to help them. Even experts use a variety of visual props, such as photos, charts, diagrams and digital presentation tools. These things make your performance more exciting for the audience and they can also help you remember what you are going to say. However, you shouldn't use too many visual materials or show too much information at once. That can be confusing or boring for the audience. The 'star' of your presentation should be you, not your materials.

## 3 Rehearse your performance

Professional musicians know how important it is to practise before a concert. Similarly, you need to practise your presentation many times before the 'big day'. Start by reading the text aloud until you know it well. Then write the main ideas on small notecards and use them to help you remember. Practise again in front of a mirror and time your presentation. If it's too long, you may need to cut some material. Finally, you can record your performance or ask a friend to watch you and then make suggestions for improvements.

## 4 Connect with your audience

On the day of your presentation, be sure to watch the audience. Are people interested or do they seem confused? Do you need to speak more loudly? Try to stay calm, but make sure to keep up your energy. If you sound like you're tired or bored, your audience will probably feel the same way. Stand up straight, act confident, and don't move around much. That can be annoying and then people won't pay attention to your words. Finally, be sure to thank your audience when you finish speaking. It's a simple but effective way to end any presentation.

## PROJECT *A presentation*

**Plan a presentation about a nature park that you want to visit. Use the questions below to help you. Practise your presentation with a partner.**

**1** What's the name of the park?
**2** Where is the nature park located?
**3** What time of year do you want to go there?
**4** What is the weather like at that time of year?
**5** What are some interesting natural sights there?
**6** What plants or animals do you hope to see?
**7** What activities do you want to do there?

**Give your presentation to the class.**

# REVIEW 4 UNITS 13–16

## VOCABULARY

**1** **Unscramble the words in the box and match them to the definitions.**

| tga | foollw | igllr | ubnr | tsir |
|---|---|---|---|---|
| sonases | rshea | obklc | pfreomcearn | |
| iunrs | iredct | lwdilife | | |

1 put someone else's message on your wall, or a friend's wall on social media
2 include someone using @ or their name on a social media post
3 stop someone from contacting you on social media
4 cook food using direct heat from above
5 cook something for too long
6 mix ingredients together
7 spring, summer, autumn and winter
8 acting, singing, dancing, or music to entertain people
9 tell actors what to do
10 animals, birds and plants in the place where they live
11 choose to see all of someone's posts on social media
12 the broken parts that are left from an old building after it has been destroyed

**2** **Complete the sentences using a word from each box.**

| air | health | historic | open | street |
|---|---|---|---|---|

| buildings | centre | conditioning | lights | spaces |
|---|---|---|---|---|

1 When I was ill, my dad took me to the ________ to see the doctor.
2 There are many ________ in the town, some more than 500 years old.
3 Can you turn up the ________? It's very warm in here!
4 None of the ________ in the town were working last night due to the power cut.
5 I love the countryside as there are so many ________ without any buildings or people.

**3** **Complete the questions with the phrasal verbs in the box. Then answer the questions.**

| catch up with | end up | move in | move out |
|---|---|---|---|
| show someone around | stay in | | |

1 Are you going out tonight, or are you going to ________?
2 Who would you like to ________ your town? Where would you take them?
3 Why might you ________ missing the last bus home?
4 If you could ________ an old friend, what would you talk to them about?
5 If you left home, would you live alone or ________ with a friend?
6 What would make you ________ of your home?

**4** **Complete the sentences by forming a suitable phrase with *in* and the words in the box.**

| advance | detail | the end |
|---|---|---|
| fact | future | general |
| particular | | |

1 I haven't looked at the information ________ yet.
2 I was going to send my grandmother an email, but, ________, I decided to phone her.
3 I love that director's movies, ________ his most recent one.
4 ________, men are taller than women.
5 You've broken another glass! Could you be more careful ________?
6 Train tickets are cheaper if you book them ________.
7 I love Taylor Swift's new album. ________, I'd say it's her best one yet!

## GRAMMAR

**1** **Rewrite the sentences in the passive. Use *by* + agent if necessary.**

1 A top advertising company created the adverts.
The adverts …
2 You can use different ingredients in this recipe.
Different ingredients …
3 Danish architect Bjarke Ingels will design these New York apartments.
These New York apartments …
4 You couldn't see anything from the tower because of the fog.
Nothing …
5 They didn't show me how to edit video clips on the course.
On the course, I …
6 People might forget traditional techniques of bread making.
Traditional techniques of …
7 They might film part of the new James Bond movie in the Australian outback.
Part of the new James Bond movie …
8 You can find thousands of recipes for healthy food online.
Thousands of recipes …

## 2 Complete this text with the missing articles. Sometimes no article is needed.

Canada is [1] ______ second largest country in [2] ______ world by area after [3] ______ Russia. It is located in [4] ______ northern part of [5] ______ North America. [6] ______ west coast of Canada faces [7] ______ Pacific Ocean, [8] ______ east coast faces [9] ______ Atlantic Ocean, and the country is also surrounded by [10] ______ Arctic Ocean to [11] ______ north. Canada is [12] ______ rich nation, and is [13] ______ member of various international organisations, such as [14] ______ G7. Canadians believe their quality of [15] ______ life is very good, and they enjoy [16] ______ very high standard of living in a beautiful natural landscape.

## 3 Report the questions and sentences.

1 'Did you buy anything in town, Ben?' Jo asked Ben …
2 'I'm planning to play tennis later, Sally.' Sally's brother told …
3 'I didn't go surfing after all.' James said …
4 'We won't have time for a coffee unless we leave at 5.30.' Louise insisted …
5 'Can I join the film-making course?' Matt asked …
6 'You didn't have your phone on, Harry.' Freddy complained …

## 4 Choose the correct option.

1 Well, my dad *called* / *is called* David.
2 Football can be *play* / *played* on the beach.
3 They *said* / *told* me I could go.
4 I went with my aunt and my cousin, – / *who* is two years old.

## 5 Correct the mistake in each sentence.

1 These things must use by the driver.
2 It is beautiful country.
3 She say she was Spanish.
4 He replied that he like this game too.

# PREPARE FOR THE EXAM

## Reading Part 5

## 1 For each question, choose the correct answer.

### Chilli peppers

Chilli peppers have probably been eaten for almost 1,000 years, and they were first brought to Europe in 1494 on explorer Christopher Columbus's ship. Portuguese traders then took chilli peppers to Asia, where they **(1)** ______ to be an important ingredient in Indian food. They are used to make many **(2)** ______ in South East Asia, too.

Today, chillies are produced in large quantities all over the world. As well as **(3)** ______ flavour and heat to meals, they **(4)** ______ healthy vitamins that are important for our diet. Some of the hottest varieties are the Scotch Bonnet and Habanero, which can really **(5)** ______ your mouth. Their bright red and orange colours give some warning of their heat. Most green and yellow chillies, on the other hand, are less likely to hurt your tongue when you **(6)** ______ into them!

| | A | B | C | D |
|---|---|---|---|---|
| **1** | **A** stay | **B** keep | **C** follow | **D** continue |
| **2** | **A** bowls | **B** dishes | **C** courses | **D** plates |
| **3** | **A** adding | **B** joining | **C** mixing | **D** putting |
| **4** | **A** consist | **B** hold | **C** contain | **D** keep |
| **5** | **A** boil | **B** grill | **C** roast | **D** burn |
| **6** | **A** cut | **B** try | **C** bite | **D** taste |

## Reading Part 6

## 2 For each question, write the correct answer. Write one word for each gap.

### Tristan da Cunha: an island far away

Tristan da Cunha is considered to be the most remote island in the world that people live on. The tiny island is located in the South Atlantic Ocean, 2,400 kilometres away from **(1)** ______ nearest continental land, South Africa. **(2)** ______ fact, it is so far away from South Africa that it takes six days to reach it by boat.

In January 2017, the island, **(3)** ______ is just 11 kilometres long, had a total permanent population of 262 people. Its only town, Edinburgh of the Seven Seas, stands in the shadow of the island's main volcano. The land is farmed **(4)** ______ the local people, and despite its tiny size, most things the island's residents need **(5)** ______ be found there: they shop at the supermarket, visit the museum, and catch up **(6)** ______ each other in the café.

# 17 GETTING THE MESSAGE

A

B

C

## ABOUT YOU

13 **Watch the video and answer the questions.**

How do you usually keep in touch with your friends?
What's your favourite way of communicating?
Do you ever have video chats? Why? / Why not?

## VOCABULARY Verbs of communication

**1** **Look at the photos. What are the people doing? What do you think has just happened? What do you think will happen next?**

**2** **Read the paragraph opposite. Match the words to situations 1–8.**

EP

1 You don't think the same way about something as your friend.
2 You want someone to realise they might be in danger or that there is a problem.
3 You think your friend has forgotten something.
4 You need to comment on the poor quality of a product or service you received.
5 You want to say sorry for something that you did wrong.
6 You aren't being serious about something. You want to have a laugh with a friend.
7 You tell someone that you will definitely do something for them.
8 You are unsure about something and are thinking about it as a result.

**3** **Complete the questionnaire on page 139. Then compare your answers and discuss your reasons.**

66 **4** **Listen to part of a radio show. Were any of your ideas mentioned?**

66 **5** **Choose the correct words. Then listen again and check.**

1 We *promised* / *complained* to give you the results of our questionnaire.
2 We *warned* / *wondered* whether teenagers often used email.
3 It's easier to laugh and *complain* / *joke* about things face-to-face.
4 They can easily send a text to *apologise* / *remind* a friend that they're meeting up.
5 They also find it easier to *disagree* / *apologise* for something in a text.
6 They *complain* / *promise* that phoning is too expensive.

What's your favourite way to communicate with your friends? Instant messages, tweets and Facebook posts are quick and easy, but if you want to **apologise** for a mistake or **complain** about a problem, isn't it better to speak on the phone or talk face-to-face? Messages are useful to **remind** someone where to meet or to **warn** them you'll be late – or to **joke** about something funny – but we **wonder** whether messages can be used in more serious situations? What do you do when you **disagree** with your best friend? Do you ever actually talk on the phone? Do the questionnaire on page 139 and find out about your communication preferences. Send us your answers and we **promise** to publish the results soon.

**By Lucy Chatter**

**6** **Read the questionnaire again. What other verbs of communication can you find?**

**7** **Discuss the questions.**

1 What things have you promised to do recently?
2 What was the last thing you apologised for?
3 How often do you disagree with your friends? Do you think it matters?

## READING

**1** **Look at the photo. Why would someone send a message in a bottle? What kind of things do they write?**

**2** **Read the article and answer the questions.**

# MESSAGE *in a* BOTTLE

Canadian Steve Thurber was walking along the beach one morning when he noticed an old bottle lying in the sand. He could see an envelope inside signed by Earl Willard and dated September 29th, 1906. Earl was on board a ship that was sailing north along the west coast of the USA and 'posted' his note during the voyage, by throwing the bottle into the sea.

If it turns out to be genuine, this message in a bottle will be the oldest ever found. However, the content of the message remains unknown, as Steve Thurber has refused to open the bottle and find out exactly what Earl wrote. There were a lot of angry comments online about this. Many people wanted to know why Steve wouldn't open the bottle and solve the mystery.

1 Who sent the message?
2 What was unusual about it?
3 What do you think the message said?
4 Why do you think Steve wouldn't open the bottle?

**3** **People write a lot of messages in daily life. Read messages 1–5. What kind of messages are they (text, email etc.)?**

**1**

Hi Paola, I'm wondering whether you'll be in the café later – I need to borrow your notes from yesterday's geography lesson to see what I missed. We've got our test next week! Max

67

**2**

Your laptop is fixed and ready to collect. We can also send it to your home for a small charge in advance. Please confirm your choice. Dolores Winter, CC Computers

**3**

Good morning Ben!
Kelly's party was fun – why didn't you come?
Mum's left money to pay for your lunch on her desk. I'm at college all day, as you know.
See you tonight. Anna

**4**

I'm grateful to everyone involved in last night's school concert – you should be very proud of yourselves! Would anyone like a recording of the performance? Please sign below if so. There'll be a small charge for this.

*Mrs Harris*

**5**

To: Giulia From: Martha Reply Forward

I can't wait to visit your city with my family in July! I don't know whether we'll have time to see each other – I'll let you know. Anyway, can you suggest somewhere for us to stay?

## PREPARE FOR THE EXAM

### Reading Part 1

**4** **Read each message in Exercise 3 again. For each question, choose the correct answer.**

**1** Why has Max sent this text?
**A** to offer to do a favour for Paola
**B** to arrange a meeting with Paola next week
**C** to request help with school work from Paola

**2** Dolores Winter says that
**A** delivery of the repaired laptop can be arranged.
**B** a new laptop model is available at CC Computers.
**C** if the laptop is delivered you must pay a fee when you receive it.

**3** In this note, Anna mentions
**A** who she met at Kelly's party last night.
**B** when their mother will be back from work.
**C** where Ben will find something he needs.

**4** **A** Mrs Harris is giving students a gift for taking part in the concert.
**B** Mrs Harris is seeing which performers would like a souvenir of the event.
**C** Mrs Harris is asking whether any student in the audience filmed the performance.

**5** **A** Martha is keen for her family and Giulia to meet.
**B** Martha would like Giulia to recommend something locally.
**C** Martha wants to ask whether she can stay with Giulia in July.

## TALKING POINTS

If you sent a message in a bottle, what would you write about?

Will we still be writing messages like these in the future? Why? / Why not?

What other methods have people used in the past to communicate?

## GRAMMAR Reported questions

**1** **Read the examples of reported questions and match them to the direct questions a–d. What do you notice about the tenses used in 1–4?**

1. Many people wanted to know why Steve wouldn't open the bottle.
2. We asked teens which activities they had done in the last 24 hours.
3. We wondered whether teens often used email.
4. We asked them if they agreed with the comments.

**a** Do you often use email?

**b** Why won't you open the bottle?

**c** Do you agree with the comments?

**d** Which activities have you done in the last 24 hours?

**2** **Complete the rules with the words in the box.**

| never | positive | question | whether | which |
|---|---|---|---|---|

When we report questions:

**a** we can use *ask*, *want to know* or *wonder* to introduce the reported ________.
**b** we use the same word order as in ________ statements.
**c** we start reported *yes / no* questions with *if* or ________.
**d** we ________ use the auxiliary verb *do* in reported *yes / no* questions.
**e** we start reported *wh*-questions with a *wh*-question word, such as ________ or *why*.

» GRAMMAR REFERENCE AND PRACTICE PAGE 163

**3** **Correct the mistake in each sentence.**

1. My mum ask them if they know about the trip.
2. I asked her if I can take someone with me on the trip.
3. You wanted to know how was the house.
4. She asked who was the owner of the wallet.
5. Joanna wanted to know what should she do to join the group.
6. He started laughing and I wonder why.
7. Have you ever wondered how many messages do we send each day?
8. They asked me did I enjoy the film.

**4** **Complete the reported questions. Make the necessary changes to pronouns, possessive adjectives and tenses.**

0 'Do you miss your aunt in Canada?'
Rob asked *me if I missed* my aunt in Canada.
1 'Will there be any food at the party?'
Rob wondered ________ any food at the party.
2 'Have you ever lost your phone before?'
Sally asked ________ phone before.
3 'Why haven't you bought yourself a new phone?'
Sally wondered ________ a new phone.
4 'When did you last see your cousin?'
Rob asked ________ cousin.
5 'How many songs have you downloaded for your trip?'
Sally asked ________ trip.

**5** » **Work in groups of three. Turn to page 139.**

## VOCABULARY Adverbs of degree: *fairly, pretty, quite, reasonably*

**1** **Read the examples and answer the questions.**

EP
1. Do you keep your bedroom **reasonably** tidy?
2. Are you **fairly** reliable as a person?
3. I'm **pretty** good at table tennis.
4. He spoke **quite** slowly.
5. We're working **reasonably** hard at the moment.
6. It's **quite** an expensive phone.

**a** Do the bold adverbs mean 'very'?
**b** How is the meaning similar or different to 'very'?
**c** What types of word follow the bold adverbs?

**2** **Complete the description. Combine adverbs from Exercise 1 with the words in the box. More than one adverb may be possible.**

| confident | happily | large |
|---|---|---|
| typical | well-behaved | |

*I'd say I'm a [1] ________ person who doesn't mind performing in front of a [2] ________ audience. I can [3] ________ do a long solo on my guitar, for example. It doesn't bother me. At school, I'm a [4] ________ student – I do most of my homework on time and I'm [5] ________ in class!*

**3** **Complete the sentences about you. Use *fairly*, *pretty*, *quite*, *reasonably* and *very*, and suitable adjectives and adverbs.**

1. I'd describe myself as … .
2. My friends would say that I'm … .
3. My bedroom is always … .
4. I usually do … in exams.

## WRITING An article (2)

**1** **Read the article. Which task does it answer, A, B or C?**

Nowadays, people spend a lot of time online. Thanks to mobile internet and wi-fi, we can easily access our social media accounts and look things up wherever we are. I often research things when I'm doing my homework, for example.

I check Snapchat many times during the day. My friends and I are always chatting on WhatsApp or other apps – it's fun and I like to find out what everyone's been doing. I don't want to miss anything! I also have an Instagram account and I post photos of food there. It's a 'foodstagram'! That's what I love doing most online.

### ARTICLES WANTED!

**A TIME ONLINE**

What do you do online?
Which is your favourite site?
How important is messaging to you?

**B MESSAGING**

How do you send messages?
Which is the best messaging app?
How many messages do you send a day?

**C POSTING PHOTOS**

Do you post photos online?
Which sites do you prefer using?
How many photos do you post a day?

**Tell us what you think.**
Write an article answering these questions and we will publish the most interesting articles in our magazine.

- Write your article in about 100 words.

### PREPARE TO WRITE

**Giving opinions**

In my opinion
(Some/Many) people say / think …
I don't think …
Other people may think … but I think …

**2** **Write a sentence giving your opinion about the following.**

1 Checking your phone during the night
2 Texting at the dinner table
3 Posting food photos
4 Grandparents on Facebook
5 Reading blogs written by other teenagers

### PREPARE FOR THE EXAM

**Writing Part 2 (An article)**

**3** **Choose one of the remaining tasks in Exercise 1 (*Messaging* or *Posting photos*). Write your article.**

- Cover all three points in the task.
- Use phrases from the *Prepare to write* box.
- Write about 100 words.
- Remember to check your spelling and grammar.

# 18 WE LOVE CELEBS!

## ABOUT YOU

14 **Watch the video and then answer the questions.**

Who's your favourite celebrity? Have you ever seen him/her? If yes, did you take a photo?

In what ways do celebrities affect the way that young people behave?

Do you think they should be good role models?

Do you enjoy reading about the lives of celebrities? Why? / Why not?

## VOCABULARY Personal feelings and qualities

68 **1 Listen to five people talking about celebrities. Match four of the speakers to the sentences.**

1 This speaker isn't really interested in the lives of celebrities.
2 This speaker thinks that celebrities should be careful about what they do because fans do the same.
3 This speaker felt sad about what the celebrities did.
4 This speaker was surprised by the celebrity.

68 **2 Listen again and complete the sentences with the words in the box.**

EP

| annoyed | charming | curious | delighted |
|---|---|---|---|
| lonely | mad (about) | nasty | professional |
| rude | shy | stressful | unexpected |

1 **Joanne** is ______ about celebrities – she wants to know all about their lives.
2 **Phil** sometimes gets ______ about the celebrities.
3 He thinks that people who are crazy about celebrities might be a bit ______.
4 **Nicole** says that she was too ______ to ask a famous person for their autograph.
5 When the celebrity had gone, she found an ______ souvenir.
6 **Andy** thinks that having your photo taken all the time must be ______.
7 But he thinks that celebrities shouldn't behave badly, or be ______ to their fans.
8 He says that most celebrities are polite, or ______.
9 Often fans copy celebrities and so this is a good reason for the celebrities to be ______ at all times.
10 **Maggie** was ______ that her favourite band had a tour date in her town.
11 She was upset that the band didn't interact with the audience. She thought they were ______.
12 Some fans were ______ because they couldn't hear the band.

**3 Which of the speakers do you agree with the most? Why?**

**4 Look at the words in Exercise 2 again. Are they generally positive or negative? Which two adjectives describe situations and not people?**

**5 Look at the photos and answer the questions. Use words from Exercise 2.**

What is happening in each picture?
How do you think the people are feeling? Why?
What do you think of their behaviour?

## READING

**1** **Which of these things do you think a celebrity might do for you?**

- be your Facebook friend
- buy you food or drink
- give you their autograph
- hang out with you
- help you when you are ill
- give you money
- send you a signed photo
- visit you if you are not well

**2** **Read the article quickly. Which ideas from Exercise 1 are mentioned?**

# CELEBRATING THE CARING CELEBS!

The charming American singer-songwriter Taylor Swift once spent two hours having lunch with a fan who was unwell. In fact she is a celebrity who regularly reaches out to her fans. She noticed a comment on social media and sent a care package to one of her fans – a box full of lovely things including a letter, a signed photo and a cheque for over $1000 to help the fan pay for her studies.

What would you do if you found a wallet? Especially one that had a lot of money in it, and that belonged to a celeb? This happened to a 17-year-old who found Thor's wallet. He was able to return the wallet to actor Chris Hemsworth on a TV show. Kind Chris then gave this young fan all the money from the wallet, and some more!

Now what about the footballer Cristiano Ronaldo? He's been in the news for football, girlfriends and … helping a young boy? Well, yes! A young fan with a serious illness was delighted when he watched Ronaldo play a game and dedicate a goal to him. But that's not the end of the story. The boy is now having his medical treatment paid for by Ronaldo. What a great thing to do!

Selena Gomez usually takes the time to stop and have a chat with her fans. We heard that once, because of a huge number of crazy reporters and photographers, she even invited some excited fans into her car! She has also used social media to stop bad behaviour like bullying. She wants her fans just to be themselves. Go Selena! People notice things like that!

And of course, Ariana Grande! What a superstar! We love her. She supports lots of charities and performs at concerts raising a lot of money for people who are ill with various diseases. She has helped raise millions of dollars for patients and their families.

Can you imagine waiting in line to see your favourite celeb and then suddenly he surprises you? That's what happened when One Direction singer Niall Horan appeared with hot chocolate for fans who had camped out all night because they wanted to see him the next day! We think he's the cutest ever!

But what do we fans really expect of our celebs? Well, we can respect them for their talent, or the way they look. We like reading about them in magazines and online. We enjoy watching their movies and we buy their music, their clothes or their perfume. We love it when they do good things, and we don't like it when they don't. But remember, show them respect and give them space. They are people, like you and me, and they just want to live their lives.

**3** **Read the article and answer the questions.**

1. How did Taylor Swift help a fan who was sick?
2. What did the actor do for the boy who found his wallet?
3. What good thing did a football player do?
4. Why did Selena Gomez invite fans into her car?
5. What good things does Ariana Grande do?
6. Why did Niall give his fans hot chocolate?
7. What does the author think it is OK for fans to do?
8. What does the author say fans should remember to do?

**4** **Match the highlighted words in the article to the meanings.**

1. see something
2. ill or sick
3. took place
4. saying or doing bad things to someone
5. slept outside in a tent

### TALKING POINTS

Why are many people so interested in the lives of celebrities?

Do the celebrities have a responsibility to be good people? Why? / Why not?

## GRAMMAR *have something done*

**1** **Read these sentences. What is the difference between them? Choose the correct words to complete the rule.**

**1** She washes her car on Sundays.
**2** She **has** her car **washed** at a garage.

> We can use *have something done* to talk about something that *we do ourselves / someone else does for us*.

**2** **Match the sentence halves.**

**1** Every day she has her emails
**2** She has her clothes
**3** In the evenings, she has her food
**4** Tomorrow she is going to have her hair
**5** She always has fresh flowers
**6** Yesterday she had her nails

**a** cut and coloured by her hairdresser.
**b** delivered in time for the weekend.
**c** read to her every 10 minutes.
**d** cooked for her by a chef.
**e** painted.
**f** chosen for her by a personal shopper.

**3** **Look at the examples and choose the correct option to complete the rule.**

When I was at the swimming pool, I **had** my phone **stolen** from my locker.
Our neighbours are so unlucky – they'**ve had** their house **burgled** twice recently.

> We also use *have something done* to talk about *victims of crime / people who commit a crime*.

» **GRAMMAR REFERENCE AND PRACTICE PAGE 164**

**4** **Correct the mistakes in the sentences.**

**1** First they have to make their car serviced at a garage.
**2** The ladies go to cut their hair at a hairdressers.
**3** I just stole my bike by a thief.
**4** I did not miss the opportunity to ask the artist if I could have our photo taken of us together with my phone.
**5** The students will be pleased to be taken some photographs.
**6** When Mum and Dad did some work on our house, the workmen made a lot of noise.

**5** **Tell your partner about five things that you have had done or would like to have done.**

*I'd love to have my hair coloured blue.*
*I had my football shirt signed by my favourite player.*

## VOCABULARY Prepositions and conjunctions

**1** **Match the words to the meanings.**

EP **1** **According to** everything you read in magazines, the life of a celebrity must be really hard.
**2** And we heard that **because of** a huge number of reporters, she invited some fans into her car!
**3** Do you think celebrities are interested in anything else **besides** their appearance?
**4** **Despite** their odd appearance, the band are really nice guys.
**5** Some celebrities look for the photographers **instead of** avoiding them.
**6** I'm not interested in news about celebrities, **unless** it's about my favourite singer, Sia.

**a** in place of
**b** not prevented by
**c** in addition to
**d** except if
**e** as a result of
**f** as said by someone

**2** **Complete the sentences with the words in the box.**

> according to   because of   besides
> despite   instead of   unless

**1** Today I bought ice cream ______ buying sweets.
**2** ______ the news, my favourite tennis player has just lost an important match.
**3** Jane cycled to school ______ the awful rain.
**4** Is that boy interested in anything ______ his computer and his phone?
**5** Cara wasn't at school today ______ her cold.
**6** ______ I get good grades, my parents won't let me go to the music festival.

## PREPARE FOR THE EXAM

### Reading Part 6

**3** **For each question, write the correct answer. Write one word for each gap.**

### So you want to be a model?

[1] ______ to top model agencies, there's plenty you can do to get seen. Wear something bright instead [2] ______ a boring pair of jeans. That's obvious, but what else can you do [3] ______ looking after your appearance if you want to be a model?

Well, you could try imagining that whenever you step outside, the cameras will be there. [4] ______ of that, you'll have to think hard about how you look. And unless you've got enough money for a whole new wardrobe, you'll have to get creative instead!

[5] ______ doing all of these things, some people just won't get seen. But don't give up! However, being a model isn't easy, so don't try to become one [6] ______ it's what you really want.

# LISTENING

**1** **Look at the pictures below and discuss what you think would be good or bad about each of the situations.**

**2** **You will hear an interview with a woman called Pattie. Read the questions and options. What do you think she will talk about?**

## PREPARE FOR THE EXAM

### Listening Part 4

**3** **For each question, choose the correct answer.**

70

1 Pattie thinks that some people who want to be famous
  **A** have little idea of how they will achieve it.
  **B** only consider the positive things about it.
  **C** are not prepared to work hard for it.

2 What does Pattie say about the paparazzi?
  **A** Famous people and journalists need each other.
  **B** Being followed by them annoys celebrities.
  **C** Building a good relationship with them isn't easy.

3 Pattie says that some fans
  **A** want too much from famous people.
  **B** behave in unusual ways towards famous people.
  **C** are disappointed when they finally meet someone famous.

4 Pattie believes that if she became famous quickly, it would be hard to
  **A** give up her private life.
  **B** ask for advice from others.
  **C** learn how to give interviews.

5 Pattie says most famous people especially enjoy
  **A** receiving free gifts from designers.
  **B** not having to do boring jobs any more.
  **C** being able to try new kinds of work.

6 Pattie's most important advice for newly famous people is to
  **A** make sure you plan for the future.
  **B** not talk to anyone you don't trust.
  **C** try to hide any negative feelings.

**4** **What do you think of Pattie's advice? Give your reasons.**

# SPEAKING Discussing a topic (2)

**1** **Read these questions from a discussion about celebrities. Decide how you might answer them.**

1 Can anyone famous really have a private life?
2 Do you agree that journalists should leave celebrities alone?
3 But what about the children of famous people?

71 **2** **Listen to two people discussing the questions. Did they mention any of your ideas?**

71 **3** **Listen again. Does one speaker say more than the other? How does each speaker involve the other in the discussion?**

71 **4** **Read the *Prepare to speak* box. Then listen again.**

**Which phrases do the speakers use to keep the conversation going?**

## PREPARE TO SPEAK

### Keeping the conversation going

What do you think?
Why do you say that?
But what about …?
Do you agree that …?
That's an interesting point.
I suppose so, although …
It depends, doesn't it?
I'm not sure, because …

## PREPARE FOR THE EXAM

### Speaking Part 4

**5** **Read the questions and discuss them with a partner. Use phrases from the *Prepare to speak* box to keep the conversation going.**

1 How much do you know about your favourite celebrity?
2 What would you like to find out about your favourite film star?
3 Would you like to be famous? Why? / Why not?
4 How would your life change if you were famous?

# CULTURE

## FAN CULTURE

**1** **Complete the table with two celebrities for each category. Talk about why each celebrity is famous.**

**FAMOUS FACES!**

Actors ..........

Singers ..........

Writers ..........

Athletes ..........

**2** **Discuss the questions.**

1 Who are your favourite celebrities?
2 Why do celebrities want fans?
3 What can celebrities do to get more fans?

**3** **Read the article on the opposite page. Match the headings (1–6) to the paragraphs (A–F).**

1 Building a fan base
2 Unhappy fans
3 Fans in the past
4 Saved by the fans
5 Fan club activities
6 Fans and advertising

**4** **Match each sentence to a paragraph in the text.**

1 Fans can use protests to support their favourite celebs.
2 Some famous people look to their fans for suggestions.
3 Celebrity fan clubs aren't a particularly new invention.
4 Stars with lots of followers can use them to earn more money.
5 Fan clubs can use technology to improve communication.
6 Some celebrities use social media to say they're sorry.

**5** **Are you a sports fan? Answer the questions.**

1 Which sports are you interested in?
2 Have you got a favourite player or team?
3 Which sportspeople are most famous in your country?

72 **6** **Listen to Akira, a football fan from Japan. How does he watch Arsenal matches?**

72 **7** **Listen again. Are the sentences true or false?**

1 Akira isn't interested in Japanese football at all.
2 He wasn't a fan of Japan in the World Cup.
3 Akira thinks Özil is a very good football player.
4 Akira watches live football when he has school the next day.
5 He and his friends discuss the matches in online forums.
6 Akira thinks it's difficult to follow your favourite players nowadays.

**8** **Read the *Useful language* phrases. Complete them with the words in the box.**

| brilliant | fan | follow | joining | live | mad |
|---|---|---|---|---|---|

### USEFUL LANGUAGE

**Talking about being a fan**

1 I'm a really big ... of (Özil).
2 I'm ... about (Katy Perry).
3 I ... my favourite band on Twitter.
4 I think (Alicia Vikander) is a ... actress.
5 I like ... in on sports forums.
6 We can have ... chats with fans from all over the world.

# FANS AND FANDOM

73

**A** There have always been celebrities and there will always be fans. In the early years of cinema, film stars had their own fan clubs, and many pop singers in the 1950s had huge crowds of fans who loved them and followed them around everywhere. This shouldn't be surprising, since the word *fan* is actually short for *fanatic* – a person who is so interested in something that they may seem a bit mad!

**B** In typical fan clubs, people can buy photos, posters and other products. They may also get discounts on tickets to films and concerts. Some clubs organise annual conferences to get together and celebrate their fandom. Modern technology also offers new ways for club members to share interests, such as online forums, fan sites and social media. They also give fans more direct contact with the celebs they love.

**C** The most successful celebrities today understand the value of a good relationship with their fan base. They upload photos and messages to keep their fans up to date, and some celebs ask their fans for advice. For example, the singer Rihanna was going to make a new remix, so she tweeted her fans and asked them who she should invite to sing with her. Then she accepted their choice.

**D** Celebrities who treat their fans well can benefit in many ways. They get more followers on social media, which lets them advertise important events and spread the word about products that they want to sell. In only a few seconds, superstars like Beyoncé and Cristiano Ronaldo can contact millions of people around the world and create interest or 'buzz' about anything they want, without paying anything.

**E** Of course, modern fandom can also have disadvantages. If fans are disappointed with a film, the bad news can spread very quickly and be bad for ticket sales. If famous people say offensive things or make mistakes in public, they may need to apologise online to avoid losing fans. In addition, celebrities may pay too much attention to their biggest and loudest fans and lose popularity with the general public.

**F** On the bright side, loyal fans can also rescue their favourite celebrities. For example, when the directors of the popular TV show *Glee* talked about replacing some of the main characters after the third season, millions of fans went crazy and started a campaign to prevent the changes. In the end, the characters continued on the show, thanks to the energetic support of their fans.

## PROJECT

*A poster about a celebrity*

**Make a poster about your favourite celebrity. Use the following list of questions to help you. Decorate your poster with photos and drawings.**

1. Who is your celebrity and why is he/she famous?
2. What are some important events in his/her career?
3. How does your celebrity communicate with fans?
4. Does your celebrity sell or advertise any products?
5. Does he/she use social media to get more publicity?
6. Do you belong to this person's official fan club?
7. Do you follow this person on any social media?

**Present your poster to the class.**

15 NOW WATCH THE CULTURE VIDEO

# 19 THE WORLD OF WORK

## ABOUT YOU

What kind of job would you like in the future? Why?
Which jobs would you **not** want to do? Why not?

## VOCABULARY Work tasks

**1** **Look at the photos of teenagers doing work experience. What do you think 'work experience' is? What kind of work do you think they are doing?**

74 **2** **Listen to four teenagers. Match each speaker to a photo.**

74 **3** **Complete the sentences with the correct form of the verbs. Listen again and check.** EP

| arrange | calculate | deal with | deliver |
|---|---|---|---|
| develop | handle | install | manage |
| organise | produce | run | update |

**Connie**

1 Our careers officer hadn't .......... a place for me.
2 They .......... the wooden doors for new houses.
3 I spent some time .......... figures in the manager's office.

**Vera**

4 We planted the 147 trees that .......... to local parks.
5 We weren't sure we could .......... the work.
6 They .......... our programme really well.

**Ali**

7 My dad .......... a TV production company.
8 The man who was .......... the project was very encouraging.
9 I even helped to .......... ideas for costumes.

**Gordon**

10 She .......... the problem immediately.
11 I saw how to .......... new software.
12 I also .......... the information about the store.

**4** **What do people in these jobs have to do? Use the verbs from Exercise 3.**

| accountant | engineer | shop assistant |
|---|---|---|
| teacher | website designer | |

## READING

### PREPARE FOR THE EXAM

#### Reading Part 2

**1** **You are going to read descriptions of eight places offering work experience to teenagers. Look at the eight titles in A–H. Answer the questions.**

1 Which ones probably include some work outside?
2 What might teens be asked to do in each place?

**2** **Read the descriptions of the eight places quickly to check your ideas.**

**3** **Read about five teenagers who are looking for work experience. Decide which place (A–H) would be the most suitable for each teenager.**

1 Leila is interested in the arts, including live music and dance, and she also has IT skills which she is happy to use. She doesn't mind travelling so that she can get necessary work experience.
2 Ben wants to avoid work where he would be sitting at a desk. He has good local knowledge and is reasonably strong, having spent lots of time doing outdoor activities such as riding and climbing.
3 Helen loves working with computers and wants to gain further experience using them in a job. She's interested in film and hopes to join a team of experts to see how they handle challenging industry projects.
4 Marco would like to experience the kind of work involved in the tourism industry. He enjoys researching topics online and is good at communicating with younger children.
5 Jade has above-average ability in maths and wants to use this skill in the area of leisure – especially in sport. She would like to find a company with easy access to the city centre.

A

B

C

D

# WORK EXPERIENCE

*Spend two weeks at a local company and learn about a job!*

## A Delivery company

If you know the area around the city quite well and enjoy travelling around, come and help us. We provide a fast delivery service for online orders and we also transfer products for other companies. We need someone to help the drivers lift heavy boxes and parcels.

## B Cruise ship

Our company is important for tourism because it provides cruises worldwide. When ships are in port, we get them cleaned and make sure cabins are ready for new passengers. You will spend 40% of your time on board helping our staff with cleaning and general repairs, and also work in the office on a busy customer service desk.

## E Football club

Every year, students on work experience get the chance to meet players at our club, which is located close to the heart of the city. Last year's students worked outside preparing the training ground, whereas this time you'll be in our financial department, learning about costs and other issues from top accountants.

## C Riding school

You'll look after one particular horse while you're here, dealing with everything from its food to its appearance and daily exercise routine. Although your work will be mostly in the fresh air, you'll be at a desk for brief periods, in order to answer phones and arrange customers' lessons.

## F Television studio

We make comedy shows, drama and wildlife programmes. Our busy IT department welcomes students with knowledge of this area. You will develop new skills and stay with a single work group, learning from experienced people coping with demanding situations, like installing systems software.

## G Primary school

We encourage secondary school students to work in our classes, reading to the youngest children and helping older ones with maths problems. If you are good at sport, why not help to teach our junior football team what you know? As the school is in the north of the city, it takes about an hour from the centre by bus.

## D Festival office

This city's cultural festival is world-famous and our small out-of-town office is open all year round, booking next year's performers. Join our friendly team, helping with general phone enquiries, printing, and design of our advertising. You will find out a lot about the entertainment industry.

## H City museum

While you don't have to know about local history, we do expect you to put your internet skills to good use! Find out interesting facts about the objects on display, which you can then pass on to kids and their parents as you guide them around the building. Many of these visitors come from other countries.

### TALKING POINTS

Do you think it is useful to gain some experience of work as a teenager? Why? / Why not?
What are the advantages and disadvantages of working indoors / outdoors?
Are some jobs more important than others? Which ones and why?

# GRAMMAR Different types of clause

**1** **Read the examples and match the clauses to the types of clause (a–c) in the rules.**

1 You'll have to be strong <u>so that</u> you can lift the heavy boxes and parcels.
2 Last year's students worked outside, <u>whereas</u> this time you'll be in our financial department.
3 <u>As</u> the school is in the north of the city, it takes about an hour from the centre by bus.

We use linking words to join clauses.

**a** **Contrast clauses**
To add different or surprising information in the same sentence, we can use the linking words *although*, *whereas* and *while*.

**b** **Purpose clauses**
To explain the purpose of something in the same sentence, we can use the linking words *so that* and *in order to*.

**c** **Reason clauses**
To explain the reason for something in the same sentence, we can use the linking words *because* and *as*.

» **GRAMMAR REFERENCE AND PRACTICE PAGE 165**

**2** **Complete the sentences with the correct word.**

1 I'll be late home ______ I've got football practice.
2 ______ I arrived very late, my friends had waited for me.
3 You need to place your order one week in advance ______ that it can be delivered on time.
4 ______ I enjoy my job, I'd like to be paid more.
5 Why don't you arrange an appointment with the careers officer in ______ to discuss your plans?
6 The report states that there was no damage to the environment, ______ actually, local wildlife suffered greatly.
7 We enjoyed this film very much, especially ______ of the brilliant acting.

**3** **Match the sentence halves and join them with a suitable linking word.**

1 People who work at a desk are often unhealthy
2 Farmers need to listen to weather forecasts
3 Accountants normally have a degree in maths
4 Some of our greatest performers have no drama training

a company directors sometimes lack financial skills.
b they admit that their acting has improved with experience.
c they don't get any exercise during the day.
d they know when to bring young animals inside.

**4** **Complete the sentences so they are true for you. Use linking words from Exercise 2.**

1 I hope to / I don't want to earn a lot of money …
2 I'm learning English …
3 I really like / dislike science …

# VOCABULARY *as* and *like*

**1** **Read the examples. Which preposition, *as* or *like*, introduces an example?**

EP

1 One guy in my group thinks he might do it as a job.
2 I did jobs like printing and photocopying.

**2** **Read the text. Match the bold examples of *as* and *like* to the uses a–d below. There are two examples of one use.**

Although we were only on work experience, my friend and I were just [1]**like** any other employee in the company – we had the same coffee breaks and were able to buy cheap meals in the canteen. Most mornings, I was working [2]**as** a receptionist on the front desk, so I had to wear smart clothes, but my friend was outside helping the gardeners, so she was able to wear things [3]**like** jeans and t-shirts. We got to know quite a few of the staff and were known [4]**as** the Terrible Twins, because we look so similar.
When we left, they gave us a big bag of souvenirs, [5]**like** coffee mugs with their company name on, mint chocolates and special pens.

a used to introduce an example
b used to mean 'similar to'
c used with a verb to talk about a job
d used with a verb to mean 'called'

**3** **Complete the sentences with *as* or *like*.**

1 When Luke worked ______ a waiter, he had to balance several things on his tray at the same time, ______ dirty plates and glasses.
2 What can you see? I think the clouds look ______ castles in the sky.
3 Everyone dressed up ______ their favourite character and went to the party by bus.

**4** » **Turn to page 140.**

## WRITING An email (3)

**1** **Read the task. Then tick (✓) the three things that Daisy wants you to write about.**

- Read this email from your penfriend Daisy and the notes you have made.

To:
From: Daisy

My aunt has offered me some work experience this summer! — *Great!*

I can either be a waiter in her busy restaurant or work outside in her garden, where she grows all the vegetables for the restaurant. Which of the two jobs should I take? — *Suggest ...*

What do you think I should do with the money I'll earn? — *Tell Daisy*

Are you going to do some work experience this summer, too? — *Yes. Say what*

Love,
Daisy

- Write a reply to Daisy, using all the notes.

**2** **Read the *Prepare to write* box. Then read the reply to Daisy's email. Which of Daisy's questions has the writer failed to answer properly? What information should you add?**

To:
From:

Hi Daisy

Thanks for your email. That's awesome news. You're lucky to have such a nice aunt!

If I were you, I'd go for the restaurant because gardening can be really hard work. You might meet some interesting people and I guess you'll get to try some of the delicious food, too!

I'm going to do some work experience at the wildlife centre near where I live, feeding the animals. I'll probably have to do some cleaning, as well. I think it'll be fun, although I won't earn any money doing that.

Anyway, let me know what you decide!

Bye,

### PREPARE TO WRITE

**An email**

When you are replying to a friend's email:

- make sure you answer all the questions the friend asks.
- organise your ideas so that the email reads clearly.
- include some longer sentences with linking words.
- remember to use short forms and informal language, such as phrasal verbs.
- remember to use an informal phrase to begin and end your email.

**3** **Complete the sentences with *although* or *because*.**

1 You'll enjoy this job ________ you enjoy working with animals.
2 It's fun working outside, ________ it's sometimes cold and wet in the winter.
3 Babysitting is fun, ________ young children can be difficult sometimes.
4 I'd love to work for a TV company ________ I might meet some famous people!

**4** **Find these things in the reply in Exercise 2:**

1 a phrasal verb meaning 'choose'
2 two more examples of informal language

**5** **Read the task below and plan your answer. Remember to plan answers to all the questions.**

- Read an email from your friend, Ben.

To:
From: Ben

Hi

In class today, we were discussing possible jobs that we might like to do in the future. — *Interesting!*

I'd love to be a firefighter one day. — *Ask why?*

What would be your perfect job? — *Explain*

How could you find out more about this type of work? — *Tell Ben*

See you soon,
Ben

### PREPARE FOR THE EXAM

**Writing Part 1**

**6** **Write your reply to Ben's email using the notes you have made.**

- Use the tips in the *Prepare to write* box.
- Write about 100 words.
- Remember to check your spelling and grammar.

# 20 MAKING PLANS

## ABOUT YOU

What do you hope to do after you finish school?
What do you plan to do in the summer holidays?

## VOCABULARY Hopes and dreams

**1** **Look at the photos. Describe them to your partner.**

**2** (76) **Listen to three teenagers talking about their plans and hopes for the future. Match the speakers to three of the photos.**

**3** (76) **Answer the questions. Then listen again and check.**

1 What did speaker 1 always dream of doing?
2 What did her mother encourage her to do?
3 Who has speaker 2 always admired?
4 What does he imagine himself doing before a game?
5 Where does speaker 3 aim to study?
6 What advice does she give to other young people?

**4** EP **Complete the sentences with the correct form of the verbs in the box.**

achieve admire aim choose dream encourage imagine try your best

1 When he was younger, my dad ______ of being an astronaut.
2 I can't ______ what it's like to work all day.
3 Max ______ to study French and Spanish when he was 14.
4 I really ______ sports stars who practise for hours.
5 Mum ______ me to take up dance classes.
6 Nelson Mandela ______ many great things in his life.
7 Jenny ______ to go running every day before school, but she found it really hard.
8 Don't be sad. You ______ and no one can ask more.

**5** **Discuss the questions.**

1 What would you like to achieve in the next five years?
2 Who do you admire most? Why?
3 What subjects do you think you will choose to study when you're older?
4 Do you dream of being famous?
5 What or who encourages you most when you have to study?
6 What do you imagine you will be doing in five years' time?
7 In what situations do you try your best?

## READING

1 What do you usually do in the long holidays? Make a list.

2 Look at the photos and the headline. What do you think the article is about?

# A meaningful summer

**The summer holidays are most definitely a time for rest and relaxation. But after the first few days of staying in, you might start to get bored. After all, watching videos on YouTube all day isn't the best way to spend your free time! How about choosing to take on a few meaningful activities these holidays? It'll be a challenge, but we think you'll have a lot of fun, and learn some incredible life skills. Whatever you choose to do, you're certainly going to make some great memories, and maybe even a bit of extra cash. Here are some ideas.**

### Home camp

Plan a week of activities as though it were a summer camp week. First, make a list of things you can do, for example, go for a cycle ride in your local park, visit a museum in the city, go swimming at the local leisure centre. Perhaps you could volunteer as well by helping out at a local charity, hospital or care home? Encourage your friends to join in the activities and then find a week when you're all free and plan what you're going to do each day. Aim to include at least two activities per day and you'll see that you have a very busy week, and certainly no time to be bored!

### Grow your own food

You don't need to live in the countryside to grow your own food. You can do this on your balcony if you live in an apartment block. You can grow fruit, vegetables and herbs. It might be an idea to begin this project earlier though, in the spring, as the plants need a few months to grow. Go to a local garden centre to get some ideas. And what better way to enjoy the food you grow than by using it in your own cooking? Why not find recipes online or ask family members to teach you how to cook their favourite dishes?

### Your own holiday business

Do you want to earn some extra pocket money this summer? The summer holidays are the perfect time to start your own 'holiday business' and gain some skills. What type of thing you can do depends on your abilities and interests. Are you good with your hands? Do you enjoy making things? You could start making your own jewellery or clothes and then sell them online. Are you good with computers and technology? Maybe you could help your friends and neighbours with their IT problems. Are you an animal-lover? You could look after your neighbours' pets while they are on holiday or offer a dog-walking service.

### Raise money with a run

There are sports activities taking place all the time, even during the summer. Have a look online and find one near you that's open to young people. Why not take part in a 5-km run, or a cycling event? If you do this, people can sponsor you and then you can give your favourite charity the money. This is a great way to do two great things – helping people and exercising!

3 **Read the article and answer the questions.**

1 Why did the writer write this article?
2 Why should the camp week have different activities?
3 What does the writer suggest for creative people?
4 Why do you need to begin the garden project early?
5 What are the advantages of taking part in a sponsored sports activity?

4 **Match the highlighted words to the definitions.**

1 help or work for an organisation without being paid
2 a building with a swimming pool and places where you can play sports
3 to give money to someone to support an activity, event or organisation
4 useful or important
5 things you do well because you have practised them

### TALKING POINTS

Which of these ideas would you like to try?
Do you think it's important to plan what you want to do? Why? Why not?
How important is luck in achieving your aims?

## GRAMMAR Verbs with two objects

**1** **Read the two examples. Which verb has two objects? Which is the direct object and which is the indirect object?**

**1** You can give your favourite charity the money.
**2** You could start making your own jewellery.

**2** **Read the examples and identify the direct object and indirect object in each one. Then choose the correct word to complete the rules.**

**1** My friend sent me this photograph.
**2** My friend sent this photograph to me.

> Some verbs can be followed by two objects, a direct object and an indirect object.
> **a** The direct object is usually a *person / thing*.
> **b** The indirect object is usually a *person / thing*.
> **c** If the *direct / indirect* object comes first, we use *to* or *for* before the indirect object.
> **d** If the *direct / indirect* object comes first, we don't use *to* or *for*.

» **GRAMMAR REFERENCE AND PRACTICE PAGE 166**

**3** **Underline the direct object and circle the indirect object in each sentence.**

**0** I sent my (cousin) an email.
**1** She gave him some flowers.
**2** He took his dad a present.
**3** The girl sent her mother a photo.
**4** My best friend told me a secret.
**5** Mum brought me a glass of juice in bed.
**6** The girls showed each other their phones.

**4** **Write the sentences with the indirect object first.**

**0** They brought some flowers for me.
*They brought me some flowers.*
**1** Jack wrote an email to his friend.
**2** She gave some flowers to the boy.
**3** She showed a photo to her friends.
**4** I bought a book for my brother.
**5** She told her story to the class.

**5** **Correct the mistake in each sentence.**

**1** Parents have to pay to them a lot of money.
**2** I will you show the photographs.
**3** Tell to me everything about our last class.
**4** I'm going to tell a story about my holiday.
**5** Can you lend to me a pencil, please?

**6** **Answer the questions with a partner.**

**1** Who did you send your last message to?
**2** What presents did people give you for your last birthday?
**3** Has anyone promised you anything recently? What was it?
**4** Who do you usually show your homework to?

## VOCABULARY Phrasal verbs

**1** **Read the examples and underline the phrasal verbs.**

**1** Encourage your friends to join in the activities.
**2** What type of thing you can do depends on your abilities and interests.

**2** **Read the sentences and match the phrasal verbs to the meanings.**

EP

**1** If you want to grow your own food, you should **go for** it!
**2** I **kept on** reading my book after midnight – it was so good!
**3** My friend Janey **got into** the national team. She was so pleased.
**4** I think it's important to **join in** group activities.
**5** Her success **depends on** her ability to practise every day.
**6** Jake's father **believed in** his ability as a surfer.
**7** Mark is trying to **work out** how he can do everything he wants to.
**8** I got to the party too late and **missed out** on all the fun.

**a** trust that someone can do something well
**b** not do or have something that you would enjoy
**c** be affected by something or someone
**d** become a member of a team or group
**e** try to get or achieve something
**f** take part in something with other people
**g** understand something after thinking very carefully
**h** continue to do something

**3** **Complete the text with the correct phrasal verbs from Exercise 2.**

Hi Frankie,

Sorry I couldn't make it to the party! I know I [1] ________ on a lot of fun. I've been really busy with training recently. Did I tell you I [2] ________ the national team?! I'm so happy! The coach said he'd always [3] ________ me, which I thought was a nice thing to say! I have worked so hard to get this far, but I can't stop now – I need to [4] ________ practising to get even better. I have to make the most of this opportunity and really [5] ________ it. My success at the next Olympic Games [6] ________ a lot of training. So I won't be able to [7] ________ the holiday activities. But let's try to see each other soon – I just need to [8] ________ when I'm free, first!

Bradley

**4** » **Work in pairs.** **Turn to page 140.**

# LISTENING

78 **1** **Listen to the introduction to a radio programme. What is it about?**

78 **2** **Now listen to the programme and write down the teens' achievements.**

| | Achievement |
|---|---|
| Chris | |
| Nathan | |
| Sophia | |
| Lucy | |
| Tom | |

78 **3** **Listen again and answer the questions.**

1 Why does Chris describe his schedule as 'crazy'?
2 What does Nathan say was the best part of his course?
3 What does Sophia say about the test day?
4 What skills did Lucy learn?
5 What useful skills did Tom learn?

# SPEAKING Discussing options (3)

**1** **Look at the pictures of activities on a summer activity course. Which activities would you like to do on holiday? Why?**

79 **2** **Read the task. Then listen to three people discussing the different activities. Decide if the sentences are true or false.**

A boy is going to do a **summer activity course** during his holidays. Here are the different things that he could do. Talk to each other about the **benefits** of these different activities and then decide which would be best.

1 Jessica thinks sleeping all summer holiday would be boring.
2 Ana thinks it's nice to learn something new in the holidays.
3 Jon thinks team activities are better than individual activities.
4 Jon doesn't think that rock climbing is a team sport.
5 The three people agree that rock climbing and painting are the best activities.

79 **3** **Read the *Prepare to speak* box, then listen again. Which phrases do you hear?**

## PREPARE TO SPEAK

### Agreeing and disagreeing

**Agreeing**
I completely agree with you.
That's (very) true.
That's an excellent idea!
I agree with you.

**Disagreeing**
I don't agree with you because …
That's quite a good idea, although …
Yes, but at the same time …

**Asking for agreement**
Do you agree with me?
Do you think the same?
Is that how you feel?
What do you think?

## PREPARE FOR THE EXAM

### Speaking Parts 3 and 4

**4** » **Work in pairs. Turn to page 140.**

**5** **Discuss the questions.**

1 What do you usually do during the summer holidays?
2 Is it important to plan what you are going to do in the summer holidays? Why? / Why not?
3 In the holidays, do you prefer to spend time with your friends or your family? Why?
4 Do you prefer spending time at home or spending time outdoors? Why?
5 Would you like to have longer summer holidays? Why? / Why not?

# LIFE SKILLS EMOTIONAL SKILLS

# MANAGING STRESS

## LIFE SKILLS

**How to manage stress**

It's normal to have some problems at school, at home or with friends. These problems can cause negative feelings, or stress. Everyone has some stress in life, but too much stress can be bad for a person's health. That's why it's important to deal with stress and reduce its effects.

**1** **What things are stressful for you? Rate the issues below from 1 (not stressful) to 4 (very stressful).**

- **a** ____ homework and school projects
- **b** ____ personal problems with friends
- **c** ____ worries about tests and exams
- **d** ____ nasty messages on social media
- **e** ____ not having enough pocket money
- **f** ____ looking good and being in style
- **g** ____ bullies and other negative people

**2** **Read the text on the opposite page. Which suggestions would be the most helpful for you?**

**3** **Match the following ideas with the tips in the text.**

1. Doing your homework at the last minute isn't a good habit.
2. Take some time to enjoy yourself after your work is done.
3. Make sure you have a good diet and get plenty of rest.
4. It's important to think about the possible causes of your stress.
5. Talking to someone about your worries can make you feel better.
6. Sports and exercise are good ways to reduce feelings of stress.

**4** **Match the highlighted words in the text to the meanings.**

1. based on good decisions
2. spend your free time in a place or with someone
3. feeling nervous or worried
4. related to school and studies
5. when you feel how something happens to you
6. have something inside or as a part

80 **5** **Listen to four people: Paul, Emma, Marco and Vicky. Match them with the problems they mention.**

arguments bullying homework money parents sisters social media sports

1. Paul ____
2. Emma ____
3. Marco ____
4. Vicky ____

80 **6** **Listen again. Answer the questions.**

1. How did Paul finally solve his problem?
2. Why hasn't Emma got very much free time?
3. Why does Marco tell his friends that he's busy?
4. What do her sisters do that annoys Vicky so much?

**7** **Work in pairs. Think of suggestions to help Paul, Emma, Marco and Vicky.**

**8** **Read the *Useful language* phrases. Complete them with your own ideas.**

## USEFUL LANGUAGE

**Describing stress**

1. I can't relax when …
2. It's annoying when …
3. I feel upset when …
4. I get stressed when …
5. I really hate it when …

# Stress-busters!

81

**There are lots of things that cause stress in our lives, such as school problems, arguments with friends and negative feelings that we sometimes have about ourselves. We all experience stress at times, but it's important to manage it properly and reduce its effects. Here are some helpful tips for dealing with stress.**

## 1 Stop and reflect

Sometimes we feel stressed without understanding the reason. For example, you might be anxious about a maths exam tomorrow because you haven't studied enough. However, your real problem isn't the exam – it's the way you organise your studies. Whenever you're stressed, you should stop and think. What is really happening? How can you improve the situation? Try keeping a diary about your problems and the possible causes.

## 2 Manage your time

Do you forget when your school projects are due? Do you wait until Sunday evening to do homework? These bad habits can cause 'last-minute' stress, as well as poor grades. It's more sensible to plan your studies, for example with a calendar. You can also divide big projects into smaller tasks that you can do in parts. In addition, you should plan your other activities, like sports and clubs. In this way, you'll always know how much time you really have.

## 3 Watch your health

Healthy habits are very important for reducing stress. Be sure to eat healthy meals with lots of fruit and vegetables. Try to get at least eight hours of sleep and don't drink too much coffee or tea in the evening. They contain caffeine, which can make you nervous. And don't check your mobile phone or use the computer before bedtime. It will keep you awake! Finally, you should do at least one hour of exercise every day. Physical activity keeps your body strong and healthy and it's also very relaxing.

## 4 Reach out for help

When you're feeling stressed, it's helpful to speak to someone who understands your situation, such as your friends and family. Sometimes it's enough to talk about your problems and share your feelings with other people. Other times, you might ask for advice or suggestions. At school, you can also speak to teachers, especially if you're having academic problems. Don't keep your worries to yourself. Remember that you're not alone!

## 5 Have some fun!

Finally, find some free time for activities that you enjoy, such as sports, hobbies and meeting with friends. Why not make plans to see a film or hang out in the park at the weekend? You can also spend some time listening to your favourite music or playing computer games, but make sure you've done your homework first! If you take some time to relax and enjoy yourself, you'll feel better, have more energy, and reduce your level of stress.

## PROJECT

*A report*

**Prepare a report about the things that are stressful for you and how you deal with that stress. Use the questions below and add more ideas of your own.**

1. When do you usually get stressed?
2. What things do you hate or find annoying?
3. How well do you manage your time?
4. Have you got healthy habits that reduce stress?
5. Who do you talk to when you feel stressed?
6. What do you do to relax and have fun?

**Share your report with a classmate and ask for suggestions to improve your work. Then revise your report and present it to the class.**

# REVIEW 5 UNITS 17–20

## VOCABULARY

**1 Unscramble the verbs in the box and use them to complete the sentences.**

| anrw | diernm | edegaisr |
|---|---|---|
| noewrd | spagoolie | sporime |

1 I'm definitely going to do my homework after dinner – I ________ !
2 I'm really sorry I didn't text you earlier. I ________ for the confusion.
3 I don't want to forget about my appointment. Can you ________ me?
4 I don't have the same opinion as you – I ________ with you.
5 Mum and Dad will be asking themselves where you are – they will ________ where you are.
6 The police will ________ us if there is any danger of flooding.

**2 Write the adjective to describe each person.**

1 I want to know all about kangaroos and other animals from Australia. c _ _ _ _ _ _ _
2 Argh! The internet isn't working, so I can't chat to my friends! a _ _ _ _ _ _ _
3 I'm really happy with my grade for my project! d _ _ _ _ _ _ _ _ _ _
4 I don't know anyone at this school. I miss my old school. l _ _ _ _ _ _
5 I don't want to talk to anyone. I feel silly. s _ _
6 Sometimes he doesn't even say hello to me when he sees me! r _ _ _

**3 Complete the sentences with the verbs in the box.**

| arrange | calculate | develop |
|---|---|---|
| handle | run | update |

1 We want to ________ a better design, which won't have so many problems.
2 It's a difficult situation and I'm not sure how to ________ it.
3 My parents want to ________ a meeting with my teachers.
4 She loves cooking and she'd like to ________ her own restaurant one day.
5 We ________ the website with new information every day.
6 I've got all the figures, so I can ________ the total.

**4 Choose the correct words to complete the sentences.**

1 If you want to do something, you should *go for* / *go at* / *try to* it.
2 I can't study any more – I have *tried the best* / *tried my best* / *done the best*.
3 I really *admire* / *imagine* / *dream* people who have more than one job – they're amazing!
4 Lara *chose* / *encouraged* / *achieved* to visit her best friend after school.
5 I *aim* / *encourage* / *dream* of being a famous sports star.
6 I *keep on* / *aim* / *imagine* to be rich by the time I am 20.

## GRAMMAR

**1 Complete the reported questions.**

1 How many celebs actually enjoy their status? I wondered …
2 Did you all enjoy the film? Mr Hamilton wanted to know …
3 Did you finish the maths homework? Margit asked me …
4 Can you speak more than one foreign language? I asked my uncle …
5 Have you seen the new James Bond movie? Julia wanted to know …
6 Where is Stefan going on Saturday? George wondered …

**2 Fill in the missing words to rewrite the sentences.**

1 The woman painted my nails. I ________ my nails ________ .
2 The man brushed the dog's hair. The dog ________ its hair ________ .
3 Someone is taking my photo. I ________ my photo ________ .
4 The garage has fixed my motorbike. I ________ my motorbike ________ .
5 Tomorrow, my aunt is going to cut my hair. Tomorrow I ________ my hair ________ .

**3** **Choose the correct linking words.**

1 I went to the shop *because* / *although* we didn't have any bread.
2 My favourite colour is red, *whereas* / *as* my best friend's is blue.
3 *As* / *Although* we have to get up early tomorrow, I'm going to bed now.
4 We're going to check in online *in order to* / *because* get the best seats.
5 I like most kinds of rice dishes, *although* / *because* I don't really like fried rice.

**4** **Put the words in order to make sentences.**

1 mum / my / a / me / new / my birthday / for / gave / bike
2 them / email / an / explaining / Susan / wrote / everything
3 showed / her / Jessica / photos / holiday / us
4 bunch / took / flowers / aunt / a / I / of / my
5 teacher / our / us / told / biology / our / grades
6 grandmother / sent / my / me / a / gift

**5** **Choose the correct option.**

1 I found a large case. I wondered *what's* / *what was* inside.
2 He started to tell me about where *did he come* / *he came* from.
3 She's *having her car washed* / *washing her car* at the garage because she doesn't have time to do it herself.
4 She asked me *if I enjoyed* / *did I enjoy* the film.

**6** **Correct the mistake in each sentence.**

1 I like the summer despite it can be too hot sometimes.
2 We play video games together. Because we both enjoy this.
3 When you write, please tell about your school.
4 Please send to me an email with the information.

## PREPARE FOR THE EXAM

### Reading Part 5

**1** **For each question, choose the correct answer.**

**Be a volunteer!**

For most of you, it will be another few years before you enter the world of work. However, you can still get prepared by **(1)** ________ suitable skills. How? By becoming a volunteer.

Young people can do anything from caring for kids to getting involved in local environmental projects. But what should you **(2)** ________ to do? A good idea is to think of something you feel **(3)** ________ about or already have an interest in, and then try your **(4)** ________ to get involved with it. As a volunteer, you need to be friendly and professional, turn up on time and be able to **(5)** ________ with problems, which are all skills that employers are looking for. So, although you might not get paid as a volunteer, in the future you could get a better job **(6)** ________ of your hard work.

| | A | B | C | D |
|---|---|---|---|---|
| **1** | **A** increasing | **B** developing | **C** producing | **D** growing |
| **2** | **A** choose | **B** select | **C** prefer | **D** want |
| **3** | **A** keen | **B** interested | **C** lively | **D** curious |
| **4** | **A** highest | **B** first | **C** best | **D** most |
| **5** | **A** support | **B** handle | **C** deal | **D** advise |
| **6** | **A** according | **B** because | **C** besides | **D** instead |

### Reading Part 6

**2** **For each question, write the correct answer. Write one word for each gap.**

**The paparazzi**

The paparazzi are photographers who take pictures of famous people. They work for themselves instead of a company, and then sell their work to newspapers and magazines. **(1)** ________ order to get photos, the paparazzi follow celebrities wherever they go. They do things **(2)** ________ waiting outside restaurants or taking photos through the window while a celebrity is **(3)** ________ their hair done.

**(4)** ________ some celebrities take advantage of the publicity to promote their latest film or song, many do not enjoy the attention they receive **(5)** ________ they are just trying to live their normal lives. Many people argue that the 'paps' cause problems by interfering too much in people's lives. **(6)** ________ to some celebrities, their private lives have been completely destroyed because of the paparazzi's actions.

# PREPARE FOR THE EXAM
## B1 PRELIMINARY FOR SCHOOLS

## READING

### Reading Part 1 Multiple-choice notices and messages (Unit 14, Unit 17)

#### EXAM INFORMATION

**Reading Part 1**

- You will read five short texts, such as notes, messages, signs, postcards, emails or labels.
- You need to read the text and then choose the answer which matches it.

#### EXAM TIPS

Read each text and think carefully about its meaning and purpose. What kind of text is it? Who has written the text? Who will read it?

**1** **Look at the example (0). What kind of text is this? Who are Jenny and Max?**

**0**

Jenny
I hope you haven't forgotten about our tennis match? I'll see you at the courts just before 3 pm, like we said. Don't forget your racket this time!
Max

**Why has Max sent this message?**

**A** to ask Jenny to bring sports equipment for him
**B** to make a new arrangement with Jenny
**(C)** to remind Jenny about their plans

**2** **Now read the exam instructions and complete the task.**

For each question, choose the correct answer.

**1**

SALE ENDS FRIDAY
All boots half price
10% off other goods (except designer bags)

**A** The shop is offering discounts for a limited period.
**B** Everything in the shop will be reduced in price until Friday.
**C** Customers buying designer bags this week will pay less.

**2**

PHOTO COMPETITION
Subject: families
Email your entries to the school secretary
There will be a prize for each year group!

**A** Only one student will be the winner.
**B** Email the secretary to find out how to enter.
**C** Take photos only on a single topic.

**3**

From: Anna To: Mark Reply Forward

As you've finished your geography homework, could I borrow your textbook overnight? Mine's disappeared! I can collect it now, if you're at home? I promise I'll return it tomorrow!

**A** Anna is asking Mark to return her textbook by tomorrow.
**B** Anna is suggesting that they do their homework together at Mark's place.
**C** Anna is checking to see if Mark will lend his textbook to her.

**4**

Hi Pippa!
I'm having a great time in the mountains. I've been snowboarding for the first time. I doubted it would be more exciting than skiing, like you said – but you were right!
See you soon! Kaz

**A** Kaz prefers skiing to snowboarding.
**B** Kaz didn't expect snowboarding to be so good.
**C** Kaz hasn't been able to try snowboarding yet.

**5**

Tom – the delivery man's coming at 11 to pick this parcel up. It's a dress I ordered online. I'm sending it back. You might have to sign something to say it's been collected.
Thanks,
Mum

**Tom's mum is asking him to**

**A** order something for her.
**B** collect something for her.
**C** give something to someone.

## Reading Part 2
## Matching people to short texts (Unit 8, Unit 19)

**1 Read the exam instructions and complete the task.**

The people below all want to find a music website they haven't seen before. Opposite are eight music website reviews. Decide which website would be the most suitable for each person.

1 George wants to watch band members from the past talking about their work and get albums that are difficult to find. He also wants to read reliable reviews by experts.
2 Ella likes writing about her favourite music and posting it online. She wants to find out about future live events and be able to download interviews with musicians which she can listen to later.
3 Bojing often invites friends round to listen to music and they try out music from bands they've heard about. He's also interested in the musicians his parents used to like and seeing pictures from concerts those bands gave.
4 Saanvi is into classical music and rock and prefers reading opinions written by people her age for advice on what to listen to. She listens to music at home rather than going to concerts.
5 Rob wants to be a radio DJ one day and he likes listening to top DJs talking about their work. He's into dance music and enjoys watching the latest dance music videos, too.

### EXAM INFORMATION
**Reading Part 2**

- You will read five short profiles followed by eight short texts.
- You need to read the profiles and then choose the text which matches it.

### EXAM TIPS
Read the profile and underline the **three** things that the person wants or needs. Then read the eight short texts and choose the one which includes **all** of the three points.

# MUSIC WEBSITES

### A THE MUSIC SCENE
This website provides advance information on various festivals and free concerts. There's also an opportunity to win a prize every month by uploading your own album reviews. You can also hear question and answer podcasts with the most famous performers of today, which you can save to your phone.

### B BEATS
This site is where you can find albums for free through its fantastic exchange service. You can also upload clips of the music you've got to offer – whether it's pop, rock, dance, metal or more traditional stuff. Buy tickets for upcoming concerts, too, via the 'What's on' page.

### C SOUND BUZZ
Although its reviews of live performances aren't always written by experienced journalists, this website has an amazing amount of unusual music to listen to, from electronic sounds to folk songs. It also provides downloadable advice from experts on how to produce demo tracks without access to a studio or a sound technician.

### D MUSIC LIVE
Watch live concerts on this brilliant new website. For a small fee, you can see a choice of performances as they're happening! You can leave a review, too, for others to read and decide whether they want to go and see the band in the future or not. See photos of the concerts, too.

### E HOT STUFF
Set up by a well-known radio presenter, this site offers brilliant suggestions for what to include in playlists for an event at home and has some free dance music downloads. There's also a gallery where you'll find photos from performances of your favourite bands from the past, but the site has no music videos, unfortunately.

### F COOL TUNES
If you like both modern and classical music, then this review site is the one for you. There are also loads of reviews on here, by teenagers rather than music journalists or DJs. This means you can find out what people like you really think is cool. Listen to clips for free!

### G MUSIC FREAKS
Some of the best music journalists write reviews for this website, which also has a good collection of video interviews with musicians who were performing twenty years ago. You won't find up-to-date news, or photos of today's celebrities – it's serious stuff! But there are links to online music stores, where you can buy rare CDs.

### H PLAY IT
This site is for anyone who's hoping to work in the music industry. Full of advice and stories from a range of experts in the industry, this is *the* place to come to find out about what's happening right now on the dance floor. Download the videos of the moment – and find out how to produce your own.

# PREPARE FOR THE EXAM
## B1 PRELIMINARY FOR SCHOOLS

**Reading Part 3 Multiple choice (Unit 3, Unit 9, Unit 13)**

**1** Read the text quickly for general meaning. Does the writer enjoy backpacking?

**EXAM INFORMATION**

**Reading Part 3**

- You will read a text followed by five multiple-choice questions.
- You need to read the text and then choose the correct answer to each question.

# TRAVELLING WITH A BACKPACK

BY ANDY ROBINSON

Why is it that the people you meet when backpacking seem to be more interesting and easygoing than your friends at home? That's my experience, anyway. Occasionally you may be unlucky and be put in a hostel room with someone you have nothing in common with. More often than not, though, you'll meet people that are fun to visit the local sights with and worth getting to know. I've spent time with people of many nationalities and have found out some fascinating things about their cultures. It's a great way to learn more about the world.

It's generally easy to make new friends while you're travelling, and you'll be able to hang around with them for a few days, until one of you leaves for the next exciting destination. Relationships of this kind are shorter but can be just as strong as friendships back home, because you do so much together in that short time. I often find I'm willing to admit things about myself that I'd never say to my close friends, safe in the knowledge that we probably won't meet again, except online.

One thing that's important when you're backpacking is to make sure you carry only essential items, so your backpack isn't too heavy. This took me a few attempts on different occasions, but I think I've finally got it right, and I travel 'light' these days. One good tip someone gave me is to take old clothes and just get rid of them when you move on, instead of washing and waiting for things to dry. Many hostels have shampoo and shower gel – you can get mini bottles in supermarkets, but I'd say don't bother. Choose a size of backpack that suits you, but do make sure it's waterproof.

I've discovered that many backpackers visit little places other tourists ignore, and by using local facilities, such as shops and guest houses, they provide those places with much-needed financial support. Most hostels or smaller accommodations allow you to stay for unlimited periods of time, which means you can take as long as you like exploring the local area. Backpackers are also kinder to the environment, because they use trains and buses rather than cars. So, what are you waiting for?!

**2** **Read the first paragraph of the text and then look at the multiple-choice question below. The highlighted parts in the text show you where the answer comes from. Choose the correct option. Why are the other options wrong?**

**1** What does Andy Robinson say about the people he meets backpacking?

**A** They generally come from one of a few particular countries.

**B** He finds it difficult to share accommodation with them.

**C** They often know more about the sights than he does.

**D** He learns interesting information by talking to them.

**3** **Now read the exam instruction and complete the rest of the task.**

For each question, choose the correct answer.

**2** According to Andy, friendships made with other backpackers

**A** are less serious than those with his friends at home.

**B** never last beyond the short time they spend together.

**C** allow him to talk about himself in an honest way.

**D** help him to decide where he would like to travel to in the future.

**3** What advice does Andy give about travelling with a backpack?

**A** Carry things you can throw away when you've finished with them.

**B** Make sure you practise packing it before you go away.

**C** It doesn't matter what kind of backpack you have.

**D** Buy small bottles to carry any liquids in.

**4** In the final paragraph, Andy suggests that

**A** backpacking can make it harder to access certain places.

**B** backpackers help to support less well-known locations.

**C** backpacking can be a disadvantage on some forms of transport.

**D** backpackers are not welcome in some types of accommodation.

**5** Which text message would Andy send to a friend?

**A** Why don't you fly out to visit me and we'll stay in a luxury hotel in one of the big resorts on the coast. I stay in them all the time.

**B** I'm glad I filled up my backpack – I've got everything I need, though it isn't easy carrying it around as I can hardly lift it!

**C** I've met some great people. Tomorrow we're going by boat to an ancient village in the mountains together.

**D** I'm leaving here tomorrow and then a few of us will hire a car and drive along the coast.

### EXAM TIPS

Read the questions and text. Underline the part of the text which gives you the answer. Then check that the other three options are definitely wrong.

### Reading Part 4 Gapped text (Unit 1, Unit 5)

**1** Read the text about Emily Hagins. What has she done since the age of 11?

**2** Read the first paragraph and options A–H. Which sentence fits in gap 1? How do you know this is the correct answer?

**3** Now read the exam instructions and complete the rest of the task.

Five sentences have been removed from the article below. For each question, choose the correct answer. There are three extra sentences which you do not need to use.

### EXAM INFORMATION

**Reading Part 4**

- You will read a text from which five sentences have been removed.
- The five sentences are placed after the text. They are not in the correct order. There are three extra sentences which are not needed.
- You need to read the text and then choose the sentence which best fits each gap.

### EXAM TIPS

Read the whole text first. Then read the options and decide which one fits best. Read the sentences directly before and after each gap carefully. When you have finished, read the whole text again and make sure it makes sense with the options you've chosen.

## EMILY HAGINS: YOUNG MOVIE-MAKER

American teenager Emily Hagins was born in the city of Philadelphia in the USA, but her family moved to the city of Austin in Texas when she was just a baby. **(1)** .................... She would often happily sit through the same movies several times at her local movie theater, including *The Muppet Movie*, which she particularly enjoyed.

When she was in second grade at school, around the age of seven, her classmates were already calling her 'Movie Girl'. A few year later, after reading *The Hobbit* by J. R. R. Tolkien for school, she became inspired by the *Lord of the Rings* movies. This was the point at which she decided she wanted to make movies herself. **(2)** .................... In his reply, he suggested a useful contact for Emily, who she later got in touch with.

Emily started her career at the age of just 11, by producing several short movies and a documentary. **(3)** .................... This was due to his job in advertising. However, although he guided her through what needed to be done, he made sure he left all the directing up to Emily.

This keen young movie-maker then went on to write the script for a full-length movie called *Pathogen*, and the filming of this took place in her home town when she was just 12. **(4)** .................... Somehow she managed to get everything done. Her efforts at directing the movie won Emily a grant from the Austin Film Society, which made it possible for her to turn the results into a finished 68-minute movie. She was the youngest ever person to receive the money.

Emily went on to produce another full-length movie, *The Retelling*, by the time she was 16. **(5)** .................... These include one called *Coin Heist*, a crime drama, which received good reviews. Emily Hagins is definitely a name to look out for in the future!

**A** Emily could only do this work at weekends and during vacations from school.
**B** He let Emily watch him while he worked and she learned about filming techniques.
**C** So, she wrote a letter to the series' director, Peter Jackson.
**D** She isn't really sure what kind of movie she'd like to produce next.
**E** After that experience as a child, Emily decided not to ask for advice again.
**F** Emily showed a strong interest in movies and movie-making at a very young age.
**G** Her father was helpful early on, having spent time with directors on movie sets.
**H** She has been making movies ever since.

## Reading Part 5 Multiple-choice cloze (Unit 4, Unit 10, Reviews 1–5)

**1** **Read the text about friendship quickly. According to the text, why do we need different kinds of friends?**

**2** **Now look at the first sentence and options A–D in question 1. Which is the correct answer? Why are the other options wrong?**

**3** **Now read the exam instructions and complete the rest of the task.**

For each question, choose the correct answer.

### THE VALUE OF friendship

Friends are some of the most important people in our lives. Many experts say that it is good to have different kinds of people within a **(1)** ________ group.

A reliable friend will always help you with a problem and **(2)** ________ your secrets. The sociable friend is the one you go out dancing with, and the smart one is who you ask to help you with your homework. Occasionally, it can be helpful to have someone to go to who is completely **(3)** ________ from your usual group of friends. This person can be honest about a difficult situation and help you to **(4)** ________ with it.

Even with only a small **(5)** ________ of close friends, we need to **(6)** ________ for sure that they will each be there to support us when we need them most.

| | A | B | C | D |
|---|---|---|---|---|
| **1** | **A** partners | **B** friendship | **C** mate | **D** relationship |
| **2** | **A** carry | **B** hold | **C** save | **D** keep |
| **3** | **A** single | **B** divided | **C** separate | **D** alone |
| **4** | **A** deal | **B** manage | **C** challenge | **D** act |
| **5** | **A** figure | **B** total | **C** number | **D** sum |
| **6** | **A** imagine | **B** hope | **C** think | **D** know |

### EXAM INFORMATION

**Reading Part 5**

- You will read a short text with six gaps and six multiple-choice vocabulary questions.
- You need to read the text and then choose the word which best fits each gap.

### EXAM TIPS

Read the whole text first for meaning. Then read the options and decide which one fits best. Read the sentence which contains each gap carefully. When you have finished, read the whole text again and make sure the word you've chosen makes sense.

# PREPARE FOR THE EXAM
## B1 PRELIMINARY FOR SCHOOLS

### Reading Part 6 Open cloze (Unit 15, Unit 18, Reviews 1–5)

**1** Read the text about the Northern Lights quickly. What are they?

**2** Look at question 1. Why is 'the' the correct answer?

**3** Now read the exam instructions and complete the task.

For each question, write the correct answer.
Write one word for each gap.

## THE Northern Lights

People who live north of the equator, might be lucky enough to see the Northern Lights. These natural 'lights', which appear in some northern areas of **(1)** *the* Earth, often appear as wide green or red lines across the sky. But how **(2)** ______ they created?

When tiny particles escape from the Sun and meet solar winds, a **(3)** ______ of these particles mix with gases which surround the Earth. This produces an interesting light show in the sky.

You are more likely to see the northern lights **(4)** ______ you live in a northern country like Iceland or Canada. However, during times of increased solar activity, **(5)** ______ is sometimes possible to see the lights in countries further south, though the colours may not be **(6)** ______ bright as they are in the north.

### EXAM INFORMATION
**Reading Part 6**

- You will read a short text with six words missing.
- You need to read the text and then decide what word best fits each gap.

### EXAM TIPS
Read the whole text first for meaning. Then look at each gap and read the sentence containing it very carefully. Think about what part of speech is needed (e.g. preposition, article, pronoun) and write the best word. When you have finished, read the whole text again and make sure the word you've chosen is correct.

# WRITING

## Writing Part 1 An email (Unit 7, Unit 15, Unit 19)

### EXAM INFORMATION

**Writing Part 1**

- You will read an email which you should reply to.
- The email has some notes which you should use to write your reply.
- You need to write about 100 words.

**1** **Read the email and the notes. Match the sentences below to each note in red.**

1. Indian food's my favourite but I like Italian and Chinese food, too.
2. We usually go to one called Resort, which does ice creams and milkshakes.
3. The café you went to sounds really good.
4. Why don't you have a barbecue? Everyone loves burgers!

**2** **Now read the instructions and complete the task.**

**Question 1**

You **must** answer this question. Write your answer in about **100** words.
Read this email from your English-speaking friend, Sam, and the notes you have made.

To:
From: Sam
Reply Forward

Hi,

We went to a really cool café in town the other day. We had some lovely fresh juice and sandwiches. — *Great!*

You said you sometimes go to cafés with your friends, too. Where do you go? — *Tell Sam*

I really like Indian food. What kind of food do you like best? — *Say what*

I'm having a party at the weekend. What kind of food should I make? — *Suggest ...*

See you soon!
Sam

Write your **email** to Sam, using **all** the **notes**.

### EXAM TIPS

Read the email carefully and think about how you could use the notes. Write your reply, making sure you use all of the notes. When you have finished, check your spelling, punctuation and grammar carefully.

## Writing Part 2 An article or a story (Unit 5, Unit 9, Unit 11, Unit 17)

### EXAM INFORMATION

**Writing Part 2**

- You should choose **one** task only: either an article **or** a story.
- There is some information to read which you must respond to.
- You need to write about 100 words.

**1** **Read the instructions for questions 2 and 3. What do you have to do?**

**2** **Now read the exam instructions and complete the task.**

Write an answer to **one** of the questions (**2** or **3**) in this part.
Write your answer in about **100 words.**

**Question 2**

You see this notice in an international English-language magazine.

ARTICLES WANTED!

**Being healthy**

Which do you think is more important: doing exercise or eating healthy food?
What do you do to stay healthy?
Tell us what you think!

**Write an article answering these questions and we will publish the best ones in our magazine.**

Write your **article** in about **100 words.**

**Question 3**

Your English teacher has asked you to write a story.
Your story must begin with this sentence:
*Jake ran towards the building as quickly as possible.*
Write your **story** in about **100 words.**

### EXAM TIPS

Read the information carefully. Then write **either** your article **or** your story, making sure you use the information given. When you have finished, check your spelling, punctuation and grammar carefully. Make sure the language you use is right for the context (e.g. formal or informal).

# PREPARE FOR THE EXAM
## B1 PRELIMINARY FOR SCHOOLS

## LISTENING

### Listening Part 1 Multiple-choice conversations with pictures (Unit 6, Unit 14)

82 **1 Look at the three pictures in question 1 below and read the question. What words do you expect to hear? Listen and check.**

83 **2 Now read the exam instructions and complete the rest of the task.**

For each question, choose the correct answer.

**1** How has the girl changed the appearance of her jeans?

**A**

**B**

**C**

**2** Which concert is the boy talking about?

**A**

**B**

**C**

**3** What happened to the girl during her hockey match?

**A**

**B**

**C**

**4** What does the boy decide to eat?

**A**

**B**

**C**

### EXAM INFORMATION
**Listening Part 1**

- You will hear seven recordings: monologues and conversations.
- There is one question for each recording and three pictures to choose from.
- You need to listen and choose the picture which answers the question.
- You will hear each recording twice.

### EXAM TIPS
Look at the pictures carefully as you listen. Choose the picture which answers the question. Check your answers when you listen to the recording the second time.

**5** Which animal are they looking at?

**A**

**B**

**C**

**6** What did the girl do yesterday?

**A**

**B**

**C**

**7** Where is the new sports shop located?

**A**

**B**

**C**

## Listing Part 2 Multiple-choice conversations (Unit 8, Unit 16)

**1** **Look at question 1 below. Who will you hear? What will he talk about? What do you need to listen for?**

84 **2** **What other words or phrases might you hear which mean the same as *stressed*, *confident* and *worried*? Listen and check.**

85 **3** **Now read the exam instructions and complete the task.**

For each question, choose the correct answer.

**1** You will hear a boy telling his friend about a cooking course.
How did he feel before he started the course?
**A** stressed about arriving on time
**B** confident in his cooking skills
**C** worried about meeting new people

**2** You will hear two friends talking about a trip to the mountains.
What did the girl enjoy most about it?
**A** relaxing at the end of each day
**B** learning a new activity
**C** winning a competition

**3** You will hear two friends talking about a film they're making.
What do they say about it?
**A** They may not finish it on time.
**B** They are pleased to have learned so much.
**C** They will be satisfied with the end result.

**4** You will hear a girl telling a friend about her father's job.
The girl thinks that the buildings her father usually designs
**A** are very expensive to produce.
**B** are not very attractive.
**C** are not very quick to create.

**5** You will hear two friends talking about writing blogs.
They agree that it is
**A** a good way to offer their opinions.
**B** harder to do than many people realise.
**C** enjoyable to receive comments on their blogs.

**6** You will hear a boy telling a friend about a journey he's going to make.
How does the boy feel about it?
**A** excited about flying for the first time
**B** curious about who he will meet on it
**C** surprised by how long the journey is

### EXAM INFORMATION

**Listening Part 2**

- You will hear six conversations.
- There is one question for each recording and three options to choose from.
- You need to listen and choose the option which answers the question.
- You will hear each recording twice.

### EXAM TIPS

Look at the options carefully as you listen. Choose the option which answers the question. Remember that you may not hear the same words that you read on the page.

# PREPARE FOR THE EXAM
## B1 PRELIMINARY FOR SCHOOLS

### Listening Part 3 Sentence completion (Unit 2, Unit 12)

#### EXAM INFORMATION
**Listening Part 3**

- You will hear a monologue which lasts for about three minutes.
- There are six sentences which you need to complete with information that you hear in the recording.
- You will hear the recording twice.

**1** **Read the notes below. What kind of information is missing in each gap?**

86 **2** **Listen to the recording for question 1. You will hear several times mentioned. Which one is correct? Why?**

87 **3** **Now read the exam instructions and complete the rest of the task.**

For each question, write the correct answer in the gap. Write **one** or **two words** or a **number** or a **date** or a **time**.
You will hear an announcement about an animal park.

#### EXAM TIPS
Read the sentences before the recording starts. Think about the kind of word or words which might be missing, but do not write anything. As you listen, complete the sentences. You may need to write one or two words, a number, a date or a time in each gap. Do **not** change the words you hear.

**Appleton Animal Park**

Summer opening times: from 9.30 a.m. to **(1)**........ p.m.

Most popular animal in the park: the **(2)**........

New activity for visitors: **(3)**........ certain animals

New animal arriving at the park soon: a **(4)**........

Name of the new café: The **(5)**........

Date of competition announcement: **(6)**........

### Listening Part 4 Multiple-choice interview (Unit 4, Unit 18)

#### EXAM INFORMATION
**Listening Part 4**

- You will hear an interview.
- There are six multiple-choice questions which you need to answer.
- You will hear the recording twice.

**1** **Read the questions below. Underline the key words in each one.**

88 **2** **Now read the exam instructions and complete the task.**

For each question, choose the correct answer.
You will hear an interview with a girl called Ruth Leyton, who plays tennis.

#### EXAM TIPS
Read the questions before the recording starts. Underline key words in the questions. This will help you to remember what you're listening for.

**1** Who suggested that Ruth should try playing tennis?
**A** one of her parents
**B** her brother
**C** a coach

**2** Before she was 11, Ruth
**A** attended training at the National Centre.
**B** did well in several tennis competitions.
**C** had tennis lessons with a friend.

**3** When she started serious tennis training, Ruth
**A** was sorry to have less free time.
**B** found the lessons very challenging.
**C** often felt too tired to do her homework.

**4** When she entered her first big competition, Ruth
**A** was disappointed not to win.
**B** watched what other players did.
**C** thought about giving tennis up.

**5** How did Ruth feel about missing an international competition?
**A** upset that she had an injury
**B** worried that she may not compete again
**C** sad that she wouldn't get to see a new country

**6** What would Ruth like to do in the future?
**A** appear on TV
**B** teach tennis to young people
**C** become the best player in the world

## SPEAKING

### Speaking Part 1 Short conversation with examiner (Unit 2, Unit 4, Unit 12)

**1** **Read the questions in Phase 1. Practise giving answers to the questions. Then ask and answer with a partner.**

**2** **Read the questions in Phase 2. Why do you think there are back-up questions?**

**3** **Now practise the whole of Part 1. Work in groups of three. One student is the examiner and the other two students are Candidate A and Candidate B. The examiner reads the script, while Candidate A and B answer the questions. Then change roles until everyone has had a turn at being the examiner.**

**Part 1 (2–3 minutes)**

*Phase 1*

**Examiner**

| | |
|---|---|
| *To both candidates* | Good morning/afternoon/evening. Can I have your mark sheets, please? I'm ............ . |
| *To Candidate A* | What's your name? How old are you? Thank you. |
| *To Candidate B* | And what's your name? How old are you? Thank you. |

| **Examiner** | **Back-up questions** |
|---|---|
| **B**, where do you live? | Do you live in [*name of town, city or region*]? |
| Who do you live with? | Do you live with your family? |
| Thank you. | |
| **A**, where do you live? | Do you live in [*name of town, city or region*]? |
| Who do you live with? | Do you live with your family? |
| Thank you. | |

*Phase 2*

| **Examiner** | **Back-up questions** |
|---|---|
| How often do you watch TV? | Do you often watch TV? |
| How do you get to school every day? | Do you take a bus to school every day? |
| Tell us about your favourite teacher. | Do you have a favourite teacher? (Who?) |
| What kind of food do you like? | Do you like English food? |
| How much time do you spend online? | Do you spend much time on the internet? |
| What hobbies do you have? | Do you have any hobbies? (What?) |
| Which do you like most: reading or listening to music? (Why?) | Do you prefer reading or listening to music? (Why?) |
| Which do you like best, Saturdays or Sundays? | Which is better, Saturday or Sunday? (Why?) |

### EXAM INFORMATION

**Speaking Part 1**

- The examiner will ask some general questions about you.
- You need to answer the questions.
- You do not need to talk to your partner.

### EXAM TIPS

You can prepare the answer to these questions in advance, so that you are ready to answer them. Don't be afraid to ask the examiner to repeat a question or say that you didn't understand it. The examiner will repeat the question for you, or ask it again in a different way so that you can understand it.

# PREPARE FOR THE EXAM
## B1 PRELIMINARY FOR SCHOOLS

### Speaking Part 2 (Unit 8, Unit 16) Describing a photo

**1** Look at the photos. What does each one show?

**2** Work in groups of three. One student is the examiner and the other two students are Candidate A and Candidate B. The examiner reads the script, while Candidate A and B answer the questions. Then change roles until everyone has had a turn at being the examiner, Candidate A and Candidate B.

Part 2 (2–3 minutes)

| | |
|---|---|
| 1A | **People eating together** |
| Examiner | Now I'd like each of you to talk on your own about something. I'm going to give each of you a photograph and I'd like you to talk about it.<br>**A**, here is your photograph. It shows people **eating together**.<br>**B**, you just listen.<br>**A**, please tell us what you can see in the photograph. |
| Candidate A | ........................................ |

**Back-up prompts**
- Talk about the people/person
- Talk about the place
- Talk about other things in the photograph

| | |
|---|---|
| Examiner | Thank you. |

| | |
|---|---|
| 1B | **People doing sport** |
| Examiner | **B**, here is your photograph. It shows people **doing sport**.<br>**A**, you just listen.<br>**B**, please tell us what you can see in the photograph. |
| Candidate B | ........................................ |

**Back-up prompts**
- Talk about the people/person
- Talk about the place
- Talk about other things in the photograph

| | |
|---|---|
| Examiner | Thank you. |

### EXAM INFORMATION
**Speaking Part 2**
- The examiner will give you a photo to talk about.
- You need to look at the photo carefully and describe what you can see.
- Your partner will be given a different photo to talk about. You do not need to talk to your partner.

### EXAM TIPS
Make sure you say as much about the photo as you can: What are the people doing? Where are they? What's the weather like? What objects can you see? If you can't remember the word for something, try to describe it in a different way. Keep talking until the examiner asks you to stop, but do **not** talk about anything which is not in the picture.

## Speaking Part 3 Discussing options (Unit 6, Unit 14, Unit 20)

**1** Look at the pictures. What can you see in each one?

**2** Work in groups of three. One student is the examiner and the other two students are Candidate A and Candidate B. The examiner reads the script, while Candidate A and B answer the questions. Then change roles until everyone has had a turn at being the examiner, Candidate A and Candidate B.

**Part 3**

| | |
|---|---|
| **Examiner** | Now, in this part of the test, you're going to talk about something together for about two minutes. I'm going to describe a situation to you.<br>**A teenager is writing to a new penfriend and is deciding what to write to him/her about.**<br>**Here are some topics the teenager could write about.**<br>**Talk together about the different topics the teenager could write about in the first email, and then decide which would be most interesting for the penfriend to read about.**<br>All right? Now, talk together. |
| **Candidates** | ........................................ |
| **Examiner** | Thank you. |

**Topics to write about**

### EXAM INFORMATION

**Speaking Part 3**

- The examiner will describe a situation to talk about with your partner.
- You will be given some pictures to look at and asked to discuss them together.
- You need to try to reach an agreement with your partner.

### EXAM TIPS

Listen carefully to the situation and look at the pictures. Discuss the pictures and situation with your partner. Make sure you give your partner time to speak and encourage him/her to speak if he/she is quiet.

# PREPARE FOR THE EXAM
## B1 PRELIMINARY FOR SCHOOLS

### Speaking Part 4 Discussing a topic (Unit 10, Unit 18, Unit 20)

**1** **Read the Part 4 questions. What is the general theme of the questions?**

**2** **Work in groups of three. One student is the examiner and the other two students are Candidate A and Candidate B. The examiner reads the script, while Candidate A and B answer the questions. Then change roles until everyone has had a turn at being the examiner, Candidate A and Candidate B.**

**Part 4**

**Examiner**
- Have you got a penfriend in another country? (What do you write to him/her about?)
- Do you like writing and receiving emails or letters? (Why?)
- How do you usually communicate with your friends? (Why?)
- Which do you prefer: making phone calls or texting? (Why?)
- What kind of information do you share with other people through phone calls or emails?

**Back-up prompts**
- How/What about you?
- Do you agree?
- What do you think?

Thank you. That is the end of the test.

### EXAM INFORMATION
**Speaking Part 4**
- The examiner will ask questions related to the topic of Part 3.
- The examiner will ask questions either to individual candidates or to both candidates.
- You need to answer the questions as fully as possible.

### EXAM TIPS
Listen carefully to the questions and say as much as you can. You may need to explain your answers. If a question is directed at you and your partner, make sure you give your partner a chance to speak. Don't be afraid to ask the examiner to repeat a question.

# EXTRA ACTIVITIES

## UNIT 1 VOCABULARY, PAGE 12

**4 Ask and answer with your partner. Give full answers.**

1 Have you bought anything interesting recently?
2 Have you visited anyone in your family recently?
3 Have you seen anything funny online recently?
4 Did you visit anywhere interesting during the school holidays?
5 Have you got anything in your bedroom that you don't use any longer?
6 Is there anyone famous you would like to meet?

## UNIT 4 GRAMMAR, PAGE 26

**6 Ask questions about your partner when he or she was 10 years old. Use phrases from the box.**

*When you were ten years old did you use to go to shopping centres alone?*

| | |
|---|---|
| belong to a sports team | text friends |
| do your homework on time | stay in every night |
| go to shopping centres alone | watch a lot of TV |
| play loads of computer games | wear make-up |
| chat with online friends | your own ideas |

## UNIT 8 VOCABULARY, PAGE 48

**4 Complete the sentences with adverbs from Exercise 3.**

1 Last year we spent our summer holiday in a ............ big house.
2 The 10-hour drive was long and we were ............ exhausted when we got there.
3 The view from the upstairs window was ............ spectacular.
4 The owner said the stone house was ............ freezing in winter.
5 Everything about the house was ............ good.
6 We visited a palace, which was ............ enormous.
7 It had a smaller building nearby, which was ............ ancient.
8 Unfortunately, the photos I took were ............ bad.

## UNIT 9 VOCABULARY, PAGE 56

**4 Read the sentences. Which are true for you? Compare your answers with your partner.**

1 I have enough money to be able to buy a new computer.
2 I spend too much time on social media.
3 I don't have enough time to do my homework every evening.
4 My favourite news website is [what?] because it's full of very interesting articles.
5 I think driverless cars are safe enough to be on the roads now.

## UNIT 10 VOCABULARY, PAGE 61

**3 Write two sentences for each phrase in the box, one true and one false. Use the topics below to help you.**

at first at its best at least at once at present at risk

animals friends and families house and homes shopping weather your own ideas

**Read your sentences to your partner. Can they guess which is true and which is false?**

# EXTRA ACTIVITIES

## UNIT 8 SPEAKING, PAGE 49

1

## UNIT 8 SPEAKING, PAGE 49

### PREPARE FOR THE EXAM

**Speaking Part 2**

**6** **Describe the picture to your partner. Use interesting adjectives, and use phrases from the *Prepare to speak* box if you don't know the right words.**

» PREPARE FOR THE EXAM PAGE 132

## UNIT 11 VOCABULARY, PAGE 66

**4** **Choose one of the compound nouns. Talk about it for 30 seconds but don't say what it is. Can the other students guess what you are talking about?**

## UNIT 12 VOCABULARY, PAGE 70

**3** **Tell your partner about a time when you:**

1 were **on board** a plane or ship.
2 behaved badly **on purpose**.
3 saw an unusual item **on sale**.
4 didn't arrive somewhere **on time**.
5 went somewhere **on foot**.
6 bought something that was **on display**.
7 wanted to be **on your own**.

## UNIT 13 VOCABULARY, PAGE 78

**3** **Discuss the questions with your partner.**

1 What do you like doing **in detail**?
2 Do you know someone who does things **in advance**?
3 How much time do you spend on social media **in general**?
4 Talk about a recent post that you liked **in particular**.
5 When was the last time someone told you to do something differently **in future**?
6 Talk about a time when you didn't want to do something but **in the end** it was OK.
7 Talk about a story you read online but which **in fact** was not true.

## UNIT 14 VOCABULARY, PAGE 82

**4** **Choose a column, 1–4.**

**You have one minute. Write as many sentences as you can for each verb. You get extra points if you can write a transitive and an intransitive example for the same verb. Good luck!**

| 1 | 2 | 3 | 4 |
|---|---|---|---|
| barbecue<br>roast<br>bite | fry<br>burn<br>stir | boil<br>taste<br>freeze | steam<br>grill<br>bake |

## UNIT 14 SPEAKING, PAGE 83

### PREPARE FOR THE EXAM

#### Speaking Part 3

**4** **Work in pairs. Read the instructions and look at the pictures below. Then talk together. Use the phrases from the *Prepare to speak* box on page 83.**

Two friends are planning to attend a one-day cooking course. Here are some different things they could learn to cook. Talk together about the different things they could cook and say which would be most useful to learn.

Things to cook

## UNIT 15 VOCABULARY, PAGE 86

### Add up your scores.

| | | | | |
|---|---|---|---|---|
| **1** | **a** 1 | **b** 4 | **c** 2 | **d** 3 |
| **2** | **a** 2 | **b** 1 | **c** 1 | **d** 4 |
| **3** | **a** 1 | **b** 2 | **c** 3 | **d** 4 |
| **4** | **a** 1 | **b** 4 | **c** 2 | **d** 3 |

### What your score says about you

**Low score (4–7)**
You love nature and being outdoors. You especially love animals and know when they are unhappy. You like walking home and being in open spaces. You're an awesome country teen!

**Medium score (8–12)**
You are a bit of both. You like the excitement of the city but not the pollution and crime. As for the country, well, that's just a bit too quiet for you. You like your facilities, and you're interested in history, too. So you are a town teen! All the good things of the city without the bad things! Rock it down, town teen!

**High score (13–16)**
You love the street lights, the sounds, and the smell of the city! It's just so exciting! You like surprises in the city but not in the countryside. All those animals? Not you at all! You are a city teen – go city you!

# EXTRA ACTIVITIES

## UNIT 15 VOCABULARY, PAGE 88

**3** **Tell your partner about:**

1. a time when you **showed** someone **around** your school.
2. someone you want to **catch up with** soon.
3. things you enjoy doing when you **stay in**.
4. when you are planning to **move out** of home.
5. a time when you **ended up** studying after midnight
6. how you welcome people when they **move in** to your area

## UNIT 16 VOCABULARY, PAGE 92

**4** **Read out the following sentences to your partner. Check your stress and intonation. Your partner has to guess the reporting verb that would be best for each situation.**

Student A

- I've got something to say. It's really important and it's really good! I got the top mark in the class. (*announce*)
- You must give me that phone. It's mine. It isn't yours. Give it back. (*demand*)
- I think you have to go straight on, then turn left. Then you get to a roundabout and the shop is on the right. You can't miss it! (*explain*)
- I know you want me to stay at home but I want to go. Everyone else is going and nothing will change my mind. Nothing you can say. I've decided. (*insist*)
- Well, there are a few things you could do. But I think it would be good to take some flowers. Why don't you get some from the flower shop on the way? (*suggest*)

## UNIT 16 SPEAKING, PAGE 93

### PREPARE FOR THE EXAM

**Speaking Part 2**

**4** **Student A:** **Look at photograph A and describe what you can see in it. Talk for about one minute.**

**Student B:** **Look at photograph B and describe what you can see in it. Talk for about one minute.**

## UNIT 17 VOCABULARY, PAGE 98

**1** Tick all the things you have done online in the last 24 hours.

- ☐ visited a social networking site
- ☐ posted your status online
- ☐ tweeted something
- ☐ used a video chat
- ☐ chatted with an online gamer
- ☐ phoned a friend
- ☐ commented on a blog

**2** It was your birthday and your mum reminds you to thank an elderly relative for a present. How do you do it?

A send them a text full of emojis
B send them an email beginning 'Dear …'
C send them a picture of yourself holding the present on Snapchat
D pick up the phone and give them a call

**3** When you update your social media status, do you use

A just a photo?
B just words?
C a photo and words?

**4** How do you usually communicate with friends? And parents?

A through a social networking site
B via email
C face-to-face
D on the phone
E by texting or instant messaging

**5** You disagree with your parents. Do you

A post your social media status as an angry face?
B phone your best friend?
C send your friends a group message?
D text a friend and ask him/her to call you?

## UNIT 17 GRAMMAR, PAGE 100

**5** Work in groups of three. Follow the instructions.

**Student A:** Choose three questions to ask Student B.
**Student B:** Answer Student A's questions.
**Student C:** Report Student A's questions and Student B's answers.

Are you fairly reliable as a person?
How much time do you spend online each day?
Have you ever chatted with someone in another country online?
Are your grandparents on social networks?
How many friends or followers do you have on social networks?
What is the most recent photo you have taken on your phone?
What is the most interesting fact you have found out online?
Which music website can you recommend?
What is your biggest fault?
What is the strangest thing you've ever done?
Do you prefer oranges or lemons?
Which films have made you laugh?
Which films have made you cry?
Do you keep your bedroom reasonably tidy?

Then change roles and repeat the activity.

# EXTRA ACTIVITIES

## UNIT 19 VOCABULARY, PAGE 110

**4** **Complete the sentences for yourself and then compare your answers with your partner.**

1. The last time I went to a fancy dress party/event, I dressed up **as** a …
2. I'd like to work **as** a … because …
3. For my next birthday, I want things **like** … because …
4. At the weekends, I usually wear things **like** …
5. In my family, I most look like …

## UNIT 20 SPEAKING, PAGE 115

### PREPARE FOR THE EXAM

#### Speaking Part 3

**4** **Look at the pictures of activities on a summer activity course. Which activities would you like to do on holiday? Why?**

A girl is going to do a **summer activity course** during her holidays. Here are the different things that she could do. Talk to each other about the **benefits** of these different activities and then decide which would be best.

**Discuss your ideas with your partner. Talk about all the ideas and agree on which is best. Use phrases from the *Prepare to speak* box on page 115.**

## UNIT 20 VOCABULARY, PAGE 114

**4** **Discuss the questions with your partner.**

1. What activities do you **join in** with at school?
2. Do you think success **depends on** ability, hard work, or both?
3. Do you have a talent? Who **believes in** you and will help you to succeed?
4. What have you **missed out on** recently? Why?
5. When was the last time you **kept on** reading a difficult book? What was the book?
6. If there was a really good university course abroad, would you **go for** it and apply, or not?
7. What (or who) do your summer holiday ideas and plans **depend on**?
8. If you see a word in English that you don't understand, how do you **work out** the meaning?
9. Have you ever **got into** a school team? What team was it?

## UNIT 16 VOCABULARY, PAGE 92

**4** **Read out the following sentences to your partner. Check your stress and intonation. Your partner has to guess the reporting verb that would be best for each situation.**

**Student B**

- Give me my pen back! It's mine – you can't use it. (*demand*)
- Mum, Dad – guess what? I got a place at university! I've got into medical school! (*announce*)
- Please, Grandma. Sit down. I can make the tea. No, I don't need any help. You just sit there. (*insist*)
- So we have to write about a book we've read. You can't write about the film, just the book. The teacher wants it in by Monday. (*explain*)
- Why don't we write about our last holiday? We all went to the same place but we had different experiences. It's exactly what we have to do! (*suggest*)

# VOCABULARY LIST

## UNIT 1

### SHOPPING

**charge** /tʃɑːdʒ/ *v* to ask an amount of money for something, especially a service or activity
**charges** /'tʃɑːdʒɪz/ *n* the amount of money that you have to pay for something, especially for a service
**discount** /'dɪskaʊnt/ *n* a reduction in price
**exchange** /ɪks'tʃeɪndʒ/ *v* to take something back to a shop and change it for something else
**online shopping** /'ɒn,laɪn 'ʃɒpɪŋ/ *n* the activity of buying things on the internet
**promotions** /prə'məʊʃənz/ *n* activities to advertise something
**purchases** /'pɜːtʃəsɪz/ *n* the act of buying something
**receipt** /rɪ'siːt/ *n* a piece of paper that proves that you have received goods or money
**refunds** /'riːfʌndz/ *n* an amount of money that is given back to you, especially because you are not happy with something you have bought
**send sth back** /send 'bæk/ *pv* to return something to the person who sent it to you, especially because it is damaged or not suitable
**serve** /sɜːv/ *v* to help customers and sell things to them in a shop
**service** /'sɜːvɪs/ *n* the work that people who work in shops, restaurants, hotels, etc. do to help customers
**shop** /ʃɒp/ *v* to buy things in shops
**spend** /spend/ *v* to use money to buy or pay for something

### *ANY*

## UNIT 2

### PERSONALITY ADJECTIVES

**annoying** /ə'nɔɪɪŋ/ *adj* making you feel annoyed
**anxious** /'æŋkʃəs/ *adj* worried and nervous
**easygoing** /'iziˈgəʊɪŋ/ *adj* relaxed and not easily upset or worried
**jealous** /'dʒeləs/ *adj* unhappy and angry because you want something that someone else has
**loyal** /lɔɪəl/ *adj* always liking and supporting someone or something, sometimes when other people do not
**reliable** /rɪ'laɪəbl/ *adj* able to be trusted or believed
**sensible** /'sensɪbl/ *adj* showing good judgment
**silly** /'sɪli/ *adj* not taking things seriously
**sociable** /'səʊʃəbl/ *adj* Someone who is sociable enjoys being with people and meeting new people.
**thoughtful** /'θɔːtfəl/ *adj* kind and always thinking about how you can help other people
**talented** /'tæləntɪd/ *adj* having a natural ability to do something well

### PREFIXES: *UN-* AND *DIS-*

**disagree** /dɪsə'griː/ *v* to have a different opinion from someone else
**disappear** /ˌdɪsə'pɪə/ *v* to become impossible to see or find
**dislike** /dɪ'slaɪk/ *v* to not like someone or something
**unhappy** /ʌn'hæpi/ *adj* sad
**uninteresting** /ʌn'ɪntərestɪŋ/ *adj* not interesting
**unkind** /ʌn'kaɪnd/ *adj* slightly cruel
**unlucky** /ʌn'lʌki/ *adj* having bad things happen to you
**unpleasant** /ʌn'plezənt/ *adj* not enjoyable or pleasant
**unreliable** /ˌʌnrɪ'laɪəbl/ *adj* If someone or something is unreliable, you cannot trust or depend on them or it.

## UNIT 3

### SPORTS PHRASES

**beat the other team** /biːt ði 'ʌðə tiːm/ *phr* to defeat or do better than someone in a competition
**enter a competition or tournament** /'entə ə ˌkɒmpə'tɪʃən ɔː 'tʊənəmənt/ *phr* to take part in a competition or tournament
**give (someone) the chance** /gɪv 'sʌmwʌn ðə tʃɑːns/ *phr* to provide someone with an opportunity to do something
**have a go at something** /hæv ə gəʊ ət 'sʌmθɪŋ/ *phr* to try something you have not done before
**join a club** /dʒɔɪn ə klʌb/ *phr* to become a member of a club
**lose a game or match** /luːz ə geɪm ɔː mætʃ/ *phr* If you lose a game or competition, the team or person that you are competing with wins.
**miss an opportunity to do something** /mɪs ən ˌɒpə'tjuːnəti tə duː 'sʌmθɪŋ/ *phr* to not use an opportunity to do something
**score a goal or point** /skɔː ə gəʊl ɔː pɔɪnt/ *phr* to get points in a game or test
**win a prize, medal, game or match** /wɪn ə praɪz 'medəl geɪm ɔː mætʃ/ *phr* to get the most points, or to get a prize, in a competition or game

### SUFFIXES: *-IST*, *-ER*, *-OR*

**canoeist** /kə'nuːɪst/ *n* a person travelling in a canoe
**climber** /'klaɪmə/ *n* someone who climbs mountains, hills or rocks as a sport
**competitor** /kəm'petɪtə/ *n* someone who is trying to win a competition
**footballer** /'fʊtbɔːlə/ *n* someone who plays football, especially as their job
**runner** /'rʌnə/ *n* someone who runs
**sailor** /'seɪlə/ *n* someone who sails ships or boats as their job or as a sport
**spectator** /spek'teɪtə/ *n* someone who watches an event, sport, etc.
**surfer** /'sɜːfə/ *n* someone who surfs
**swimmer** /'swɪmə/ *n* someone who swims
**winner** /'wɪnə/ *n* someone who wins a game, competition or election

# VOCABULARY LIST

## UNIT 4

### EXTREME WEATHER

**blow** /bləʊ/ *v* If the wind blows, it moves and make currents of air.

**earthquake** /ˈɜːθkweɪk/ *n* a sudden movement of the Earth's surface, often causing severe damage

**fall down** /fɔːl daʊn/ *v* to fall onto the ground

**flood** /flʌd/ *n* a situation in which a lot of water covers an area that is usually dry, especially when a river becomes too full

**flow** /fləʊ/ *v* If something such as a liquid flows, it moves somewhere in a smooth, continuous way.

**lightning** /ˈlaɪtnɪŋ/ *n* a sudden flash of light in the sky during a storm

**pour** /pɔː/ *v* to rain a lot

**rise** /raɪz/ *v* to increase in level

**shake** /ʃeɪk/ *v* to make quick, short movements from side to side or up and down

**snowstorm** /ˈsnəʊstɔːm/ *n* a storm when a lot of snow falls

**tornado** /tɔːˈneɪdəʊ/ *n* an extremely strong and dangerous wind that blows in a circle and destroys buildings as it moves along

### PHRASAL VERBS

**blow away** /bləʊ əˈweɪ/ *pv* to be moved or make something move on a current of air

**burn down** /bɜːn daʊn/ *pv* to destroy something, especially a building, by fire, or to be destroyed by fire

**clear up** /klɪə ʌp/ *pv* If the weather clears up, the cloud and rain disappear.

**come out** /kʌm aʊt/ *pv* If the sun, the moon, or a star comes out, it appears in the sky.

**fall down** /fɔːl daʊn/ *pv* to fall to the ground

**put out** /pʊt aʊt/ *pv* to stop something burning

## UNIT 5

### VERBS FOR MAKING THINGS

**create** /kriˈeɪt/ *v* to make something happen or exist

**customise** /ˈkʌstəmaɪz/ *v* to change something to make it suitable for a particular person or purpose

**decorate** /ˈdekəreɪt/ *v* to make something look more attractive by putting things on it or around it

**design** /dɪˈzaɪn/ *v* to draw or plan something before making it

**fix** /fɪks/ *v* to repair something

**mend** /mend/ *v* to repair something that is broken, torn, or not working correctly

**rebuild** /ˌriːˈbɪld/ *v* to build something again after it has been damaged

**recycle** /ˌriːˈsaɪkl/ *v* to put used paper, glass, plastic, etc. through a process so that it can be used again

**sew** /səʊ/ *v* to join things together with a needle and thread

### TIME ADVERBS

## UNIT 6

### HEALTH VERBS

**ache** /eɪk/ *v* If a part of your body aches, it is painful.

**beat** /ˈbiːt/ *v* When your heart beats, it makes regular movements and sounds.

**bleed** /bliːd/ *v* to have blood coming from a place in your body

**blink** /blɪŋk/ *v* to open and close your eyes quickly

**blow your nose** /bləʊ jə ˈnəʊz/ *pv* to clear your nose by forcing air through it

**breathe** /briːð/ *v* to take air into and out of your lungs

**burn** /bɜːn/ *v* to be hurt by fire or heat

**cough** /kɒf/ *v* to make air come out of your throat with a short sound

**cut** /kʌt/ *v* to injure yourself on a sharp object that makes you bleed

**injure** /ˈɪndʒə/ *v* to hurt a part of your body

**recover** /rɪˈkʌvə/ *v* to become healthy or happy again after an illness, injury, or period of sadness

**yawn** /jɔːn/ *v* to take a deep breath with your mouth wide open, because you are tired or bored

### WORDS WITH *SOME*, *ANY*, *EVERY* AND *NO*

## UNIT 7

### MUSIC

**celebrity** /səˈlebrəti/ *n* a famous person

**clip** /klɪp/ *n* a short part of a film or television programme

**concert hall** /ˈkɒnsət ˌhɔːl/ *n* a large building in which concerts are performed

**DJ** /ˈdiːˌdʒeɪ/ *n* someone who plays music on the radio or at discos

**festival** /ˈfestɪvəl/ *n* a series of events, performances, etc. that often takes place over several days

**gig** /gɪg/ *n* a performance of pop or rock music

**guitarist** /gɪˈtɑːrɪst/ *n* someone who plays the guitar, especially as their job

**live** /laɪv/ *adj* A live performance is done with an audience.

**lyrics** /ˈlɪrɪks/ *n* the words of a song

**music channel** /ˈmjuːzɪk ˈtʃænəl/ *n* a television channel that shows music videos and programmes about music

**musician** /mjuːˈzɪʃən/ *n* someone who plays a musical instrument, often as a job

**music video** /ˈmjuːzɪk ˈvɪdiəʊ/ *n* a short film made to go with a popular song

**production** /prəˈdʌkʃən/ *n* the job of controlling how a film, play, programme, or musical recording is made

**sound technician** /saʊnd tekˈnɪʃən/ *n* someone who works with the equipment in a recording studio

**studio** /ˈstjuːdiəʊ/ *n* a room where television/radio programmes or musical recordings are made

### WORD FAMILIES

**achieve** /ə'tʃiːv/ *v* to succeed in doing something good, usually by working hard
**achievement** /ə'tʃiːvmənt/ *n* something good that you have done that was difficult
**advertise** /'ædvətaɪz/ *v* to tell people about a product or service, for example in newspapers or on television, in order to persuade them to buy it
**advertisement** /əd'vɜːtɪsmənt/ *n* a picture, short film, song, etc. that tries to persuade people to buy a product or service
**entertain** /ˌentə'teɪn/ *v* to keep someone interested and help them to have an enjoyable time
**entertainer** /ˌentə'teɪnə/ *n* someone whose job is to entertain people by singing, telling jokes, etc.
**entertaining** /ˌentə'teɪnɪŋ/ *adj* interesting and helping someone to have an enjoyable time
**entertainment** /ˌentə'teɪnmənt/ *n* shows, films, television, or other performances or activities that entertain people
**music** /'mjuːzɪk/ *n* a pattern of sounds that is made by playing instruments or singing, or a recording of this
**musical** /'mjuːzɪkəl/ *adj* relating to music
**musician** /mjuː'zɪʃən/ *n* someone who plays a musical instrument, often as a job
**perform** /pə'fɔːm/ *v* to entertain people by acting, singing, dancing, etc.
**performance** /pə'fɔːməns/ *n* acting, singing, dancing, or playing music to entertain people
**performer** /pə'fɔːmə/ *n* someone who entertains people
**record** /'rekɔːd/ *n* a flat, round, plastic disc that music is stored on, used especially in the past
**record** /rɪ'kɔːd/ *v* to store sounds or pictures using electronic equipment, a camera, etc. so that you can listen to them or see them again

## UNIT 8

### AMAZING ARCHITECTURE

**brand new** /brænd njuː/ *adj* completely new
**classic** /'klæsɪk/ *adj* typical
**cosy** /'kəʊzi/ *adj* comfortable and warm
**fresh** /freʃ/ *adj* new or different from what was there before
**historic** /hɪ'stɒrɪk/ *adj* important in history or likely to be important in history
**modern** /'mɒdən/ *adj* relating to the present time and not to the past
**original** /ə'rɪdʒənəl/ *adj* special and interesting because of not being the same as others
**spectacular** /spek'tækjələ/ *adj* extremely good, exciting, or surprising
**traditional** /trə'dɪʃənəl/ *adj* following the customs or ways of behaving that have continued in a group of people or society for a long time
**unusual** /ʌn'juːʒuəl/ *adj* different and not ordinary, often in a way that is interesting or exciting

### STRONG ADJECTIVES AND ADVERBS

**absolutely** /ˌæbsə'luːtli/ *adv* used with strong adjectives to mean 'very'
**ancient** /'eɪnʃənt/ *adj* from a long time ago
**brand new** /brænd njuː/ *adj* completely new
**enormous** /ɪ'nɔːməs/ *adj* extremely large
**exhausted** /ɪg'zɔːstɪd/ *adj* very tired
**extremely** /ɪk'striːmli/ *adv* very
**freezing** /'friːzɪŋ/ *adj* very cold
**incredibly** /ɪn'kredɪbli/ *adv* very
**spectacular** /spek'tækjələ/ *adj* extremely good, exciting, or surprising
**terrible** /'terəbl/ *adj* very bad, of low quality, or unpleasant

## UNIT 9

### TECHNOLOGY

**charge** /tʃɑːdʒ/ *v* to put electricity into something's battery
**connection** /kə'nekʃən/ *n* something that joins things together
**display** /dɪ'spleɪ/ *n* electronic information that is shown on a computer screen
**experiments** /ɪk'sperɪmənts/ *n* tests, especially scientific ones, that you do in order to learn something or discover if something is true
**fuel** /'fjuːəl/ *n* a substance that is burned to provide heat or power
**invention** /ɪn'venʃən/ *n* something that has been designed or created for the first time
**plug in** /plʌg 'ɪn/ *pv* to connect a piece of electrical equipment to an electricity supply
**power** /paʊə/ *n* energy, usually electricity, that is used to provide light, heat, etc.
**pump** /pʌmp/ *n* a piece of equipment that forces liquid or gas to move somewhere
**satellite** /'sætəlaɪt/ *n* a piece of equipment that is sent into space around the Earth to receive and send signals or to collect information

### *ENOUGH, TOO, VERY, NOT ... ENOUGH*

## UNIT 10

### NATURE AND WILDLIFE

**creature** /'kriːtʃə/ *n* anything that lives but is not a plant
**crop** /krɒp/ *n* a plant such as grains, fruits or vegetables that is grown in large amounts by farmers
**endangered** /ɪn'deɪndʒəd/ *adj* animals that may soon not exist because there are very few alive
**environment** /ɪn'vaɪrənmənt/ *n* the air, land and water where people, animals and plants live
**habitat** /'hæbɪtæt/ *n* the natural environment of an animal or plant
**human** /'hjuːmən/ *n* a man, woman or child
**hunting** /'hʌntɪŋ/ *n* chasing and killing animals for sport or food

# VOCABULARY LIST

**jungle** /'dʒʌŋgl/ *n* an area of land, usually in tropical countries, where trees and plants grow close together
**landscape** /'lændskeɪp/ *n* the appearance of an area of land, especially in the countryside
**population** /ˌpɒpjə'leɪʃən/ *n* all the people or animals living in a particular area
**rainforest** /'reɪnˌfɒrɪst/ *n* a forest with a lot of tall trees where it rains a lot

### PHRASES WITH *AT*

**at first** /ət 'fɜːst/ *phr* at the beginning of a situation or period of time
**at its best** /ət ɪts best/ *phr* at the highest level of achievement or quality
**at least** /ət liːst/ *phr* as much as, or more than, a number or amount
**at long last** /ət lɒŋ lɑːst/ *phr* finally
**at once** /ət wʌns/ *phr* at the same time
**at present** /ət 'prezənt/ *phr* now
**at risk** /ət rɪsk/ *phr* being in a situation where something bad is likely to happen

## UNIT 11

### SCHOOL

**attend** /ə'tend/ *v* to go regularly to a particular school
**boarding school** /bɔːdɪŋ skuːl/ *n* a school where students live and study
**break up** /breɪk 'ʌp/ *v* When schools or colleges break up, the classes end and the holidays begin.
**degree** /dɪ'griː/ *n* a qualification given for completing a university course
**do well** /duː wel/ *phr* to be successful
**do badly** /duː 'bædli/ *phr* to be unsuccessful
**education** /ˌedʒʊ'keɪʃən/ *n* the process of teaching and learning in a school or college, or the knowledge that you get from this
**primary** /'praɪməri/ *adj* of or for the teaching of young children, especially those between five and eleven
**qualifications** /ˌkwɒlɪfɪ'keɪʃənz/ *n* the skills, qualities, or experience that you need in order to do something
**secondary** /'sekəndri/ *adj* relating to the education of children approximately between the ages of 11 and 18
**undergraduate** /ˌʌndə'grædʒuət/ *n* a student who is studying for their first university degree
**Year** /jɪə/ *n* the year of education that a child is in

### COMPOUND NOUNS

**classroom** /'klɑːsruːm/ *n* a room in a school where students have lessons
**blackboard** /'blækbɔːd/ *n* a large board with a dark surface that teachers write on
**break time** /breɪk taɪm/ *n* a short period of rest
**bus stop** /'bʌs ˌstɒp/ *n* a place where a bus stops to allow passengers to get on and off
**head teacher** /hed 'tiːtʃə/ *n* the person in charge of a school
**homework** /'həʊmwɜːk/ *n* work that teachers give students to do at home
**lunchtime** /'lʌnʃtaɪm/ *n* the time when lunch is eaten
**school bus** /'skuːl ˌbʌs/ *n* a bus for taking children to and from school
**textbook** /'tekstbʊk/ *n* a book about a particular subject, written for students
**timetable** /'taɪmˌteɪbl/ *n* a list of dates and times that shows when things will happen
**whiteboard** /'waɪtbɔːd/ *n* a large white board that teachers write on

## UNIT 12

### TRAVEL

**abroad** /ə'brɔːd/ *adv* in or to a foreign country
**be held up** /bɪ held 'ʌp/ *phr* be late or delayed
**check in** /tʃek 'ɪn/ *pv* show your ticket at an airport to say that you have arrived for your flight
**go away** /gəʊ ə'weɪ/ *pv* to leave your home in order to spend time in a different place, usually for a holiday
**land** /lænd/ *v* If you land, your flight arrives at its destination.
**reach** /riːtʃ/ *v* to arrive somewhere
**sail** /seɪl/ *v* to travel in a boat or a ship
**set off** /set ɒf/ *pv* to start a journey
**tour** /tʊə/ *n* a visit to and around a place
**unpack** /ʌn'pæk/ *v* to take things out of a bag, box, etc.

### PHRASES WITH *ON*

**on board** /ɒn bɔːd/ *phr* on a boat, train, aircraft, etc.
**on display** /ɒn dɪ'spleɪ/ *phr* If something is on display, it is there for people to look at.
**on foot** /ɒn fʊt/ *phr* If you go somewhere on foot, you walk there.
**on my/your/his own** /ɒn maɪ/jə/ɪz 'əʊn/ *phr* alone
**on purpose** /ɒn 'pɜːpəs/ *phr* intentionally
**on sale** /ɒn seɪl/ *phr* available to buy in a shop
**on time** /ɒn taɪm/ *phr* not early or late

## UNIT 13

### SOCIAL MEDIA

**block** /blɒk/ *v* If you block someone on social media, they can no longer see your page or contact you.
**comment** /'kɒment/ *v* to write something in response to a social media post
**follow** /'fɒləʊ/ *v* If you follow someone on social media, you choose to see everything that they post.
**like** /laɪk/ *v* to show that you have read, and that you like a social media post
**post** /pəʊst/ *v* to put something on a website or social media page
**share** /ʃeə/ *v* to put someone else's message on your social media page, or a friend's social media page

**tag** /tæg/ *v* If you tag someone in a social media post, you include their name or username.
**take down** /teɪk 'daʊn/ *pv* to remove something from social media or the internet so that it cannot be seen any more

### PHRASES WITH *IN*

**in advance** /ɪn əd'vɑːns/ *phr* before a particular time
**in detail** /ɪn 'diːteɪl/ *phr* including every part of something
**in fact** /ɪn 'fækt/ *phr* really
**in future** /ɪn 'fjuːtʃə/ *phr* beginning from now
**in general** /ɪn 'dʒenərəl/ *phr* usually, or in most situations
**in particular** /ɪn pə'tɪkjələ/ *phr* especially
**in the end** /ɪn ði 'end/ *phr* finally, after something has been thought about or discussed a lot

## UNIT 14

### VERBS FOR COOKING

**bake** /beɪk/ *v* to cook something such as bread or a cake with dry heat in an oven
**barbecue** /'bɑːbɪkjuː/ *v* to cook food on a barbecue
**bite** /baɪt/ *v* to cut something using your teeth
**boil** /bɔɪl/ *v* to cook food in water that is boiling
**burn** /bɜːn/ *v* If something you are cooking burns, it cooks too much.
**freeze** /friːz/ *v* to make food last a long time by making it very cold and hard
**fry** /fraɪ/ *v* to cook something in hot oil or fat or to be cooked in hot oil or fat
**grill** /grɪl/ *v* to cook food on a flat, metal structure over a fire
**roast** /rəʊst/ *v* If you roast food, you cook it in an oven or over a fire, and if food roasts, it is cooked in an oven or over a fire.
**steam** /stiːm/ *v* to cook something using steam (= the gas that water makes when you heat it)
**stir** /stɜː/ *v* to mix food or liquid by moving a spoon, or similar object, round and round in it
**taste** /teɪst/ *v* to put food or drink in your mouth to find out what its flavour is like

### TRANSITIVE AND INTRANSITIVE VERBS

## UNIT 15

### ARTIFICIAL AND NATURAL WORLD

**air conditioning** /eə kən'dɪʃənɪŋ/ *n* a system that keeps the air cool in a building or car
**bug** /bʌg/ *n* a small insect
**facilities** /fə'sɪlətiz/ *n* buildings, equipment, or services that are provided for a particular purpose
**health centre** /'helθ ˌsentə/ *n* a building with several doctors and where people go to visit them
**historic buildings** /hɪ'stɒrɪk 'bɪldɪŋz/ *n* old buildings that are likely to be important in history
**modern architecture** /'mɒdən 'ɑːkɪtektʃə/ *n* buildings using the newest ideas, design, technology, etc.
**open spaces** /əʊpən 'speɪsɪz/ *n* land, especially in a town, that has no buildings on it
**pollution** /pə'luːʃən/ *n* damage caused to water, air, etc. by harmful substances or waste
**ruins** /'ruːɪnz/ *n* the broken parts that are left from an old building or town
**season** /'siːzən/ *n* one of the four periods of the year: winter, spring, summer or autumn
**street light** /striːt laɪt/ *n* a light on a tall post next to a street
**valley** /'væli/ *n* an area of low land between hills or mountains
**wildlife** /'waɪldlaɪf/ *n* animals, birds and plants living in their natural environment

### PHRASAL VERBS

**catch up with someone** /kætʃ 'ʌp/ *pv* to meet someone you know after not seeing them for a period of time and talk about things you have done
**end up** /end 'ʌp/ *pv* to finally be in a particular place or situation
**move in** /muːv 'ɪn/ *pv* to begin living in a new home
**move out** /muːv 'aʊt/ *pv* to stop living in a particular home
**show someone around** /ʃəʊ 'sʌmwʌn ə'raʊnd/ *pv* to lead someone through a place
**stay in** /steɪ 'ɪn/ *pv* to stay in your home

## UNIT 16

### FILM

**animated** /'ænɪmeɪtɪd/ *adj* An animated film is one in which drawings and models seem to move.
**appear** /ə'pɪə/ *v* to perform in a film, play, etc.
**come out** /kʌm 'aʊt/ *pv* If a book, album, film, etc. comes out, it becomes available for people to buy or see.
**direct** /daɪ'rekt/ *v* to tell the actors in a film or play what to do
**director** /dɪ'rektə/ *n* someone who tells the actors in a film or play what to do
**musical** /'mjuːzɪkəl/ *n* a play or film in which singing and dancing tell part of the story
**performance** /pə'fɔːməns/ *n* acting, singing, dancing or playing music to entertain people
**recording** /rɪ'kɔːdɪŋ/ *n* sounds or moving pictures that have been recorded, or the process of recording
**role** /rəʊl/ *n* a part in a play or film
**soundtrack** /'saʊndtræk/ *n* the music used in a film

### REPORTING VERBS

**announce** /ə'naʊns/ *v* to tell people about something officially or with force or confidence
**demand** /dɪ'mɑːnd/ *v* to ask for something in a way that shows that you do not expect to be refused
**explain** /ɪk'spleɪn/ *v* to make something clear or easy to understand by giving reasons for it or details about it
**insist** /ɪn'sɪst/ *v* to demand that something must be done or that you must have a particular thing
**suggest** /sə'dʒest/ *v* to express an idea or plan for someone to consider

# VOCABULARY LIST

## UNIT 17

### VERBS OF COMMUNICATION

**apologise** /ə'pɒlədʒaɪz/ *v* to tell someone that you are sorry about something you have done
**complain** /kəm'pleɪn/ *v* to say that something is wrong or that you are annoyed about something
**disagree** /ˌdɪsə'griː/ *v* to have a different opinion from someone else about something
**joke** /dʒəʊk/ *v* to say funny things, or not be serious
**promise** /'prɒmɪs/ *v* to say that you will certainly do something or that something will certainly happen
**remind** /rɪ'maɪnd/ *v* to make someone remember something, or remember to do something
**warn** /wɔːn/ *v* to tell someone that something bad may happen in the future, so that they can prevent it
**wonder** /'wʌndə/ *v* to want to know something or to try to understand the reason for something

### ADVERBS OF DEGREE: *FAIRLY, PRETTY, QUITE, REASONABLY*

## UNIT 18

### PERSONAL FEELINGS AND QUALITIES

**annoyed** /ə'nɔɪd/ *adj* slightly angry
**charming** /'tʃɑːmɪŋ/ *adj* pleasant or attractive
**curious** /'kjʊəriəs/ *adj* wanting to know or learn about something
**delighted** /dɪ'laɪtɪd/ *adj* very pleased
**lonely** /'ləʊnli/ *adj* unhappy because you are not with other people
**be mad (about)** /biː mæd (ə'baʊt)/ *adj* to love someone or something
**nasty** /'nɑːsti/ *adj* unkind
**professional** /prə'feʃənəl/ *adj* showing skill and careful attention
**rude** /ruːd/ *adj* behaving in a way that is not polite
**shy** /ʃaɪ/ *adj* not confident, especially about meeting or talking to new people
**stressful** /'stresfʊl/ *adj* making you stressed
**unexpected** /ˌʌnɪk'spektɪd/ *adj* Something that is unexpected surprises you because you did not know it was going to happen.

### PREPOSITIONS AND CONJUNCTIONS

**according to** /ə'kɔːdɪŋ tə/ *prep* as said by someone or shown by something
**because of** /bɪ'kɒz əv/ *prep* as a result of someone or something
**besides** /bɪ'saɪdz/ *prep* in addition to something or someone
**despite** /dɪ'spaɪt/ *prep* used to say that something happened or is true, although something else makes this seem not probable
**instead of** /ɪn'sted əv/ *prep* in place of someone or something
**unless** /ən'les/ *conj* except if

## UNIT 19

### WORK TASKS

**arrange** /ə'reɪndʒ/ *v* to make the necessary plans and preparations for something to happen
**calculate** /'kælkjəleɪt/ *v* to discover an amount or number using mathematics
**deal with** /diːl wɪð/ *pv* to take action in order to achieve something or to solve a problem
**deliver** /dɪ'lɪvə/ *v* to take something to a person or place
**develop** /dɪ'veləp/ *v* to make something new such as a product
**handle** /'hændl/ *v* to deal with something
**install** /ɪn'stɔːl/ *v* to put software onto a computer
**manage** /'mænɪdʒ/ *v* to be in control of an office, shop, team, etc.
**organise** /'ɔːgənaɪz/ *v* to plan or arrange something
**produce** /prə'djuːs/ *v* to make or grow something
**run** /rʌn/ *v* to organise or control something
**update** /ʌp'deɪt/ *v* to add new information

### *AS* AND *LIKE*

## UNIT 20

### HOPES AND DREAMS

**achieve** /ə'tʃiːv/ *v* to succeed in doing something good, usually by working hard
**admire** /əd'maɪə/ *v* to respect or approve of someone or something
**aim** /eɪm/ *v* to intend to achieve something
**choose** /tʃuːz/ *v* to decide to do something
**dream** /driːm/ *v* to imagine something that you would like to happen
**encourage** /ɪn'kʌrɪdʒ/ *v* to make someone more likely to do something, or make something more likely to happen
**imagine** /ɪ'mædʒɪn/ *v* to create an idea or picture of something in your mind
**try your best** /traɪ jə best/ *pv* to make the greatest effort possible

### PHRASAL VERBS

**believe in** /bɪ'liːv ɪn/ *pv* to be confident that something is effective or right
**depend on** /dɪ'pend ɒn/ *pv* If something depends on someone or something, it is influenced by them, or changes because of them.
**go for** /'gəʊ fə/ *pv* to try to achieve something
**get into** /get 'ɪntu/ *pv* to succeed in being chosen or elected for a position in a school or other organisation
**join in** /dʒɔɪn 'ɪn/ *pv* to become involved in an activity with other people
**keep on** /kiːp 'ɒn/ *pv* to continue to do something, or to do something again and again
**miss out** /mɪs 'aʊt/ *pv* to not do or have something that you would enjoy, or something that other people do or have
**work out** /wɜːk 'aʊt/ *pv* to understand something or decide something after thinking very carefully

# GRAMMAR REFERENCE AND PRACTICE

## UNIT 1 COUNTABLE AND UNCOUNTABLE NOUNS; DETERMINERS

### Countable and uncountable nouns

- Countable nouns can be singular or plural.
  *card → cards phone → phones*
- A few countable nouns have irregular plurals.
  *child → **children** woman → **women***
  *person → **people***
- Uncountable nouns are always singular.
  *bread, information, news, homework, money, water*
- We can use other phrases to count these nouns.
  ***a slice of** bread*
  ***a great deal of** money*
  ***two glasses of** water*
- Some nouns can be both countable and uncountable.
  *There's **a** strange **noise** coming from that box.*
  *Can you hear that **noise**?*
  *There's **a hair** in my soup!*
  *I've got long **hair**.*
  *Do you want **a coffee**?*
  ***Coffee** is my favourite drink.*

### Determiners: *some, (not) any, no, (not) many, (not) much, plenty of, (not) a lot of, several*

- We use ***some, any, no, plenty of, (not) a lot of*** with plural countable nouns and uncountable nouns. Note that we can use ***a lot of*** and ***lots of*** with the same meaning in positive sentences.
  *I've got **some biscuits** and **some cheese**.*
  *We haven't got **any apples** or **any milk**.*
  *There are **no oranges** and the shop has **no fruit juice**.*
  *I've bought **plenty of vegetables** and **cheese**.*
  *There are **a lot of people** here today but there is**n't a lot of food**.*
- We use ***any*** in questions and negative sentences. In positive sentences, we use ***no***.
  *Is there **any cake**?*
  *There is **no cake**.*
  *I **don't** need **any help**.*
- We sometimes use ***some*** in questions when we offer something and if we expect the answer to be *Yes*.
  *Would you like **some tea**?*
- We use (***not***) ***many*** with countable nouns, in positive and negative sentences and questions.
  ***Many students** enjoy meeting in this café.*
  *We **don't** have **many places** to meet our friends.*
  *Do you go to **many parties** during the holidays?*
- We use (***not***) ***much*** with uncountable nouns in negative sentences and questions. We use ***a lot of*** in positive sentences and questions.
  *My brother is**n't much help** around the house.*
  *My sister always gives me **a lot of help**.*
  *Do you watch **much / a lot of sport** on television?*
- We use ***several*** with plural countable nouns.
  *I've got **several** friends in the States.*

## Practice

**1 Choose the correct word(s) in each sentence.**

1 How *much / many* teenagers came to the party?
2 Toby has been to that club *many / any* times.
3 I haven't got *a lot of / several* homework tonight, so I can watch a film when I finish it.
4 I went out twice at the weekend, so I've got *no / any* money to spend today.
5 Sarah goes to France quite often. I think she has *several / much* friends there.
6 I can't find *any / many* information about the times of the trains.
7 We haven't got *no / much* bread, but there's *several / plenty of* cake.
8 Do you know what's happening at the school? Have you heard *many / any* news today?

**2 Six of the sentences are incorrect. Rewrite them in the correct form.**

1 Angela has coloured her hairs pink. It's great.
2 Do you prefer coffee or fruit juice?
3 We had several fun when we went to the beach.
4 Did you get much help with your homework?
5 I put any sugar in my tea, but it tastes sweet.
6 Don't make a lot of noises when you come in late.
7 There's no any place for children to play around here.
8 We had much trouble with our car on holiday.

**3 Complete the conversation with the words in the box. You can use the words more than once.**

| a lot of | any | much |
|---|---|---|
| no | several | some |

**Katie:** Dad, I haven't got [1] ________ money. Can you lend me [2] ________?
**Dad:** Haven't you got [3] ________ money from your birthday? [4] ________ people gave you money, didn't they?
**Katie:** I had to spend [5] ________ it on things for school at the beginning of term, and I bought Mum [6] ________ perfume last week, so I've got [7] ________ money left now. It isn't [8] ________ fun going out when you can't even buy an ice cream.
**Dad:** OK, here you are.
**Katie:** Thanks, Dad. You're a star.

# GRAMMAR REFERENCE AND PRACTICE

## UNIT 2 -ING FORMS

- The *-ing* form of the verb (***being, knowing, seeing, having, running***, etc.) is sometimes called the present participle or the gerund.
- We can use the *-ing* form:
  - after verbs which mean *like* and *don't like*: ***like, love, enjoy, dislike, hate, not mind, can't stand.***
    *I **love going out** with my friends.*
    *We all **hate revising** for a test.*
    *Marie **doesn't mind helping** other students with maths.*
    *My dad **hates being** late for work.*
    *My mum **can't stand doing** housework.*
  - after some adjective + preposition phrases which say how well people do things or how they feel about doing them: ***good at, bad at, keen on, interested in, crazy about, afraid of, tired of.***
    These adjectives follow the verb ***be***.
    *My brother**'s good at singing**.*
    *We **are crazy about dancing**.*
    ***I'm interested in learning** languages.*
    *Our cats **are afraid of getting** wet.*
  - as part of the subject of a sentence. The subject usually goes at the start of a sentence.
    ***Playing online games** is a fun thing to do.*
    ***Keeping in touch with friends** is easy, because of the internet.*

### Practice

**1 Complete the text. Use the *-ing* form of the verbs in the box.**

| annoy | eat | give | grow |
|---|---|---|---|
| listen | see | sit | tell |

I stayed with my cousins last weekend. I enjoyed [1] ________ them all, except my cousin Arash. He knows I can't stand [2] ________ to his stupid jokes but he likes [3] ________ them and he enjoys [4] ________ me.

I helped my aunt make lunch. I don't mind [5] ________ her some help because she's very kind. She's a good cook, so everyone loves [6] ________ her food.

After lunch, we watched an old film. My uncle doesn't like [7] ________ inside in the afternoon, so he went into his garden. He loves [8] ________ things in his garden, like fruit trees, and he brought us some apples to eat. They were really good.

**2 Complete the sentences with the correct preposition.**

1 All the students in my class are crazy ________ playing tennis.
2 Are you good ________ keeping secrets?
3 I cycle home through the city centre because I'm afraid ________ going through the park after dark.
4 We're not really interested ________ learning about politics.
5 I'm quite keen ________ understanding how machines work, so I'm not bad ________ mending things.

**3 Complete the second sentence so that it means the same as the first. Use *is/are*, the words in brackets + the *-ing* form of the verb.**

0 James makes friends easily. (good at)
James is *good at making friends.*
1 Lisa gets up early because she doesn't want to miss her bus. (afraid of)
Lisa gets up early because she ________
2 Nick doesn't want to play football any longer. (tired of)
Nick ________
3 Keira plays video games all the time. (crazy about)
Keira ________
4 Rupert wants to go to Africa. (keen on)
Rupert ________
5 Some people find it difficult to remember new vocabulary. (bad at)
Some people ________
6 We would like to learn Chinese. (interested in)
We ________

**4 Put the words in order to make sentences.**

0 football / good exercise / playing / is
*Playing football is good exercise.*
1 friends / with / studying / fun / is
2 staying in touch / is / old friends / difficult sometimes / with
3 things / about / worrying / is / a waste of time
4 often / is / useful / listening / other people's ideas / to
5 best thing / is / to do / with friends / hanging out / the

# UNIT 3 PRESENT SIMPLE AND CONTINUOUS

## Present simple

| | | |
|---|---|---|
| Positive | I, You, We, They **play** / **study** | He, She, It **plays** / **studies** |
| Negative | I, You, We, They **don't play** / **study** | He, She, It **doesn't play** / **study** |
| Questions | **Do** I, you, we, they **play** / **study**? | **Does** he, she, it **play** / **study**? |

We use the **present simple**:

- to talk about something we do regularly, or things that usually happen.
  *Most evenings, we* ***play*** *video games after dinner.*
  *My sister* ***doesn't get*** *home from school till four o'clock.*
  *What time* ***do*** *you* ***start*** *school?*
  *Our teacher usually* ***helps*** *us with grammar.*
- for facts and things which are generally true.
  *My brother* ***doesn't live*** *near us.*
  *Swimming* ***helps*** *you keep fit.*
- for systems and processes.
  *The Earth* ***goes*** *around the sun.*
  *Water* ***freezes*** *when it* ***gets*** *cold.*
- for state verbs (verbs which describe what we like, think and feel). These are not normally used in a continuous form.
  ***believe***, ***dislike***, ***hate***, ***know***, ***like***, ***love***, ***prefer***, ***remember***, ***think***, ***understand***, ***want***, ***wish***
  *Sam* ***thinks*** *this is the best café in town.*
  *Jonah* ***doesn't know*** *where his phone is.*
  *I* ***remember*** *my first ever holiday.*

## Present continuous

| | |
|---|---|
| Positive | I**'m (am) watching** / **running**<br>You, We, They**'re (are) watching** / **running**<br>he, she, it**'s (is) watching** / **running** |
| Negative | I**'m not (am not) watching** / **running**<br>You, We, They **aren't ('re not / are not) watching** / **running**<br>He, She, It **isn't ('s not / is not) watching** / **running** |
| Questions | **Am** I **watching** / **running**?<br>**Are** you, we, they **watching** / **running**?<br>**Is** he, she, it **watching** / **running**? |

**We use the present continuous:**

- to talk about things that are happening now.
  *We****'re sitting*** *on the train at the moment.* (= now)
- for future plans and arrangements that we are sure about.
  *I****'m meeting*** *some friends after school.* (= I arranged it in the past.)

## Practice

**1 Choose the correct form of the verbs.**

1 My brother *runs* / *is running* for the school bus every morning because he *doesn't wake up* / *isn't waking up* in time.
2 *I think* / *I'm thinking* some video games are good for your brain, but *I don't play* / *I'm not playing* them very often.
3 *Do you believe* / *Are you believing* all the stories in the news?
4 *I have* / *I'm having* my break now. Our teacher *always gives* / *is always giving* us a break between lessons.
5 My parents *visit* / *are visiting* some friends at the moment, so *I stay* / *I'm staying* with my grandma.
6 *I usually have* / *I'm usually having* lunch with a friend, but tomorrow *I have* / *I'm having* lunch with my brother.

**2 Complete the email. Use the present simple or continuous form of the verbs.**

Hi Marco,
I'm here in Brighton and I [1] ________ (have) a great time. We [2] ________ (have) classes every morning from 9 till 12. My flat is near the school, so I [3] ________ (get up) at 8.30 and [4] ________ (buy) a coffee on the way in. There are some good guys in my class and we all [5] ________ (go) to the park and [6] ________ (eat) lunch at a café there. The waiter sometimes [7] ________ (give) us free ice creams. In the afternoons we [8] ________ (choose) what we [9] ________ (want) to do. This afternoon I [10] ________ (go) to the beach and tomorrow I [11] ________ (play) volleyball in a match against another language school. What [12] ________ (you/do) at the moment? [13] ________ (you / revise) for your exams? [14] ________ (you / remember) last summer, when we went to the lake? Perhaps we can go again this year. Anyway, I [15] ________ (come) to Brescia with my dad after my English course, so I can see you then.
Milo

# GRAMMAR REFERENCE AND PRACTICE

## UNIT 4 PAST SIMPLE; *USED TO*

### Past simple

- The past simple is usually formed by adding *-ed* to the infinitive.
  *open → opened*
- Many common verbs are irregular, and the past simple doesn't end in *-ed*.
  e.g. ***break → broke; feel → felt; put → put; rise → rose; run → ran; say → said; take → took; think → thought***
- We form negatives and questions with ***did*** and ***didn't (did not)*** + the infinitive.
  *I **didn't open** the window.*
  ***Did** she **lock** the car?*
- The verb ***to be*** has two forms in the past: ***was/ wasn't*** and ***were/weren't***.
  *I **wasn't** in school yesterday.*
  ***Were** you late today?*
- We use the past simple to talk about:
  - single completed actions or events in the past.
    *I **grew up** in California.*
    *I **didn't learn** to drive there.*
    ***Did** your mum **work** in the film studios?*
  - something that happened at a particular time in the past.
    *I **went** to a football match **last night**.*
    *My friends **didn't send** me a card **on my birthday**.*
    ***Did** you **find** your phone **when you went home**?*
  - things that happened regularly in the past.
    *I **went** to my last school by bike every day.*
    ***Didn't** you **catch** the bus on rainy days?*

### Practice

**1 Complete the conversation. Use the past simple form of the verbs in the box.**

| be | cost | go | find | happen |
|---|---|---|---|---|
| have | pay | spend | try | want |

**Kiki:** Hi, Kay. What [1] ________ to you yesterday afternoon? I [2] ________ calling you several times, but your phone [3] ________ off.

**Kay:** I [4] ________ with my mum to the shopping mall. She [5] ________ to get a new bag, and I [6] ________ these amazing boots in a sale.

**Kiki:** They're really cool! How much [7] ________ they ________?

**Kay:** I [8] ________ £35 for them – they only [9] ________ one pair left in my size! I [10] ________ all my birthday money on them.

**2 Complete the story in the past simple.**

Last winter we [1] ________ (not / have) very cold weather but it [2] ________ (rain) nearly every day for a month. After three weeks, the river [3] ________ (rise) and the water [4] ________ (start) coming in to people's gardens. As the water [5] ________ (continue) to rise, the school [6] ________ (offer) some families with young children accommodation. They [7] ________ (sleep) on the floor of the hall, and the children [8] ________ (think) it was a great adventure. Luckily most of the houses [9] ________ (not flood) and people [10] ________ (be) able to go home the next day.

### *used to*

- We use ***used to*** + verb to talk about habits or situations in the past which are not the same now.
  *We **used to live** in a small flat.* (= We don't live in a small flat now.)
  *They **used to cycle** everywhere.* (= They don't cycle everywhere now.)
  ***I didn't use to like** camping.* (= I enjoy it now.)

| | |
|---|---|
| **Positive** | I, He, She, We, You, They **used to go** |
| **Negative** | I, He, She, We, You, They **didn't use to go** |
| **Questions** | **Did** I, he, she, we, you, they **use to go?** |

### Practice

**3 Complete the sentences. Use the correct form of *used to* and the verb in brackets.**

1. We ________ to school before the road got so busy. (walk)
2. My dad ________ me a story every night before I went to sleep. (tell)
3. At my old school, we ________ sport every day. (do)
4. My parents ________ me to go out in the evenings. (not / allow)
5. ________ when they were young? (your brothers / fight)
6. I ________ practising the guitar but now I do. (not / like)

**4 How has the world changed in the last 40 years? Complete the sentences. Use *used to* or *didn't use to* and the verbs in the box.**

| carry | catch | get | go | have |
|---|---|---|---|---|

1. Computers were the size of cars, and of course people ________ them at home.
2. There was no internet, so students ________ information online, they had to go to a library.
3. Not everyone had a car and more people ________ buses or walk to work.
4. There were no mobile phones, so people ________ a phone with them all the time.
5. Air travel was extremely expensive, so only rich people ________ abroad for their holidays.

## UNIT 5 PAST SIMPLE AND CONTINUOUS

### Past simple

- The verb *be* has two forms in the past: ***was/wasn't*** and ***were/weren't***.
  *It **was** cold yesterday.*
  ***Were** there many people at the party?*
- Other past simple verbs are usually formed by adding *-ed* to the infinitive.
  ***open → opened***
- Many common verbs are irregular, and the past simple doesn't end in *-ed*.
  e.g. ***think → thought; take → took; put → put***
- We form negatives and questions with ***did*** and ***didn't*** (***did not***) + the infinitive.
  *I **didn't open** the window.*
  ***Did** she **lock** the car?*
- We use the past simple to talk about completed actions and things that happened in the past.
  *I **lived** in Russia.*
  ***Did** the river **flood** last winter?*
  *I **didn't go** to a party last weekend.*

### Past continuous

- All verbs form the past continuous with the past tense of the verb ***be*** + present participle.

| | |
|---|---|
| I, He, She, It **was**<br>You, We, They **were** | **eating.**<br>**sleeping.** |
| I, He, She, It **wasn't (was not)**<br>You, We, They **weren't (were not)** | |
| **Was** I, he, she, it<br>**Were** you, we, they | **eating?**<br>**sleeping?** |

- We use the past continuous:
  - to talk about actions and situations in progress at a certain moment in the past.
    *It **was raining** all night.*
  - to describe the background to a story.
    *We **were travelling** with some friends and **visiting** lots of great cities.*
  - to talk about actions in progress that are interrupted by a short action in the past simple.
    *I **was waiting** for a bus when you texted.*
    *At the time the exam started, I **was sitting** in a traffic jam.*
  - We don't use **state verbs** (verbs which describe what we like, think and feel) with the past continuous.
    ***believe, hate, know, like, love, mean, need, own, prefer, understand, want***
    ~~*I wasn't liking the film. I wasn't understanding it.*~~
    *I **didn't like** the film. I **didn't understand** it.*

## Practice

**1 Complete the text. Use the past continuous form of the verbs.**

The sun [1] ________ (shine) and some teenagers [2] ________ (sit) in the park. One girl [3] ________ (sing) quietly to her friends and two boys [4] ________ (take) selfies. They [5] ________ (not / play) loud music and they [6] ________ (not / shout).
However, some older people thought they [7] ________ (not / behave) well and complained. 'What [8] ________ (we / do) wrong?' asked the teenagers, but no one could tell them.

**2 Choose the correct form of the verbs.**

1 We *watched / were watching* a film on my computer when it suddenly *stopped / was stopping* working.
2 I *didn't notice / wasn't noticing* what time my sister *came / was coming* home because I *played / was playing* a video game in my room.
3 I *learned / was learning* quite a few words of Spanish in the six months I *travelled / was travelling* in South America.
4 My brother *went / was going* to Africa last year and *climbed / was climbing* Mount Kilimanjaro.
5 Guess who we *saw / were seeing* when we *drove / were driving* to the funfair!
6 *Did you text / Were you texting* when you *walked / were walking* across the road? Please don't! It's dangerous!
7 How many nights *did you sleep / were you sleeping* in the open when you *went / were going* to that adventure camp?
8 I only left the kitchen for a moment, but I came back to find that my toast *burned / was burning*.

**3 Complete the conversation. Use the past simple or past continuous form of the verbs.**

**Barbara:** What [1] ________ (you / do) in the hall cupboard for so long?
**Rhiannon:** I [2] ________ (look) for my winter boots.
**Barbara:** [3] ________ (you / find) them?
**Rhiannon:** No, but I'm sure I [4] ________ (put) them there last spring. I remember when I [5] ________ (tidy) my room, I [6] ________ (decide) I [7] ________ (not / want) to keep them there in the summer.
**Barbara:** I guess Alex [8] ________ (move) them. He [9] ________ (use) that cupboard for his sports gear for a few months, until he [10] ________ (stop) going to the gym.
**Rhiannon:** Well, I hope he [11] ________ (not / throw) my favourite boots away! They [12] ________ (cost) a lot of money!

## UNIT 6 MODALS: OBLIGATION, NECESSITY AND ADVICE (1)

### *must, should, ought to*

- The form of these modal verbs does not change. They go before the infinitive of another verb.
  *I **must have** a shower.*
  *You **should eat** more vegetables.*
  *He **ought to wear** a coat.*
  *We **mustn't go** into the house.*
  *She **shouldn't worry** so much.*
- We don't often use ***ought not to***.

### *have to*

- This modal verb does change its form. It goes before the infinitive of another verb.

| | | |
|---|---|---|
| I, You, We, They | **have to** | work. |
| | **(don't have to)** | |
| He, She, It | **has to** | |
| | **(doesn't have to)** | |
| **Do** I, you, we, they | **have to** | work? |
| **Does** he, she, it | | |

### Obligation and necessity

- ***Must*** and ***have/has to*** mean that it is absolutely necessary to do something.
  *You **must rest** your leg for five days.*
  *I **have to** leave home at seven o'clock to get the bus.*
- ***Mustn't*** means that it is very important not to do something.
  *You **mustn't go** into that room.*
  *He **mustn't cycle** without a helmet.*
- ***Don't/Doesn't have to*** means that it is not necessary to do something.
  *I **don't have to get** to school before eight.*
  *My mother **doesn't have to work** at weekends.*

### Advice

- ***Should*** and ***ought to*** mean that it is a good idea to do something. They are not as strong as ***must*** and ***have to***.
  *You **should try** to relax before your exam.*
  *We **ought to finish** our homework before we go out.*
- ***Shouldn't*** means that it is a bad idea to do something. It is not as strong as ***mustn't***.
  *You **shouldn't go** out when you've got homework to do.*
  *I **shouldn't eat** sweets before a meal.*

## Practice

**1 Do the pairs of sentences mean the same? Write *S* for same or *D* for different. If they are different, can you explain why?**

1 a You should get up early and go for a run.
  b You must get up early and go for a run.
2 a I have to buy some new jeans.
  b I must buy some new jeans.
3 a Alan doesn't have to go out this evening.
  b Alan shouldn't go out this evening.
4 a We ought to buy some fruit for our lunch.
  b We have to buy some fruit for our lunch.
5 a You mustn't open that parcel till your birthday.
  b You don't have to open that parcel till your birthday.
6 a In my opinion, Jo should apologise to Amy.
  b In my opinion, Jo ought to apologise to Amy.
7 a Paul must remember to take his phone with him.
  b Paul has to remember to take his phone with him.

**2 Choose the correct modal verb.**

1 You look very sleepy. You *shouldn't / don't have to* go to bed so late when you have to get up early the next day.
2 You *must / mustn't* use your phone during the exam or the teacher will take it away from you.
3 I *ought to / shouldn't* finish this work before dinner, but I'm so hungry I can't wait any longer.
4 My dad *doesn't have to / mustn't* come home at lunchtime because there's a good restaurant near his office.
5 We *don't have to / have to* post this parcel before six o'clock or it won't arrive in time for Jane's birthday.

**3 Complete the text with the modals in the box.**

| don't have to | have to | |
|---|---|---|
| mustn't | ought to | shouldn't |

I belong to a photography club and it's very interesting. We use all kinds of cameras, some old and some new. There's a darkroom for people who work with black and white film. You [1] ________ pay for darkroom time when you book it because it's quite popular and people get annoyed if it's booked and then not used. You [2] ________ wear old clothes in the darkroom because you'll probably make marks on them.
You [3] ________ buy special equipment, you can borrow it, but you [4] ________ borrow anything without signing for it. I've got some great pictures from a trip we took to a mountain village, including some wonderful photos of people. Of course, you [5] ________ really photograph people without asking permission, but usually they don't mind if you ask politely.

# UNIT 7 PRESENT PERFECT AND PAST SIMPLE

FOR THE PAST SIMPLE FORM SEE GRAMMAR REFERENCE, UNIT 4, PAGE 150

## Past simple

We use the past simple to talk about completed actions which began and ended in the past. Sometimes we say when they happened.
*We **spent** hours in the recording studio **yesterday**.*
*I **didn't finish** my song.*
***Did** they **learn** lots of songs **last weekend**?*

### Practice

**1 Complete the email. Use the past simple form of the verbs.**

Hi
I really [1] ________ (enjoy) the course I [2] ________ (do) last week. I [3] ________ (meet) some amazing people and [4] ________ (make) some new friends. We [5] ________ (work) hard during the day but we [6] ________ (have) fun in the evenings. We [7] ________ (not / go) to bed until after midnight every night.

[8] ________ (you / find) the music I [9] ________ (tell) you about when I [10] ________ (text) you? I [11] ________ (find) some more tracks by the same singer. They [12] ________ (be) on the internet. I [13] ________ (listen) to them last night, and I thought her voice [14] ________ (be) beautiful.
See you soon x

## Present perfect

- We form the present perfect with ***has/have*** + the past participle.
- We use the present perfect to talk about something that started in the past and has a link to the present.
  *We**'ve spent** hours in the recording studio.*
  *I **haven't made** a recording.*
  ***Have** you **seen** this website?*

### Practice

**2 Complete the conversation. Use the present perfect form of the verbs.**

**Emma:** Mum, [1] ________ (you / see) my phone?
**Mum:** No, I [2] ________ (not). [3] ________ (you / look) in your bag?
**Emma:** Yes, I [4] ________ (look) everywhere! I think someone [5] ________ (steal) it.
**Mum:** I bet you [6] ________ (not check) your bed.
**Emma:** OK, I'll look. Oh! It's there! I [7] ________ (find) it! Thanks, Mum!

## Present perfect with *just, already, yet, ever*

- We use ***just, already, yet, ever*** with the present perfect.
- ***Just*** usually goes after *has/have* and before the main verb.
  ***I've just arrived.*** (= a few moments ago)
- ***Already*** can go after *has/have* and before the main verb, or at the end of the sentence. We don't use it in negative sentences.
  ***I've already made** one recording.* (= I made it some time before now.)
  ***I've made** one recording **already**.*
- We use ***yet*** in negative sentences and questions. It goes at the end of the sentence. It means 'up to now'.
  *I **haven't finished** this recording **yet**.* (= I'm still making it now.)
  ***Have** you **made** a recording **yet**?* (= I think you plan to make one around now.)
- We use ***ever*** in questions and it goes before the main verb. It means 'at any time in the past up to now'.
  ***Have** you **ever made** a recording?* (= at any time in your life)

### Practice

**3 Rewrite the sentences. Put the words in brackets in the correct position.**

1 The course has finished. (already)
2 Have you visited a recording studio? (ever)
3 Have you met your new teacher? (yet)
4 The singer has arrived. (just)
5 I haven't listened to that track. (yet)

**4 Choose the correct form of the verbs in this telephone conversation.**

**Ana:** Mina, [1] *have you ever bought / did you buy* clothes online or do you always go to a shop?
**Mina:** [2] *I've done / I did* it many times. [3] *I've found / I found* a new website last week and ordered some jeans and a jacket. [4] *They've just arrived / They just arrived* but [5] *I haven't tried / didn't try* them on yet because I want to have a shower first.
**Ana:** [6] *I've ordered / I ordered* a T-shirt from a website last weekend, but it [7] *hasn't arrived / didn't arrive* yet.
**Mina:** [8] *Have you paid / Did you pay* for it at the same time?
**Ana:** Yes, [9] *it's cost / it cost* $50. [10] *There's been / There was* a special offer at the weekend.

# GRAMMAR REFERENCE AND PRACTICE

## UNIT 8 COMPARATIVE AND SUPERLATIVE ADJECTIVES

We can form comparative and superlative adjectives in many ways.

- With one-syllable adjectives, add *-er* and *-est*.
  *new* → *newer* → *(the) newest*
  *light* → *lighter* → *(the) lightest*
- with one-syllable adjectives ending in **e**, add *-r* and *-st*.
  *nice* → *nicer* → *(the) nicest*
- With one-syllable adjectives ending in a vowel + consonant, we usually double the consonant and add *-er* and *-est*.
  *big* → *bigger* → *(the) biggest*
- With adjectives ending in a consonant + *-y*, change the *-y* to *-ier* and *-iest*.
  *tidy* → *tidier* → *(the) tidiest*
  *funny* → *funnier* → *(the) funniest*
- For adjectives with two or more syllables, we usually use ***more*** and ***the most***.
  *active* → *more active* → *(the) most active*
  *modern* → *more modern* → *(the) most modern*
- A few common adjectives are irregular.
  *good* → *better* → *(the) best*
  *bad* → *worse* → *(the) worst*
  *far* → *further/farther* → *(the) furthest / farthest*
- Adjectives which are made from two words use ***more*** and ***the most***.
  *user-friendly* → *more user-friendly* → *(the) most user-friendly*

### Comparative structures

- When we want to say something is more than another thing, we usually use the comparative adjective + ***than***.
  *Your bike is* ***newer than*** *mine.*
  *The grammar book was* ***more useful than*** *the dictionary.*
- When we want to say that one thing is less than another thing, we can use:
  - ***less*** + adjective + ***than***.
    *My bike* ***is less new than*** *yours.*
    *The dictionary* ***was less useful than*** *the grammar book.*
  - ***not as*** adjective + ***as***
    *My bike* ***isn't as good as*** *yours.*
    *The dictionary* ***wasn't as useful as*** *the grammar book.*
- When we want to say that two things are the same, we can use ***as*** + adjective + ***as***.
  *My bedroom is* ***as big as*** *my brother's bedroom.*

### Superlative structures

- When we want to say that one thing is better, worse, etc. than everything else, we can use superlatives.
  *Your bike is* ***the newest*** *in the race and mine is* ***the oldest***.
  *The grammar book was* ***the most useful***. (of all the books I used)
  *The dictionary was* ***the least useful***.
- We often use ***the*** or a possessive before a superlative.
  ***The fastest*** *runner in our school is Amy.*
  *Amy is the* ***school's most successful*** *runner.*
  *Game shows are* ***my least favourite*** *TV programmes.*

### Practice

**1 Complete the sentences. Use the comparative form of the adjectives, adding *not as … as*, *less* or *than* where necessary.**

1 I want to change into ________ (smart) clothes before my interview. The clothes won't make me ________ (intelligent) but they might make me feel ________ (confident)!
2 The modern part of the house is ________ (new) the rest of it, so it has ________ (big) windows and ________ (good) heating.
3 This phone looks ________ (modern) mine, but I'm not impressed because it's ________ (expensive) and ________ (easy) to carry because it's bigger.
4 I prefer this café. The other one is ________ (not / comfortable) this one, and the waiters here are ________ (friendly) too.

**2 Complete the sentences. Use the superlative form of the adjectives, and use *the* or *the least* where necessary.**

1 My sister is the world's ________ (bad) cook; she can't follow ________ (simple) recipe.
2 This website is ________ (useful) of all the ones I've looked at. It gives no real information at all.
3 I've just spent all morning sorting out my room. It's now ________ (tidy) it has ever been!
4 This phone is ________ (cheap) in the shop, but it's also ________ (easy) to use, so it isn't good value.
5 Shall I wear my ________ (good) boots or will it rain, do you think?
6 Rob's ________ (kind) boy in the class, and he's also one of ________ (funny), so he's probably ________ (popular) too.

**3 Complete the second sentence so that it has the same meaning as the first. Use the words in brackets.**

1 My new phone and my old one are the same.
My new phone is ________ (good) the old one.
2 My sister's room is larger than mine.
My room ________ (big) as my sister's.
3 I prefer old buildings to new ones.
I think old buildings ________ (good) new ones.
4 I've never seen such a nice building.
This is ________ (beautiful) building I have ever seen.
5 This chair is the most uncomfortable one in the room.
This is ________ (comfortable) chair in the room.

## UNIT 9 FUTURE FORMS; FUTURE CONTINUOUS

### Present continuous for plans

We use the present continuous, usually with the time mentioned, for definite future arrangements.
*Charlie **is leaving** on Tuesday.*
*What **are you doing** in the holidays?*

### *will*

We use ***will***:
- for general predictions about the future.
  *The price of phones **will fall**.*
  *Smart watches **won't do** everything laptops can do.*
- for offers and promises relating to the future.
  ***I'll help** you set up the new equipment.*

### *going to*

We use ***going to***:
- for personal plans relating to the future (this is like the present continuous).
  *Charlie **is going to leave** soon.*
  *What **are you going to do** after school?*
- for firm intentions.
  *We**'re going to drive** to the south coast.*

### Future continuous

- We form the future continuous with ***will/won't*** + ***be*** + ***-ing***.
  ***I'll be working***
  ***He won't be playing***
  ***Will you be living …?***
- We use the future continuous to talk about something that is certain to be happening at a particular time in the future.
  ***I'll be working** for my dad next year.*
  *He **won't be playing tennis** tomorrow morning.*
  ***Will you be working** all weekend?*

### Practice

**1** **Complete the conversation. Use the future continuous form of the verbs.**

**Evita:** I'm going to England with my brother for six weeks.
**Harry:** [1] ________ you ________ (stay) in London or [2] ________ you ________ (move) around from place to place?
**Evita:** We [3] ________ (spend) a few days in several big cities and we [4] ________ (visit) as many of our English friends as we can.
**Harry:** How [5] ________ you ________ (travel)?
**Evita:** We [6] ________ (use) public transport most of the time but for the last week we [7] ________ (borrow) a friend's car. I [8] ________ (not / drive) because I'm not old enough to have an international licence. But I [9] ________ (speak) English more than my brother because I [10] ________ (not / worry) about making mistakes when I talk, like he always does.

**2** **Choose the correct form of the verbs.**

1. I can't stop now, *I'll meet / I'm meeting* my mum at the station in fifteen minutes.
2. In the next few years, technology *is making / will make* a lot of difference to the lives of people in isolated communities.
3. Let me fix your phone for you. I *won't damage / won't be damaging* it.
4. Our teacher says *we'll be using / we'll use* the new science laboratories for the rest of this term.
5. *Are you going to play / Will you play* volleyball this afternoon or can you help me with the shopping?

**3** **Complete the conversation. Use the verbs in the correct form: present continuous, *will*, *going to* or future continuous. Sometimes more than one form is possible.**

**Evan:** What time [1] ________ (we / have) dinner tonight, Mum?
**Mum:** About seven. Do you have any plans?
**Evan:** I [2] ________ (watch) the match at Tom's house later. Is that OK with you?
**Mum:** Yes, of course. You [3] ________ (not / go) to school tomorrow. But do you think you [4] ________ (get) home very late?
**Evan:** Yes, probably, but I promise I [5] ________ (not / make) a noise.
**Mum:** Please be very quiet. Your sister [6] ________ (sleep) after 10 pm because she has to get up early in the morning. She [7] ________ (not be) happy if you wake her up.
**Evan:** Don't worry, I [8] ________ (be) really quiet.

# GRAMMAR REFERENCE AND PRACTICE

## UNIT 10 CONDITIONAL SENTENCES

### Zero conditional

- We form the zero conditional with:
  - ***if*** + present tense + comma + present tense.
    *If a lioness **has** cubs to protect, she **is** more dangerous.*
  - present tense + ***if*** + present tense.
    *A lioness **is** more dangerous **if** she **has** cubs to protect.*
- We use the zero conditional to describe real events or situations that actually happen.
  *Wild animals **aren't** dangerous **if** people **behave** sensibly.*
- ***If*** usually means the same as **when** in zero conditional sentences.
  *A lioness **is** more dangerous **when** she **has** cubs to protect.*

### Practice

**1 Complete the sentences with the correct form of the verbs.**

1. Beautiful places often ________ too crowded if they ________ popular tourist resorts. (get / be)
2. If people ________ rude to me, I ________ no notice of them. (be / take)
3. Travelling to see wildlife ________ a great holiday if you ________ watching nature documentaries. (be / enjoy)
4. When we ________ trees, we ________ animals' environment. (cut down / destroy)

### First conditional

- We form the first conditional with:
  - ***if*** + present tense + comma + ***will/won't***.
    ***If** she **thinks** her cubs are in danger, a lioness **will attack**.*
  - ***will/won't*** + ***if*** + present tense.
    *A lioness **will attack if** she **thinks** her cubs are in danger.*
- We use the first conditional to imagine what is likely to happen.
  ***If** the forests **disappear**, the weather **will be** more extreme.*

### Practice

**2 Choose the correct form of the verbs.**

1. If we *won't do / don't do* something soon, we *will lose / lose* many wild animals.
2. If conservation work *will be / is* successful, there *will be / are* more animals in the wild.
3. Many of our rare birds *will disappear / disappear* if there *won't be / aren't* safe places for them to nest.
4. Future generations *don't see / won't see* any wild animals if we *won't look after / don't look after* them.

### Second conditional

- We form the second conditional with:
  - ***if*** + past tense + comma + ***would***.
    ***If** politicians **cared** about the rainforests, they'd **(would) do** more to protect them.*
    ***If** people **cared** about their planet, they **wouldn't pollute** the sea.*
  - ***would*** + ***if*** + past tense.
    *Politicians **would do** more to protect the rainforests **if** they **cared** about them.*
    *There **wouldn't be** any apples **if** bees **didn't exist**.*
- We use the second conditional to describe something in the present or future which is unlikely to happen or is imaginary.
  ***If** I **had** a garden, **I'd grow** lots of fruit.*
  (= I don't have a garden so I don't grow fruit.)
  *We **wouldn't eat** honey **if** we **didn't like** it.*
  (= We like honey so we eat it.)

### Practice

**3 Complete the sentences using the second conditional.**

1. Cities ________ cleaner if people ________ cars for short journeys. (be / not use)
2. If more people ________ this nature reserve, there ________ more money to spend on conservation. (visit / be)
3. Raising money for wildlife projects ________ easier if people ________ how important the work is. (be / understand)
4. Some animals ________ if people ________ them. (not survive / not protect)

### *unless*

- We can use ***unless*** instead of ***if … not*** in conditional sentences.
  *We wouldn't eat honey **unless** we **liked** it.* (= **if** we **didn't like** it)
  ***Unless** we **do** something to protect the rainforests soon, they will all disappear.* (= **If** we **don't do** something soon …)

### Practice

**4 Rewrite the sentences using *unless*. Start with the words given.**

1. We will lose the rainforests if we don't do more to protect them.
   We will ________________________
2. If we don't look after the planet, future generations will suffer.
   Future generations will ________________________
3. I wouldn't support conservation work if I didn't think it was important.
   I wouldn't ________________________

## UNIT 11 PAST PERFECT

- We form the past perfect with ***had*** + the past participle.
  *had looked* *hadn't looked* *had he looked?*
  *had written* *hadn't written* *had he written?*
- We use the past perfect to talk about events or actions which happened some time before another action or event in the past.
- The past perfect usually makes the order of the events clearer and gives background information. The main past action is usually in the past simple.
  *I'**d** never **been** to a live concert so I was really excited when we went to one last weekend.*
- We often use words such as ***before*** or ***after*** in sentences with the past perfect.
  *I'**d seen** the film **before** but I enjoyed seeing it again.*
  ***After** we'**d sung** Happy Birthday, my sister opened her presents.*

### Practice

**1 Last Saturday the students of Park School gave a surprise party for their head teacher when she retired. Write sentences about what they had and hadn't done when the head teacher arrived on the afternoon of her last day.**

1 decorate the school hall ✓
They ______
2 do their usual lessons ✗
They ______
3 eat lunch ✗
They ______
4 prepare a special meal ✓
They ______
5 write a song to sing her ✓
They ______

**2 Last summer Leo left school and went on holiday with some friends. Look at the things he had planned to do before he left home. Write questions and answers.**

0 running shoes? ✗ / swimming trunks ✓ (pack)
*Had he packed his running shoes?*
*No, he hadn't packed his running shoes but he had packed his swimming trunks.*
1 sun block? ✗ / shampoo ✓ (buy)
2 his driving test? ✗ / all his exams ✓ (pass)
3 a hotel room ✗ / a seat on the train ✓ (book)

**3 Complete the text. Use the past perfect form of the verbs.**

When I first came into my new classroom in the village school, the students were sitting in rows. My previous job [1]______ (be) in a modern school in the capital city, where the students [2]______ (always / sit) in a circle. I asked the students to stand up and move their desks. After we [3]______ (arrange) the desks in a circle, I asked them to sit down and began the lesson.

After we [4]______ (try) the new arrangement for several days, I asked the students what they thought about it. Here's what they said: 'We were surprised because we [5]______ (not / sit) in a circle before. We [6]______ (always / sit) in rows and the lessons [7]______ (often / seem) boring. Now we have more discussions and everyone joins in.'

Luckily the head teacher agreed with them! 'I [8]______ (not / realise) that moving the furniture could make such a difference,' he said.

**4 Choose the correct form of the verbs.**

1 When John arrived late for his exam he *was / had been* upset because nobody *told / had told* him the time *changed / had changed*.
2 The school team *never played / had never played* in a real stadium before, and they *were / had been* very excited to see so many spectators when they ran out onto the pitch.
3 I was at a boarding school before I *went / had been* to university, so I knew how to look after myself, but some of my classmates *were never / had never been* away from home and *found / had found* it hard to manage without their parents at first.
4 Last Friday our teacher *gave / had given* us a test in biology. I *was / had been* able to answer the questions because I *saw / 'd seen* a documentary on the subject just a week before, not because I *revised / 'd revised*. In fact I *forgot / 'd forgotten* that we *had / had had* a test that day!
5 It *was / had been* my birthday yesterday. I was sad, because no one wished me a happy birthday. It seemed that everyone *forgot / had forgotten*. But, when I *got / had got* home, all my friends were there! I was very surprised. No one *told / had told* me anything about it, but my friends *all planned / had all planned* a surprise party. They *bought / had bought* a cake and presents, and it was really amazing. I *felt / had felt* so happy.

# GRAMMAR REFERENCE AND PRACTICE

## UNIT 12 MODALS: OBLIGATION, NECESSITY AND ADVICE (2)

### Advice

- We use ***should / shouldn't*** + verb to give advice to someone, and when the speaker believes something is the right thing to do.
  *You **should arrive** at the airport early.*
  *You **shouldn't take** too much hand luggage.*

### Practice

**1 Give advice to the people in the following situations. Use *should(n't)* + the words in brackets.**

1 Adam's got to catch a train in twenty minutes but he can't walk to the station.
You ________ (call a taxi).
2 Amina has a test in school tomorrow. Her sister wants her to play a video game.
You ________ (revise). You ________ (play with your sister).
3 Dmitri is going out later. He's used his phone a lot already today.
You ________ (charge it).
4 Tex wants to mend his bike. He's wearing his best sweater.
You ________ (change your sweater).

### Obligation and necessity

- We use ***need to*** + verb when we believe something is important, but not a rule or law.
  *You **need to keep** your passport in a safe place.*
- We use ***have to*** + verb when something is necessary because it is a rule or the law.
  *You **have to get** a visa.*
  *You **have to show** your passport when you enter the country.*

### Lack of obligation

- When something is not necessary, we use:
  - ***don't have to*** + verb.
    *You **don't have to pay** for your food on this flight.*
  - ***needn't*** + verb (*needn't* is not followed by *to*).
    *You **needn't take** an umbrella – it won't rain.*
  - ***don't need to*** + verb.
    *You **don't need to get** to the airport early.*

### Practice

**2 Choose the correct verbs.**

1 You *need to / needn't* finish your homework, then you can relax.
2 You *have to / needn't* tell the teacher today if you want to go on the school trip.
3 You *shouldn't / should* clean your teeth before you go to the dentist.
4 You *don't have to / need to* walk to school – I can give you a lift.
5 You *needn't / should* buy a drink – I've already got one for you.
6 You *should / needn't* pack your bag the night before you leave, so that you'll be ready when the taxi arrives.
7 You *needn't / shouldn't* forget to switch all the lights off before you leave.
8 I *don't need to / shouldn't* take a passport with me because I'm not flying to a different country.

**3 Do the pairs of sentences mean the same? Mark *S* for same or *D* for different. If they are different, can you explain why?**

1 **a** You need to book in advance to get a cheap ticket.
**b** You don't have to buy your ticket in advance, but it costs more on the day.
2 **a** You don't have to take a lot of cash with you.
**b** It's sensible to take plenty of money with you.
3 **a** You shouldn't buy tickets on the internet from people you don't know.
**b** It's a bad idea to buy tickets on the internet from people you don't know.
4 **a** You should try to stay with your friends if there are big crowds.
**b** You have to stay with your friends if there are a lot of people there.
5 **a** You have to be with an adult if you're under 16, or you can't go in.
**b** People aged under 16 can only go in if they're with an adult.
6 **a** You don't have to take a phone.
**b** You needn't take a phone.
7 **a** You should buy travel insurance before you go.
**b** My advice is to buy insurance before you travel.
8 **a** You need to be at the airport at least two hours before your flight leaves.
**b** The airline says that you must be at the airport two hours before you fly.

## UNIT 13 THE PASSIVE

We form the passive with the verb *be* + the past particle. If we want to talk about the past or the present, we change the form of *be*.

### The present simple passive

- We form the present simple passive of a verb with *is* or *are* + the past participle.
  *Millions of photos* ***are posted*** *online every day.*
  *These toys* ***aren't sold*** *in supermarkets.*

### The past simple passive

- We form the past simple passive of a verb with *was* or *were* + the past participle.
  *This picture* ***was drawn*** *to illustrate a story.*
  *The artists* ***weren't told*** *what to paint.*

### Modal passives

- Modal verbs like ***can, could, must, may*** and ***might*** are often used in passive structures. We form them with a modal verb + ***be*** + past participle.
  *The writer of the poem* ***can't be identified.***
  *The students* ***may be allowed*** *to film the show.*
  *Tickets* ***must be booked*** *in advance.*

### The agent

- The person or thing that performs an action is called **the agent**. The agent of the passive verb is the subject of an active verb.
  *Someone sent Sam a letter.* (*Someone* is the subject and the agent.)
  *Sam* ***was sent*** *a letter.* (*Sam* is the subject, but not the agent.)
- We often use the passive in English when:
  - we do not know who performs (or performed) the action.
    *My bag* ***was taken*** *while I was sunbathing.*
    *A lot of clothes* ***are made*** *in small factories.*
  - it isn't important who performs (or performed) the action.
    *My new phone* ***was delivered*** *yesterday.*
    *This room* ***must be cleaned*** *immediately.*
  - we want to emphasise the subject of the passive verb.
    *I* ***was asked*** *to sing at the end-of-term concert!* (It was me who was asked, not someone else.)
    *Your brother* ***must be invited*** *to the party.* (The focus is on *your brother*.)
- We can use ***by*** if we need to make it clear who the agent is in a passive sentence.
  *My friends gave me lots of presents on my birthday.* (active)
  *I* ***was given*** *lots of presents* ***by my friends*** *on my birthday.* (passive)
  *The photographer didn't pay that model very much.* (active)
  *That model* ***wasn't paid*** *very much* ***by the photographer.*** (passive)

### Practice

**1 Rewrite the sentences using the active form of the verb.**

1. The school blog is edited by a group of senior students.
2. This kind of box can't be opened by young children.
3. This software isn't often used by designers nowadays.
4. The paintings in my room were done by my grandfather.

**2 Rewrite the sentences using the passive form of the verb. Only include the agent if it is important.**

1. Several celebrities attended the party.
2. Nobody could find the ball at the end of the match.
3. I made all these cakes.
4. My aunt designed these shoes for a famous singer.
5. Software can change the shape of a model's eyes in a photo.
6. The editor of the magazine couldn't identify the writer of the poem.
7. Our parents may allow us to go to a concert if we tidy our rooms.

**3 Choose the correct form of the verbs.**

1. If you want to take a good photo, you need enough light. Photos *can't take / can't be taken* in the dark.
2. Smartphones *used / are used* by many people these days to take photos. However, if you want to take really good-quality photos, then you *should buy / should be bought* a good camera.
3. When you go on holiday, it's a good idea to take lots of photos. These *can share / can be shared* online, so your friends *can see / can be seen* all the interesting places you've visited.
4. If you want to take photos of people, remember that you *should ask / should be asked* their permission first.
5. Remember to save your photos carefully. Lots of photos *delete / are deleted* by accident. Don't let this happen to you.
6. You can edit your photos. This *can do / can be done* online, or by using special software. But be careful. If your photos *edit / are edited* too much, they *might look / might be looked* strange.

# GRAMMAR REFERENCE AND PRACTICE

## UNIT 14 RELATIVE CLAUSES

### Defining relative clauses

- Defining relative clauses give essential information about the things, places or people we are talking about. They are never separated from the rest of the sentence by commas.
  *The cakes **that my brother makes** are really good.*
  We need the words *that my brother makes* to know which cakes the speaker is talking about.
- To begin a relative clause, we use the pronouns ***who*** (for people), ***which*** (for things), ***that*** (for things and people), ***whose*** (belonging to) and ***where*** (for places).
  *There's the girl **who** won the cookery competition.*
  *She showed me the recipe **which** she invented.*
  *I can email the recipe **that** I told you about.*
  *That's the boy **whose mum** designs sunglasses.*
  *This is the place **where** I bought my book.*
- ***Who, which*** or ***that*** can be the subject or the object of the relative clause.
  *The woman **who/that** runs the café is very friendly.* (*who/that* is the subject)
  *There's the chef **who/that** I told you about.* (*who/that* is the object)
  *He showed me a recipe **which/that** he often uses.* (*which/that* is the object)
- We can leave out ***who, which*** or ***that*** if it is the object of the defining clause.
  *The cakes **(which/that)** my brother makes are really good.*
  *There's the chef **(who)** I told you about.*
  *He showed me a recipe **(which/that)** he often uses.*
  *I can email the recipe **(which/that)** I told you about.*
- We cannot leave out ***who, which*** or ***that*** if it is the subject.
  *The woman **who** runs the café is very friendly.*

### Practice

**1 Complete the sentences with *who*, *which*, *where* or *whose*.**

1 The first restaurant ________ I worked was in London.
2 Do you remember the name of the chef ________ restaurant we visited?
3 I've never met anyone ________ could cook as well as my mum.
4 The dishes ________ I like best are the ones ________ use fresh ingredients.
5 I like working with people ________ are interested in food from different countries.
6 The friend ________ saucepan I borrowed will be angry when he sees I've burned it.

**2 Look at the sentences in Exercise 1.**

a Where can you use ***that*** instead of the word you chose?
b Where can you leave out the relative pronoun?

### Non-defining relative clauses

- We use non-defining relative clauses to give more information about the things or people we are talking about. Non-defining relative clauses are always separated from the rest of the sentence by commas.
  *The cakes on this plate, **which my brother helped to make**, are really good.*
  If we take out *which my brother helped to make*, we still know which cakes the speaker is talking about.
- Non-defining relative clauses begin with the relative pronoun ***who*** (for people), ***where*** (for places), ***which*** (for things) or ***whose***, but never ***that***.
  *My brother, **who** is an excellent cook, has written a cookbook.*
  *The recipes, **which** he tested carefully, require lots of special ingredients.*
  NOT ~~*The recipes, that he tested carefully, …*~~
  *My grandparents, **whose** kitchen he uses, are proud of what he's done.*
- We can never leave out the relative pronoun in a non-defining clause.

### Practice

**3 Rewrite the pairs of sentences using non-defining relative clauses.**

1 My grandma taught me to make cakes. She worked in a restaurant when she was young.
2 We lit the barbecue half an hour before the guests arrived. We had bought it the day before.
3 My friend Darren brought us some fresh fish. Darren's dad is a keen fisherman.
4 This Thai food is mild enough for anyone to eat. It doesn't have any chillies in it.
5 These sausages are all burnt. I was cooking them for my lunch.

**4 Explain the difference in meaning between the pairs of sentences.**

1 a The biscuits which my brother made were all eaten.
  b The biscuits, which my brother made, were all eaten.
2 a The students who had not had lunch wanted to find a café.
  b The students, who had not had lunch, wanted to find a café.
3 a The lettuces which weren't fresh were thrown away.
  b The lettuces, which weren't fresh, were thrown away.
4 a The bread which was freshly baked smelled delicious.
  b The bread, which was freshly baked, smelled delicious.

## UNIT 15 ARTICLES: *A/AN*, *THE* AND ZERO ARTICLE

### The indefinite article *a/an*

We use *a/an* before a singular countable noun:

- when we mention something for the first time.
  *I live in **a flat** near the city centre.*
- when we mention someone's job or what they do.
  *My mum's **a doctor**, my dad's **an architect** and my brother's **a student**.*

### The definite article *the*

We use *the* before any noun:

- when we mention something for the second time.
  *Our flat is near a park. **The park** has several tennis courts.*
- when there is only one of something.
  *My brother likes swimming in **the sea**.*
- when we talk about particular people or things.
  ***The school** I go to is not far away.*
- which is the name of a group of mountains, and states and countries that are plural.
  ***the Urals**, **the United Arab Emirates***
- which is the name of a desert, ocean or river.
  ***the Sahara, the Pacific, the Amazon***

### The zero article

We do not use an article:

- before an uncountable noun or a plural countable noun, when we talk about that thing in general.
  ***Volleyball** is my favourite sport.*
  ***Teenagers** are usually interested in **sport**.*
- with the names of towns, countries and continents, individual islands, mountains and lakes.
  ***New Zealand**, **Rome**, **Europe**, **Sicily**, **Mount Fuji**, **Lake Issyk Kul***

### Practice

**1 Match the sentence halves.**

1 When she finishes university, my sister wants to be
2 In my English lessons, we all like
3 I'm learning a lot in
4 In my village, there's a post office, a few shops and
5 I saw some shoes and a bag in a shop today – I liked the shoes, but I didn't like
6 I can't carry all this shopping in my hands – I need

a a school.
b the teacher.
c the bag.
d a teacher.
e school.
f a bag.

**2 Choose the correct article or no article.**

1 *The* / – town where I grew up is on *the* / – River Loire.
2 My brother has gone to *the* / – Chile for a mountaineering expedition in *the* / – Andes.
3 There was *a* / *the* thunderstorm yesterday, and my cat hid under my bed because he's terrified of *the* / – loud noises.
4 Our maths teacher was *a* / *the* soldier before she trained to be *a* / *the* teacher.
5 On Fridays, my friends and I all meet in – / *a* café near *the* / – central bus station to drink *the* / – coffee and chat. *A* / *The* café isn't great, but *the* / – music they play there is amazing.
6 *The cheese* / *Cheese* is nice, but too much can give you *the* / – spots.
7 When we went to *the* / – Canada last year, we stayed in – / *a* hostel in *the* / – Vancouver and we also camped near *the* / – Lake Louise in *the* / – Rocky Mountains.

**3 Complete the email with *a/an*, *the* or – if no article is necessary.**

We had a great holiday in [1] ________ West Indies last February. We went to [2] ________ Grenada and stayed in [3] ________ hotel near [4] ________ amazing beach of white sand. [5] ________ hotel had [6] ________ beautiful garden with [7] ________ good sports facilities, and we played [8] ________ tennis every morning. We also did [9] ________ tour of [10] ________ island and wandered round [11] ________ market in [12] ________ St Georges, which is [13] ________ capital. But the best thing was swimming in [14] ________ warm sea every day when [15] ________ sun was rising over [16] ________ mountains behind our hotel.

**4 Find the mistakes with articles in the sentences and correct them.**

1 The petrol is very expensive in this country.
2 I'm not very interested in the science, but I enjoy learning a new language.
3 A football match we watched last night was very exciting and my team won!
4 I went to good sports club when I was on holiday.
5 The vegetables are an important part of a balanced diet.
6 I was so embarrassed in the meeting yesterday when I realised phone that was ringing was in my bag!

# GRAMMAR REFERENCE AND PRACTICE

## UNIT 16 REPORTED SPEECH

### Verbs in reported speech

- The tense of the verbs in direct speech changes when the reporting verb (*said, told, explained*, etc.) is in the past tense.

| Direct speech | | Reported speech |
|---|---|---|
| **present simple** *'I **enjoy** watching films.'* | → | **past simple** *He said he **enjoyed** watching films.* |
| **present continuous** *'That girl **is acting** well.'* | → | **past continuous** *He said that girl **was acting** well.* |
| **past simple** *'She **studied** at film school.'* | → | **past perfect** *He said (that) she**'d (had) studied** at film school.* |
| **present perfect** *'I **haven't seen** her before.'* | → | **past perfect** *He said he **hadn't seen** her before.* |
| ***will*** *'She**'ll** be famous one day.'* | → | ***would*** *He said she**'d (would)** be famous one day.* |
| ***can*** *'She **can** sing well too.'* | → | ***could*** *He said she **could** sing well too.* |

- We do not change ***could, would, should, might, used to*** or the past perfect when they are reported.
  *'You **could visit** her website.'*
  *→ He said I **could visit** her website.*
  *'She **used to be** in a TV series.'*
  *→ He said she **used to be** in a TV series.*
  *'She **hadn't appeared** on TV before that.'*
  *→ He said she **hadn't appeared** on TV before that.*

### Pronouns in reported speech

- Pronouns sometimes have to change when they are reported.
  *'**I** enjoy watching films,' said Tom.*
  *→ Tom said **he** enjoyed watching films.*
  *'**You** can watch a film after dinner,' said the boys' mum.*
  *→ The boys' mum said **they** could watch a film after dinner.*

### Reporting verbs

- We introduce reported speech with reporting verbs like ***said, told, insisted, announced, demanded, explained***, etc.
  *She **said** she enjoyed acting.*
- There must be an object after ***told***.
  *She **told us** she enjoyed acting.*
- Reporting verbs are often followed by ***that***.
  *She **said that** she enjoyed acting.*
  *She **told us that** she enjoyed acting.*
  *She **explained that** she enjoyed acting.*
- ***Insisted, suggested*** and ***demanded*** can be followed by ***that … should do*** instead of a past tense.
  *'You must give us your autograph.'*
  *→ We insisted that she **gave** us her autograph.*
  *We insisted **that** she **should give** us her autograph.*
  *'Let's watch the film again.'*
  *→ I suggested **that** we **should watch** the film again.*

### Practice

**1 Change the sentences from reported to direct speech.**

1. The director told the actors he would pay them a lot of money.
   The director said, '________'
2. One of the stars insisted that she needed a special diet.
   One of the stars said, '________'
3. The camera operator complained that the lights were too weak.
   The camera operator said, '________'
4. The leading actor told me he didn't enjoy working with that director.
   The leading actor said, '________'
5. The make-up artist explained that the star was feeling ill.
   The make-up artist said, '________'
6. The actors told the director they hadn't worked in such a beautiful place before.
   The actors said, '________'
7. The writer said he'd completed the film three years ago.
   The writer said, '________'

**2 Complete the reported sentences.**

1. 'We made a film at school last term.'
   The students announced that ________
2. 'We're making another one this term.'
   They told us ________
3. 'I hadn't been in a film before.'
   The leading actor said he ________
4. 'I enjoy directing but I don't like acting.'
   The director explained that she ________
5. 'Everyone must learn their words by next week.'
   Our drama teacher insisted that ________
6. 'You can't be in the film because you didn't learn your words.'
   The teacher told me that ________
7. 'We've learned a lot in drama classes.'
   The students said ________
8. 'I will finish making the film soon.'
   The director said she ________

## UNIT 17 REPORTED QUESTIONS

- The word order of a reported question is the same as a positive statement, not a question.
  *'What's the time?*
  *→ She asked me **what the time was**.*
- The verbs change after a reporting verb in the past tense, in the same way as in reported statements.
- The auxiliary verbs ***did***, ***didn't*** are not used in reported questions.
  *'When did you get up today?'*
  *→ He asked me **when I got up today**.*
  *(NOT ~~... when did I get up today~~.)*
- Pronouns change in the same way as in reported statements.
- For reported ***yes/no*** questions we use ***if*** or ***whether***.
  *'**Are** you busy?'*
  *→ She asked **if I was** busy.*
  *'**Did** he **send** an email?'*
  *→ I asked **whether** he'**d sent** an email.*
  *'**Do** you often **play** video games?'*
  *→ He asked **whether** we often **played** video games.*
  *'**Have** you **seen** my website?'*
  *→ She asked **if I'd seen** her website.*
- For reported ***Wh-*** questions, the reported question starts with the same question word as the direct question.
  *'**What** time is it?'*
  *→ She asked **what** time it was.*
  *'**When** are you coming home?'*
  *→ He asked **when** we were coming home.*
  *'**Where** can I charge my phone?'*
  *→ He asked **where** he could charge his phone.*
  *'**Which** websites have they looked at?'*
  *→ I asked **which** websites they'd looked at.*

### Reporting verbs

- We can introduce reported questions with verbs like ***ask***, ***want to know*** or ***wonder***.
  *'Are you busy?'*
  *→ She **asked** if I was busy.*
  *'Did he send an email?'*
  *→ I **wanted to know** whether he'd sent an email.*
  *'Do you often play video games?'*
  *→ He **wondered** whether we often played video games.*
- The reporting verb ***asked*** is sometimes followed by a noun or pronoun.
  *'What time is it?'*
  *→ She **asked the nurse** what time it was.*
  *'When are you coming home?'*
  *→ He **asked us** when we were coming home.*
  *'Which websites have they looked at?'*
  *→ I **asked them** which websites they'd looked at.*

## Practice

**1 Change the questions from reported to direct speech.**

1. My friends asked me why I hadn't texted anyone all day.
   They said, '________?'
2. They wanted to know whether I was coming out with them.
   They said, '________?'
3. I asked them what time they were leaving.
   I said, '________?'
4. My brother asked me if he could come with us.
   He said, '________?'
5. My dad wanted to know whether I had finished my homework.
   He said, '________?'
6. My mum wondered how long I would be out.
   She said, '________?'
7. My sister asked whether I wanted a lift to town.
   She said, '________?'

**2 Change the questions into reported speech.**

1. Why haven't you texted me?
   My mum wanted to know ________
2. Have you seen my car keys?
   My dad wondered ________
3. Where will you stay in London?
   My teacher asked me ________
4. How many tweets have you sent today?
   The reporter asked the actor ________
5. Why is everyone shouting at me?
   The footballer wondered ________
6. Do students often use the website?
   We wanted to know ________
7. Can you get superfast broadband in your town?
   The filmmaker asked us ________

**3 Find and correct six mistakes in the reported questions in this email.**

Hi Jan,
I went to see a careers adviser yesterday. He asked me what were my favourite subjects and did I prefer playing video games or taking part in sport. He wanted to know what languages did I speak and which foreign countries I visited in my life. He asked could you imagine working in an office. He also wanted to know how much did I want to earn. He didn't suggest a career, but he helped me to think more clearly about the decisions I have to make in the next two years.
Hope you're well. Write soon,
Kai

# GRAMMAR REFERENCE AND PRACTICE

## UNIT 18 *HAVE SOMETHING DONE*

- We use a form of ***have*** + object + the past participle. The past participle describes the action that was done.

| | |
|---|---|
| *I'm **going to have** my hair*<br>*We **had** our hair*<br>*They**'ve never had** their hair*<br>*You **should have** your hair*<br>*He**'ll** probably **have** his hair*<br>*She needs to **have** her hair* | ***coloured** / **cut** / **done**.* |

- We use ***have something done*** to talk about something that someone else does for us.
  *We want **to have** our hair **cut**.* (= We want someone ***to cut*** our hair for us.)
  *I'm **going to have** my hair **done**.* (= Someone ***is going to do*** my hair for me.)
- We do not usually mention who the person is that does something for us, unless it's important.
  *I **had** my hair **done**.* (= Someone, probably a hairdresser, ***did*** my hair for me.)
  *I **had** my hair **coloured by my mum**.* (emphasises that my mum did it for me)
- We can use ***get*** instead of ***have*** in more informal situations.
  *I'm **going to have/get** my bike **fixed** this weekend.*
  *My parents **had/got** their photo **taken** in front of Buckingham Palace.*

### Practice

**1** **Read the sentences. Tick (✓) the sentences in which the speaker did the action, and not someone else.**

1 I had my windows cleaned last week. They look much cleaner now.
2 I delivered the letter and then went home.
3 I had my photo taken. I needed it for a passport.
4 Unfortunately, I had my bike stolen yesterday.
5 I repaired my computer, and now it's working.
6 I checked my blood pressure, and there's nothing wrong with it.

**2** **Match the sentence halves.**

1 Do you go to the supermarket every week?
2 What did your brother do for his girlfriend's birthday?
3 Is that your grandfather in the picture?
4 Your living room looks different from last time I visited you.
5 Your mum's car looks very smart!
6 Where's your computer?

a Yes, we've just had it decorated.
b I'm having it checked for viruses at a shop in town.
c No, we have our food delivered.
d Yes, she's had it washed at last.
e Yes, he had his portrait painted and my dad had it framed.
f He had flowers delivered to her.

**3** **Correct the mistake in each sentence.**

1 I'd love to my hair coloured. I think it would look good.
2 I have to have my car serviced last week, because it was making a strange noise.
3 My daughter had her face paint and she thought it was funny.
4 I my computer fixed, because I know how to do it myself.
5 Lots of famous people have books wrote about them.

**4** **These people want someone to do something for them. Complete what they say. Use *have* + object + past participle of the verbs in brackets.**

1 My room is a boring colour. I want to ________. (paint)
2 My phone isn't working properly. I'll ________ at the shop. (fix)
3 My little sister can't reach the front door bell. We're going to ________. (move)
4 Our kitchen is very old-fashioned. We'd like to ________. (modernise)
5 I can never find clothes to fit me. I wish I could ________ for me by a personal shopper. (choose)
6 My computer is so slow. I need to ________. (check)

**5** **Complete the sentences. Use the correct form of *have* + the words in brackets.**

1 I ________ at a nail bar. Do you like them? (just / my nails / do)
2 We ________ after our last party. (all the carpets / clean)
3 I bought some jeans but I need to ________. (them / shorten)
4 You must ________. (your bike / repair)
5 ________ in your new dress yesterday? (you / your photo / take)
6 When was the last time you ________? (your / eyes / examine)

# UNIT 19 DIFFERENT TYPES OF CLAUSE

## Contrast clauses

- We can join clauses which give different or surprising information about something with words like ***although***, ***whereas*** and ***while***.
- ***Although*** and ***whereas*** can go in the middle of a sentence, or at the beginning for extra emphasis.
  *I enjoyed my holiday job* ***although*** *it was hard work.*
  ***Although*** *my holiday job was hard work, I enjoyed it.* (= my holiday job was hard work but I enjoyed it)
  *I prefer to get up early,* ***whereas*** *most of my friends like to sleep late.*
  ***Whereas*** *most of my friends like to sleep late, I prefer to get up early.* (= unlike most of my friends, I like to get up early)
- ***While*** usually goes at the beginning of a sentence.
  ***While*** *I don't enjoy going for a run, I know it's good for me.* (= I don't enjoy going for a run but I know it's good for me)

## Purpose clauses

- We can use a clause beginning with ***so that*** or ***in order to*** when we want to explain the purpose of something in the same sentence.
- ***In order to*** can go in the middle of a sentence, or at the beginning for extra emphasis. It is followed by the infinitive form of the verb.
  *I want to work in an office* ***in order to*** *learn about business software.*
  ***In order to*** *learn about business software, I want to work in an office.*
- ***So that*** goes in the middle of a sentence. It is followed by an object.
  *I want to work in an office* ***so that I*** *can learn about business software.*

## Reason clauses

- We can use a clause beginning with ***because*** or ***as*** when we want to explain the reason for something in the same sentence.
- ***Because*** and ***as*** can go in the middle of a sentence, or at the beginning for extra emphasis.
  *I needed to get a job* ***because*** *I wanted to save money for my holiday.*
  ***Because*** *I wanted to save money for my holiday, I needed to get a job.*
- ***As*** has the same meaning as ***because***.
  *I decided to walk to work* ***as*** *it was a fine morning.*
  ***As*** *it was a fine morning, I decided to walk to work.*

## Practice

**1 Do the pairs of sentences mean the same? Mark *S* for same or *D* for different. If they are different, can you explain why?**

**1 a** I need to get good exam results because I want to go to college.
**b** The reason I need good exam results is that I want to go to college.
**2 a** My dad likes to read on holiday, whereas my mum prefers going for a swim.
**b** My mum enjoys going for a swim when my dad is reading.
**3 a** It's important to leave early so that we avoid the rush hour traffic.
**b** In order to avoid the rush hour traffic, we need to leave early.
**4 a** While most teenagers enjoy parties, not all of them like dancing.
**b** Teenagers who can't dance don't enjoy parties.
**5 a** The company offers good training programmes in order to attract the best students.
**b** The company wants to attract the best students, so they offer good training programmes.
**6 a** As I don't enjoy swimming, I'm not so keen on seaside holidays.
**b** I quite like seaside holidays although I don't like swimming.
**7 a** Although it was a cold day, the sun was shining.
**b** It was a cold day, but the sun was shining.

**2 Match the sentence halves and join them with linking words from the box. Can any of the words fit in more than one place?**

although as because
in order to so that whereas

**1** I can afford new trainers
**2** I passed the exam
**3** Most students have long summer holidays
**4** It's a good idea to talk to a careers advisor
**5** I've got the afternoon off
**6** We're usually given half an hour

**a** some of the questions were really hard.
**b** I was paid yesterday.
**c** you know what kind of jobs might suit you.
**d** I worked late yesterday evening.
**e** medical students have to work all through the year.
**f** prepare for our final race.

# GRAMMAR REFERENCE AND PRACTICE

## UNIT 20 VERBS WITH TWO OBJECTS

- An active verb usually has a subject and often has a direct object.
- The direct object is usually a thing.

| Subject | Verb | Direct object |
|---|---|---|
| *I* | *sent* | *a text.* |
| *Maisie* | *wrote* | *a note about the volleyball match.* |

- Some verbs can have two objects – a direct object and an indirect object.
- The indirect object is usually a person.
- When the direct object comes first, we say ***to*** or ***for*** before the indirect object.

| Subject | Verb | Direct object | Indirect object |
|---|---|---|---|
| *I* | *sent* | *a text* | *to my aunt.* |
| *Maisie* | *wrote* | *a note about the volleyball match* | *for the teacher.* |

- When the indirect object comes first, we don't use ***to*** or ***for***.

| Subject | Verb | Indirect object | Direct object |
|---|---|---|---|
| *I* | *sent* | *my aunt* | *a text.* |
| *Maisie* | *wrote* | *the teacher* | *a note about the volleyball match.* |

- Verbs which can have two objects include: ***bring, buy, cook, choose, fetch, give, lend, make, offer, owe, pay, send, show, take, teach, tell, throw, write.***

### Practice

**1 Complete the sentences with *to* or *for*.**

1 I bought some flowers ____ my mum.
2 Did you show your presents ____ your friends?
3 Alex gave a silver necklace ____ his girlfriend.
4 Bettina told her story ____ the police officer.
5 Dad paid ten euros ____ the taxi driver.
6 Give that phone ____ me now!
7 Charlie cooked a pizza ____ himself.
8 Debbie taught a new song ____ the children.
9 Can you fetch a clean towel ____ me?
10 My brother showed his notebook ____ the teacher after the lesson.

**2 Rewrite each sentence in Exercise 1 with the indirect object before the direct object.**

1 *I bought my mum some flowers.*

**3 Write the words in the correct order.**

1 twenty dollars / Wilfred / his / owes / sister
____
2 Yolanda / cake / a / I'll / for / nice / choose
____
3 you / me / a / make / sandwich / can / ?
____
4 threw / the / sister / to / Tom / his / ball
____
5 of / mum / photo / gave / Zoe / a / herself / her
____
6 Paul / has / to / address / his / you / texted / new
____

**4 Rewrite each sentence in Exercise 3, changing the order of the direct and indirect objects. You will need to add or leave out *to* or *for*.**

1 *Wilfred owes twenty dollars to his sister.*

# LIST OF IRREGULAR VERBS

| Infinitive | Past simple | Past participle | Infinitive | Past simple | Past participle |
|---|---|---|---|---|---|
| be | was, were | been | leave | left | left |
| beat | beat | beaten | learn | learned/learnt | learned/learnt |
| become | became | become | lend | lent | lent |
| begin | began | begun | lie | lay | lain |
| bleed | bled | bled | lose | lost | lost |
| break | broke | broken | make | made | made |
| bring | brought | brought | mean | meant | meant |
| build | built | built | meet | met | met |
| burn | burnt/burned | burnt/burned | pay | paid | paid |
| buy | bought | bought | put | put | put |
| catch | caught | caught | read | read | read |
| choose | chose | chosen | ride | rode | ridden |
| come | came | come | ring | rang | rung |
| cost | cost | cost | rise | rose | risen |
| cut | cut | cut | run | ran | run |
| dig | dug | dug | say | said | said |
| do | did | done | see | saw | seen |
| draw | drew | drawn | sell | sold | sold |
| dream | dreamed/dreamt | dreamed/dreamt | send | sent | sent |
| drink | drank | drunk | shine | shone | shone |
| drive | drove | driven | show | showed | shown |
| eat | ate | eaten | shut | shut | shut |
| fall | fell | fallen | sing | sang | sung |
| feel | felt | felt | sit | sat | sat |
| fight | fought | fought | sleep | slept | slept |
| find | found | found | speak | spoke | spoken |
| fly | flew | flown | spell | spelled/spelt | spelled/spelt |
| forget | forgot | forgotten | spend | spent | spent |
| get | got | got | stand | stood | stood |
| give | gave | given | steal | stole | stolen |
| go | went | gone/been | swim | swam | swum |
| grow | grew | grown | take | took | taken |
| have | had | had | teach | taught | taught |
| hear | heard | heard | tell | told | told |
| hide | hid | hidden | think | thought | thought |
| hit | hit | hit | throw | threw | thrown |
| hold | held | held | understand | understood | understood |
| hurt | hurt | hurt | wake | woke | woken |
| keep | kept | kept | wear | wore | worn |
| know | knew | known | win | won | won |
| lead | led | led | write | wrote | written |

**Acknowledgements**

The authors would like to acknowledge everyone involved in the first edition and thank everyone who worked on the second edition, particularly Greg Clarke, Verity Cole and Alyson Maskell.

The authors and publishers are grateful to the following for reviewing the material during the writing process:

Argentina: Diana Ogando; Italy: Claudia Cantaluppi; Mexico: Cristina Godard; Spain: Estefanía Avilés

**The authors and publishers acknowledge the following sources of copyright material and are grateful for the permissions granted. While every effort has been made, it has not always been possible to identify the sources of all the material used, or to trace all copyright holders. If any omissions are brought to our notice, we will be happy to include the appropriate acknowledgements on reprinting and in the next update to the digital edition, as applicable.**

Key: U = Unit, LS = Life Skills, C = Culture, EA = Extra Activities, PE = Prepare for the Exam

Text
**U9**: Steve Rees, Minddrive, org for the quote by Steve Rees. Reproduced with permission. Copyright © 2013 All Rights Reserved; **U16**: Evan Hara for the text about Evan Hara. Copyright © Evan Hara. Reproduced with permission of Evan Hara.

Photography
The following images are sourced from Getty Images.

**U1:** Hoberman Collection/Universal Images Group; Michel Gunther/Biosphoto; Loop Images/Universal Images Group; Rawpixel/iStock/Getty Images Plus; joe daniel price/Moment; Bojan89/iStock/Getty Images Plus; tiler84/iStock/Getty Images Plus; flyfloor/iStock/Getty Images Plus; artJazz/iStock/Getty Images Plus; **U2:** Klaus Vedfelt/DigitalVision; Tomwang112/iStock/Getty Images Plus; SeventyFour/iStock/Getty Images Plus; Vladimir Godnik; herkisi/iStock/Getty Images Plus; mikeinlondon/iStock Editorial/Getty Images Plus; **C1:** mikeinlondon/iStock Editorial/Getty Images Plus; View Pictures/Universal Images Group; David Crespo/Moment; **U3**: nycshooter/E+; Liderina/iStock/Getty Images Plus; Fotosearch; FatCamera/E+; Henry Lederer/Taxi; Image Source; Alexandre Loureiro/Getty Images Sport; Clive Brunskill/Getty Images Sport; Jeff Greenberg/Photolibrary; Ole Graf/Corbis; Lynn Koenig/Moment; **U4:** Massimo Mei/Moment; Matt Cardy/Getty Images News; Don Emmert/AFP; Bloomberg; Saeed Khan/AFP; **LS1:** lisafx/iStock/Getty Images Plus; targovcom/iStock/Getty Images Plus; Gang Zhou/E+; Ron Levine/DigitalVision; Hero Images; **U5:** Ben Pipe Photography/Photolibrary; whitemay/iStock/Getty Images Plus; Suradech14/iStock/Getty Images Plus; Desiree Navarro/WireImage; MsDancy/iStock/Getty Images Plus; Laurence Mouton/PhotoAlto Agency RF Collections; **U6:** PeopleImages/E+; Steve Debenport/E+; Sue Barr/Image Source; **C2**: Claus Andersen/Getty Images Sport; Eliot J. Schechter/National Hockey League; Brent Just/Getty Images Sport; Westend61; William Manning/Corbis Documentary; **U7:** archives/Vet; Olaf Herschbach/EyeEm; Wavebreak Media Ltd/Getty Images Plus; shironosov/iStock/Getty Images Plus; Hybrid Images/Cultu; Jeff Kravitz/AMA2017/FilmMagic, Inc; BJI/Blue Jean Images; **U8**: karamysh/iStock/Getty Images Plus; Hisham Ibrahim/The Image Bank; Wojtek Radwanski/AFP; Omar Marques/Anadolu Agency; Frederick Florin/AFP/Getty Images; **LS2:** Witthaya/iStock/Getty Images Plus; Rob Lang/Archive Photos; Juanmrgt/iStock/Getty Images Plus; Michael Klippfeld/Moment; Rui Almeida Fotografia/Moment; **U9**: Adam Berry/Getty Images News; joel-t/iStock Editorial/Getty Images Plus; Noah Berger/AFP; kenex/DigitalVision Vectors; Sjo/iStock Unreleased; alexsl/iStock/Getty Images Plus; **U10:** Sue Flood/The Image Bank; CraigRJD/E+; boryak/E+; up close with nature/Moment Open; Yuri Tutov/AFP; Jami Tarris/Photolibrary; Wild Horizon/Universal Images Group; Franco Banfi/WaterFrame; **C3:** Tier Und Naturfotografie J und C Sohns/The Image Bank; kellyvandellen/iStock/Getty Images Plus;

Vicki Jauron, Babylon and Beyond Photography/Moment; Khanh Ngo Photography/Moment;

Lloyd Park/Dorling Kindersley; Jeff R Clow/Moment; Lucy von Held/Blend Images; Jason Magerkorth/iStock/Getty Images Plus; Canon_Bob/iStock/Getty Images Plus; Coneyl Jay/Stone; Steve Debenport/E+; **U11:** Chen Jie/The Beijing News/Visual China Group; Juice Images; Rachel Watson/DigitalVision; Cancan Chu/Getty Images News; **U12:** John Seaton Callahan/Moment; Arnold Media/Taxi; den-belitsky/iStock/Getty Images Plus; Marco Bottigelli/AWL Images; sturti/E+; Ken Welsh/Perspectives; Thomas Trutschel/Photothek; **LS3:** yuoak/DigitalVision Vectors; yuoak/DigitalVision Vectors; Ryan Creary/All Canada Photos; Peter Unger/Lonely Planet Images; Nicholas Rigg/Photographer's Choice RF; Busakorn Pongparnit/Moment; **U13:** Imagesbybarbara/E+; subman/E+; Caiaimage/Robert Daly; CoffeeAndMilk/E; Hugh Threlfall/Alamy Stock Photo; marioaguilar/iStock/Getty Images Plus; Supersmario/iStock/Getty Images Plus; **U14:** LauriPatterson/iStock/Getty Images Plus; Rocky89/iStock/Getty Images Plus; sbossert/E+; Tetra Images/Brand X Pictures; **C4:** Henry Lederer/Photodisc; kali9/iStock/Getty Images Plus; Ana Francisconi/EyeEm; David Sacks/The Image Bank; LeoPatrizi/E+; **U15:** Dado Daniela/Moment; Federica Grassi/Moment; Phil/Mome; Ferrantraite/E+; **U16:** Miguel Tovar/LatinContent WO; Kevin Frayer/Getty Images News; **LS4:** Pearl Bucknall/Photolibrary; VisitBritain/Britain on View; Erik Isakson; ColorBlind Images/Iconica; Hill Street Studios/Blend Images; Photograph taken by Henrik Moschner/Moment Open; Steve Debenport/iStock/Getty Images Plus; **U17:** martin-dm/E+; William King/The Image Bank; Visut Thepkunhanimit/EyeEm; MOAimage/Moment; Kaz Mori/The Image Bank; Westend61; **U18:** Neil Mockford/Alex Huckle/GC Images; Helios de la Rubia/Real Madrid; Phil Walter/Getty Images Entertainment; Justin Tallis/AFP; Andreas Rentz/Getty Images Entertainment; Michael Stewart/WireImage; Steve Granitz/WireImage; Caiaimage/Chris Ryan/OJO+; Hoxton/Tom Merton; skynesher/iStock/Getty Images Plus; Christian Vierig/Getty Images Entertainment; **C5:** Bettmann; Jenny Jones/Lonely Planet Images; Joey Foley/WireImage; Odd Andersen/AFP; Josiah Kamau/BuzzFoto/FilmMagic; **U19:** moodboard/Cultura; Hill Street Studios/Blend Images; Blend Images – KidStock/Brand X Pictures; Compassionate Eye Foundation/Steven Errico/DigitalVision; fotokostic/iStock/Getty Images Plus; Sidekick/iStock/Getty Images Plus; Mikael Vaisanen/Corbis; SolStock/E+; Calvin Chan Wai Meng/Moment Open; **U20:** Monty Rakusen/Cultura; PeopleImages/DigitalVision; Image Source; AJ_Watt/E+; gbh007/iStock/Getty Images Plus; MadKruben/iStock/Getty Images Plus; carterdayne/iStock Editorial/Getty Images Plus; **LS5:** PT Images; Juanmonino/iStock/Getty Images Plus; ajr_images/iStock/Getty Images Plus; Photodisc; Moncherie/iStock/Getty Images Plus; Alys Tomlinson/Cultura; Mikolette/E+; **PE:** Jupiterimages/Photolibrary; Ronnie Kaufman/Larry Hirshowitz/Blend Images; Thomas Barwick/Taxi;
**EA:** Franck-Boston/iStock/Getty Images Plus; Marc Romanelli/Blend Images; guruXOOX/iStock/Getty Images Plus.

The following photographs have been sourced from other library/sources.

**U2**: Courtesy of Camden Market; Courtesy of Carnaby London; **U5**: WENN Ltd/Alamy Stock Photo; Marilyn Barbone/Shutterstock; novkota1/Shutterstock; **U8**: Hugh Threlfall/Alamy Stock Photo; WENN Ltd/Alamy Stock Photo; **U11**: Reuters/Beawiharta; epa european pressphoto agency b.v./Alamy Stock Photo; Douglas Peebles Photography/Alamy Stock Photo; Chris Hammond Photography/Alamy Stock Photo; Nicram Sabod/Shutterstock; **U15**: Andrew Palmer/Alamy Stock Photo; **U16**: © Disney; STAR WARS: The Last JediTM & © Lucasfilm Ltd. LLC.; © Evan Hara; **C5**: dpa picture alliance/Alamy Stock Photo.

Front cover photography by suttisukmek/iStock/Getty Images Plus.

Illustration
Martin Sanders (Beehive Illustration); Chris Chalik (The Bright Agency); Ludovic Salle (Advocate Art).

Audio
The following audio is sourced from Getty Images.

Vitaliy Arkhanhelski/SoundExpress.

URLS
The publisher has made every effort to ensure that the URLs for external websites referred to in this book are correct and active at the time of printing. However, the publisher takes no responsibility for the websites and can make no guarantees that sites will remain live or that their content is or will remain appropriate.

**The publishers are grateful to the following contributors:** cover design and design concept: restless; typesetting: emc design Ltd; audio recordings: produced by Leon Chambers and recorded at The SoundHouse Studios, London; Life Skills and Culture sections: Robert Quinn; Grammar reference section: Louise Hashemi and Andrew Reid.